LOVE
IS NOT
BLIND
YOU ARE

Open Your Eyes
Win The Game of Love
Be Happy

With the 4Cross Love Framework and Checklist

Shelly LaVigne ♥ The Love Investigator

Sign up for a Love Investigation

I am taking cases. Whether you need help discovering your
position, relating to others, or you want to talk about navigating
your game of love, I am here for you!

The time has come for you to be a champion in love!

Make your appointment on my website

4Crosslove.com/appointment

Dedication

To every person out there who has suffered, struggled, and floundered in the game of love, you shall no longer.

I, Shelly LaVigne, your trusted, curious, and friendly Love Investigator, am here to help you win the game of love with my secret.

The 4Cross Love Checklist!

Table of Content

Preface

Welcome to a transformative journey into the heart of human connections with *Love Is Not Blind—You Are*, masterfully penned by Shelly LaVigne. As a seasoned explorer and dedicated Love Investigator, Shelly offers not just insights but a navigational compass through the complexities of romance using the groundbreaking 4Cross Love Framework.

This book emerges from a simple yet profound truth: our struggles in love stem not from love's blindness but from our own. Armed with the 4Cross Love Framework—a revolutionary guide that distills human characteristics into four positions (North, East, South, and West)—Shelly helps us clearly understand the cycle of human communication and the roles we and our partners inherently embody.

Each of us plays the game of love from one of these positions, which influences everything, from our communication styles to our needs and reactions. Understanding this unlocks smoother, more fulfilling relationships.

This is your personal love playbook, meticulously crafted by Shelly, who has not only studied but lived this framework. Her insights are illuminating, her narratives fascinating, and her observations grounded in reality. This book will challenge how you reflect, understand, and ultimately navigate the complex yet rewarding landscape of love.

With detailed descriptions, on-point observations, and engaging exercises that use the poignant Netflix show *Love Is Blind*, she will guide you through the revolutionary 4Cross Love Checklist with precision. Shelly will help you see what's happening in plain sight every day. She empowers you to identify your position and leverage this knowledge to enhance not only romantic relationships but all forms of interpersonal dynamics.

The goal? To shed the veils of confusion and misinterpretation that often cloud our interactions. Equipped with humor, empathy, and unwavering curiosity, you'll decode the complexities of love and human behavior. This book isn't merely an exploration of how we love but a monumental idea that we can love better, love smarter, and love with a profound sense of understanding.

You will not be disappointed as you embark on this expedition into the depths of the 4Cross Love Framework. Under Shelly's expert guidance and with the exacting 4Cross Love Checklist in hand, you will learn how to apply these principles practically and personally. Enhance your relationships, deepen your connections, and see your world with new, abundantly clear vision. With eyes wide open.

Welcome to the clarity of love, where we are no longer blind but beautifully aware. Let the investigation begin!

Introduction

If you've ever felt like a fool in the game of love, take solace, for I was the fool of all fools. Not a hopeless romantic or a clueless lovebird, but a brute.

In grade school, I believed that clobbering my potential suitors, literally and figuratively, would have them flocking to me. I had broken my wrist barrel racing, so it seemed like a good idea to hit one of my suitors on the head with my cast while playing soccer at recess. I got a time-out. Since that didn't work, my next move was hitting the tetherball so hard that it would smack them in the face before they could respond. My coup de grace—pulling their pants down while on the monkey bars—surely that would work! When that failed, I tried antagonizing and ridiculing, expecting boys to like me for . . . me, my brash and clever self.

No Such Luck.

In high school, my ignorance persisted, though I tempered my brashness with a touch of finesse. This subtlety drew a few young men into my orbit. My prowess in sports earned me some credit, and being relatively good-looking and kind enough landed me the title of homecoming queen. Yet, in the game of love, I was a loser. Confused, really. The boys I desired ignored me, while those who liked me were crushed by my lack of grace or simply weren't thrilling enough. *What is going on?* I wondered. I told myself, *this shouldn't be so hard!*

High school dating was a comedy of errors. A true tragicomedy. Maybe you can relate?

As I grew up, I was never given any advice that made any sense. The game being played among my peers was amateur hour without a clue. My grandparents were awkward and stoic. If there was any example, I thought I could follow, it was my parents'. I believed they were doing quite well, although they did fight a lot. My mom worried incessantly about finances while my dad was scheming the next big idea. The only thing that was clear was that I was left to my own devices. And I was not well equipped.

Off to college I went on a volleyball scholarship. During my first summer home, my older sister invited me to a beach fire. She said with a deep sense of sorrow, "Dad is cheating on Mom with the nurse taking care of Aunt Eloise." She'd discovered this after following him on one of his many suspicious visits. It was devastating news, especially with Mom battling breast cancer. We struggled over the question of whether to tell her or not tell her. We told her. She knew but didn't want to know.

I was furious—*lop off his head with a machete* furious! How could he betray the woman who supported him even through their many struggles? His cruelty was unthinkable. He even suggested she didn't deserve anything in a divorce because she "hadn't done anything."

The Audacity.

Little did I know that this experience would lead me to start doubting love. I doubted marriage, commitment, family, everything. I saw how much my mom suffered, tolerated mistreatment, and continued to hope that what was happening to her wasn't that bad. She would often say, "Well, there are so many people who have it worse." And I suppose she was right. But I have come to realize that my mom was a devoted, loyal, and sometimes stubborn South. And my dad, a dominant, clueless, and self-centered North.

Hold up, you may be thinking. *North? South? What's that all about?*

I'm going to show you what I mean. Because this book is about a framework that has changed my view of love forever.

It was then and there that I started my investigation into the game of love. I wasn't aware of it, but in those moments of disbelief, confusion, and utter pain that I was feeling through my dear mother's suffering, I vowed to find the answers to the irrational behavior that led to the collapse of my parents' marriage and our family. I wondered, *How could love turn into this?*

So, of course I studied political science in college. Really? Good lord, what was I thinking? I wish I had at least considered philosophy, sociology, or psychiatry because clearly, those areas have uncovered all the answers to the questions of love. Right? That's obviously why everyone is doing so well emotionally, the divorce rate is so low, and everyone is getting along.

Throughout college, I floundered in love. I was a directionless wanderer in a game without rules. My mom's health declined as the cancer spread. We, her daughters, were there for her, but my father was not. The divorce was finalized as my mom faded. She met my now husband but never her grandchildren. She would have been the most loving, amazing cookie-baking, noggin-kissing grandmother ever.

Not too long after that, I started butting heads with my husband. Perhaps I should have constructed a tetherball court.

He and I got along just fine, but something was off, and we both knew it. The marriage started a little off, but we denied it because, you know, we loved each other. I felt like I was entering another common disaster, but somehow, this was different enough. I was old enough. I was in love enough. It was time. I could find a way. Plus, he was really handsome, smart, and completely different than anyone I had dated. I was flying blind, and he was running into me, hoping to find a way for the both of us. We moved. We changed the color of the walls. We had two adorable girls. We kept going, but we were always searching. We didn't know what we were looking for, but we thought there had to be an answer to the mystery of love and life's odd way of trying to show us what it meant.

And then it hit us. The *BIG* piece. The missing piece.

On a mountain in Colorado, we met a man—John Cundiff—who had a remarkable, transformational idea. We listened and trained for hours on the phone. Through years of researching the human condition, he had come up with an answer to the cycle of human communication and interaction—or love, as I saw it. He took a different approach. A business approach.

I, however, have always seen it as the best way to understand the game of love that I had ever heard. I have been reorganizing, studying, and honing this discovery for over ten years to figure out a way to offer what I now call The 4Cross Love Framework. And with this framework comes the revolutionary tool, The 4Cross Love Checklist. I have had my own comedy of errors in doing so, but I promise you, it has been worth every moment because I am about to unveil the most profound tool for understanding and winning the game of love that you have ever seen.

The 4Cross Love Framework has granted me immense personal grace, acceptance, and love. My husband, our children, and I use it daily to navigate all relationships. It has truly helped me see what has been happening from the moment I met my husband. I finally realized why our relationship felt off, and now I am able to course correct and reconcile as we go. We have found common ground, understanding, and grace. I see the patterns, the cycle, and our own inner concerns in everything we do. I can see it in our children. They see it in their friends. I see it everywhere.

I'm 100 percent confident that the 4Cross Love Framework and Checklist will help you see the game of love hidden in plain sight, unwrap the brilliant gift of self-awareness, and realize true love. You will find your person or come to truly love the one you're with.

I, Shelly LaVigne, your Love Investigator, will guide you through the often hilarious, sometimes maddening, but oh-so-worth-it world of love and relationships, armed with the 4Cross Love Framework.

This framework isn't a personality test. It's a biological compass that points to your heart's true desires and uncovers your interpersonal dynamics. It is the secret to understanding the game of love.

This journey will equip you with the insight to navigate the game of love with agility, to see the forces behind attraction, and to understand the realities of human communication and connection. You'll receive a precise step-by-step 4Cross Love Checklist to help you check off all the essential things you need in order to choose the best mate for you or learn to love the person you are with. This book will show you how to play the game of love with the 4Cross Love Framework as your guide.

So, if you're ready to dive into the 4Cross Love Framework, keep an open mind, hold onto your skepticism (it's healthy), and prepare to be amused, enlightened, and possibly a bit gob smacked. Because love is about to get a whole lot clearer and, dare I say, even more exciting.

Here Is What You Will Learn in This Book

Part 1:

I reveal the 4Cross Love Framework, and we embark on an adventure to explore the four positions in the game of love: North, East, South, and West.

Each position is a world of its own, filled with unique allure, charm, and quirks. We delve deep into these positions, revealing their distinct characteristics, strengths, and challenges.

You'll discover the unique attributes and perspectives of these positions and realize that every interaction in the cycle of human communication is influenced by your position and those around you. You'll see the patterns, the plays, and, ultimately, your role in the fascinating game of love.

The end of Part I is all about you. You figure out your position, what drives you, what you value, what has happened for you in the past, and what you need going forward. You need to figure out your position in the game of love in order to go about playing the game of love effectively. Identifying your position is the basis for it all.

Part 2:

I introduce you to the greatest tool ever known when it comes to finding true love: the 4Cross Love Checklist! Together, we go through each part of the checklist so you know exactly what it is and how to use it to choose your best mate or love the one you're with and win the game of love! After we tackle each point of the checklist, we will discuss why opposites attract and what that means for you in choosing a mate or learning to love the one you're with in a new way.

Part 3:

I use the profound Netflix sensation *Love Is Blind* to investigate and reveal the positions of each coupling case by case. This showcases the four positions in their most vulnerable and strategic moments. Analyzing each coupling will show you what position they are playing in the game of love and why it turned out for them the way it did. If you can watch the show, you'll witness the raw, unfiltered aspects of these positions and gain a deeper understanding of their strengths and weaknesses while accumulating incredible knowledge in the game of love.

The show gives us a brilliant way to see the four positions in a very emotional, sped-up, stressful dilemma. Can you fall in love blindly, connect physically, live together, and then get married—yes, married! —in a matter of thirty-eight days? Talk about a recipe for creating drama, facing yourself, and finding the truth.

If only they had known the 4Cross Love Framework and followed the 4Cross Love Checklist!

You won't believe how interesting, apparent, ironic, and tragically comedic all of it becomes after you watch even one season!

Then we will go into sexual relationships by 4Cross position, what it's like to be a North, East, South, or West from their perspective. The how might each position might be red flagging. How each position may be projecting their concern onto others, without knowing it and then how each position procrastinates. It is fascinating!

Lastly, if you want to dig deeper and learn the game of love faster there are exercises and activities.

This approach to love is revolutionary and transformational. It is the recipe for true love.

The 4Cross Love Checklist makes sense only once you've grasped the four positions, identified your own, and realized the cycle of human communication and coordination. Otherwise known as the 4Cross Love Framework.

When you see these dynamics play out in *Love Is Blind*, you'll learn to recognize the positions in real life and play better by navigating the game of love with finesse. Like any game, practicing, learning, and taking responsibility for yourself are key. It works only if you follow the 4Cross Love Checklist.

In the conclusion, I provide a holistic view of how to continue playing the game of love like a champion and ensure a lifetime of happiness.

Get ready to master the game of love and live happily ever after!

Part 1

CHAPTER 1

The Game of Love

"Love is a game that two can play and both wins."

Eva Gabor

Welcome, brave adventurers, to the ultimate quest: the game of love.

The board in the game of love is a compass. The four positions—North, East, South, and West—are the four positions in the game of love. You are one of the positions. Your quest is to figure out which one you are so you can play the game of love from your position effectively.

Each player's position dictates their perspective, influencing how they move across the board, how they see the landscape, and how they interact with others on the board.

This board is filled with opportunities for connection, challenges that test resolve, and milestones that mark personal growth. As you play, you encounter various spaces, such as dates, connections, decision-making, shared experiences, challenges, and moments of vulnerability. Each space offers a chance to learn, grow, and advance toward the ultimate goal: finding and maintaining true love.

The Pieces: That's You

You are you, and that's the beauty of it. You are born to live, breathe, and be a spectacular version of yourself as you see things from your position. What a relief. Now, let's make the most of it.

Each position has unique traits, strengths, challenges, and ways they go about navigating life. By understanding these positions, you'll unlock the secrets to your own behavior and the behavior of those around you. Knowing your position and being able to identify the positions of others is your key to success.

The 4Cross Love Framework is the four positions in the game of love and the cycle of human communication. It is the secret to the game of love and the recipe for every love connection or delusional disaster you have ever had.

The 4Cross Love Framework isn't a personality model; it's how you operate in love through good times and bad. It is the compass that points to your heart's desires, showing you how you interact with others.

Why the 4Cross Love Framework Is So Profoundly Different Than Personality Tests

The 4Cross Love Framework offers a unique approach to understanding relationships and personal interactions, setting itself apart from traditional personality tests in several profound ways. While personality tests focus on categorizing individual traits and behaviors, the 4Cross Love Framework delves deeper into the biological and elemental aspects of human *interactions*, providing a more holistic and dynamic view of relationships.

Here are the key differences that make the 4Cross Love Framework profoundly different and impactful:

Elemental and Biological Foundations

Elemental Influence: The 4Cross Love Framework is rooted in the elemental forces of nature—Air, Fire, Earth, and Water—symbolizing 09(North, East, South, and West) corresponds to these elements, offering a rich metaphorical understanding of how individuals operate and relate to each other.

Biological Basis: Unlike personality tests, which often rely on self-reported data and subjective interpretations, the 4Cross Love Framework considers the biological and innate aspects of human behavior. These positions are not personality types. They are deeply ingrained biological orientations that influence how we connect, communicate, and relate. This means that the 4Cross positions—North, East, South, and West—are not merely aspects of one's personality that can change over time or through experience. You cannot change the way someone sees and plays the game. You can only learn how to read them. They are fundamental biological orientations that inherently shape how individuals perceive the world and interact with others. These positions influence the way people connect with others, how they communicate, and how they relate in relationships and social settings.

For instance, as a North, my view of relationships is guided by my concern for certainty. I want to know the facts and deal with them accordingly. This is how I operate, and I know it. Because I know this about myself and recognize this reality, I can navigate with self-awareness, which allows me to be myself without doubt. This biological basis is how we naturally think. Once we are aware of it, we can work with it and not against it or ignorant of it. It's our human nature.

In essence, this concept suggests that each person's position is a core part of their being, influencing their behaviors, motivations, and interactions on a deep level. Understanding these positions can help you better navigate your relationships and interactions by recognizing your and others' inherent tendencies and needs.

Relationship-Centric Approach

Focus on Interactions: The 4Cross Love Framework places a strong emphasis on relationships and how different positions interact with one another. It provides insights into compatibility, potential conflicts, and ways to enhance harmony in relationships, making it highly practical for improving interpersonal dynamics.

Dynamic Interactions: Rather than static personality traits, the framework explores the dynamic interplay between different positions. It acknowledges that relationships are fluid and ever changing, and it offers strategies for adapting and thriving in these evolving contexts.

Practical Applications

Actionable Insights: The 4Cross Love Framework offers practical advice and actionable strategies tailored to each position. Whether it's enhancing communication, balancing traits, or navigating stress, the framework provides concrete steps to improve interactions and relationships.

Scenarios and Examples: By incorporating everyday scenarios and real-life examples, the framework helps you visualize how your position influences your actions and decisions. This practical perspective makes it easier to implement the insights in daily life.

Emphasis on Growth and Balance

Balancing Strengths and Challenges: The framework highlights the strengths of each position and addresses the potential challenges and pitfalls. It encourages you to embrace your strengths while working on areas that need improvement, promoting personal growth and balance.

Guidance for Self-Discovery: It provides a pathway for self-discovery, helping you understand your intrinsic nature and how you can leverage your unique traits to build fulfilling relationships and a balanced life. This focus on self-awareness and growth sets it apart from more static personality assessments.

By exploring the dynamic interplay of the four positions—North, East, South, and West—the framework provides a deep and nuanced perspective on love and human connection, empowering you to navigate the complexities of relationships with greater insight and harmony.

Here's why it matters. Making the biggest life decision of all—who to marry—based on personality tests is like trying to play chess without knowing the rules, what each piece does, how they move, or what the objective is. The 4Cross Love Framework, on the other hand, is a complete system that guides you through the waves of human interaction with precision, leaving you with confidence in its instruction and granting you the gift of finding true love.

How the Game of Love Is Played

The game of love is played through a continuous four-step cycle of human communication and action. This cycle happens regardless of a person's position. Understanding and mastering this cycle is essential for successfully navigating the board and advancing in the game.

Ignition (North): Each transaction in every unique game begins with an initiation, where communication is opened or an idea is suggested. This can be as simple as a smile, a message, or an invitation.

Exploration (East): Once the initial contact is made, players enter the exploration phase. This is where deeper communication happens—sharing stories, interests, and values. Each player gathers information to better understand the other.

Execution (South): This phase involves deciding on and executing plans and actions together. It could be going on dates or working on shared goals. Collaborative actions build a strong foundation for the relationship.

Evaluation (West): After actions are taken, evaluation follows. Players reflect on what worked, what didn't, and how they feel about the experience. Based on the evaluation, players make adjustments. They tweak their communication styles, modify their actions, and realign their expectations.

This cycle repeats continuously, with each stage building on the previous one, fostering deeper connections and greater understanding. This allows each individual to build relationship strategies for every person they come into contact with. Mastering this cycle of human communication and action allows players to navigate the game of love with skill, adaptability, and resilience, leading to a more fulfilling and harmonious journey toward true love.

This cyclical process of ignition, exploration, execution, and evaluation is emblematic of the broader dynamics of human interaction and communication, which are evident in both grand endeavors and everyday decisions. It underscores the diverse perspectives and inherent concerns associated with each of the four positions—North, East, South, and West—and highlights the intricate dance of collaboration and conflict that shapes our interactions and decisions.

Understanding the underlying principles of the 4Cross Love Framework and the inherent perspective of each position offers a lens through which we view and navigate the complexities of relationships and decision-making.

This insight provides a valuable perspective for making more informed, empathetic, and strategic choices in love and beyond. It moves beyond the blindness that often accompanies our most significant life decisions because not only are we unaware of our positional attributes, but we simply don't see our role in the cycle of interaction and coordination.

So, let me break down the cycle of interaction and coordination in terms of the positions themselves. When an idea is proposed—say, the prospect of finding dinner—it starts the cycle at the North position, no matter who came up with the idea. Then the cycle moves clockwise to the East, where possibilities are explored, then to South, where the idea is executed, and then to West, where the idea is analyzed and evaluated. Then, back to the North, with all things accounted for and considered.

For example, the North idea: "I'm hungry. Let's go get some dinner."

The East possibility: "Okay, where shall we go? Italian? Bar and grill? Or perhaps Thai?" The answer is, "Thai, I want Thai."

The South implementation: They try a Thai place.

The West evaluation: Was it good? Did the restaurant make the Pad Thai the way they like it? Will they go back?

This cycle of interaction and coordination happens in various forms every day, all day.

If you are not aware of this cycle and think that your perspective (position) is the most important aspect in the cycle of communication in your relationships, you will be lost and confused. And isn't that how it feels in the game of love?

Let's go over this more so you can grasp what's happening in front of you every day with people who play these positions.

Playing the Positions

The cycle of interaction among the four positions in the 4Cross Love Framework begins with North, where an idea or initiative is proposed. The North's role is characterized by leadership, decisiveness, and strategic thinking. People in the North position often take the initiative in starting new projects or discussions.

Next, the cycle moves to East, which brings in possibilities, creativity, and adaptability. East's contribution involves exploring various ways to implement an idea, adding creativity, energy, and social dynamics to the mix. People in the East position is vital for brainstorming and negotiating a range of options or solutions.

The cycle then progresses to South, where the focus shifts to implementation and action. South embodies action, support, and cooperation. This position is where the actual work gets done; it's about turning the ideas and possibilities generated by North and East into reality. People in the South position ensure that tasks are completed and efforts are coordinated effectively.

Finally, West evaluates the outcomes and processes. West is characterized by standards, organization, and analytical thinking. People in the West position review what has been accomplished, assess the efficiency of the approach, and suggest improvements or refinements for the future. West's role is crucial for learning from experiences and enhancing future interactions and projects.

This cycle of interaction creates a dynamic and continuous flow of ideas, possibilities, action, and reflection, allowing for effective collaboration and progress. Ideally, each position contributes uniquely, ensuring that initiatives are well conceived, creatively enriched, effectively executed, and thoroughly evaluated.

While people in the North position are often associated with the inception of ideas due to their natural inclination toward innovation and leadership, the process of interaction and implementation of these ideas is not limited to North alone. In other words, any position can and will come up with ideas, but the natural sequence in the process of coordination remains consistent.

The framework emphasizes a collaborative cycle that involves all four positions, allowing for a dynamic flow of ideas and actions that moves clockwise from North to East to South to West, regardless of who initiated the idea.

People in the North position, with their characteristic drive, may frequently initiate projects or concepts, but the actualization of these ideas necessitates the involvement and contributions of all the other positions. East people, with their adaptability, explore the possibilities and engage with the idea, enhancing it with creativity and external perspectives. People in the South position, known for their support, then take the reins to implement and execute the plan, grounding the idea with practical steps and hard work. Finally, people in the West position, with their analytical skills, evaluate the outcomes, refine the processes, and ensure the sustainability and efficiency of the project.

Each position brings unique strengths and perspectives to the table. Through a coordinated effort in completing the cycle, ideas can be effectively brought to fruition and evaluated for long-term success in all areas of a relationship.

It is through this realization that you can gain insight into how relationship success can happen. You can see your role and the role of others, how each person shows up in the game of love, and how differently each person navigates their relationships based on their concerns being met or not.

Couples

Now, I'm sure you're realizing that in a romantic relationship, there are only two people playing two positions in the game. The key is knowing your position, how you play best, who you play best with, and how to effectively coordinate the cycle of interaction.

You can play the role of all four positions and see that the cycle flows in the clockwise direction, allowing all four positional requirements to be accounted for. The key is knowing that you play best from your position and acknowledging that your mate plays best from theirs.

When you are coupled with someone, you represent two of the four positions in the 4Cross Love Framework. Typically, but not always, these positions are opposites. You might find yourselves at complementary angles, like a North and an East, or a South and a West. While it's possible to share the same position, it's less common in romantic partnerships due to our biological attraction to differences. These differences bring complementary benefits to relationships, enhancing genetic diversity, resource allocation, personal growth, and relationship stability.

The complementary dynamic in such relationships creates a balance where each partner's strengths support the other's needs, leading to a more harmonious and fulfilling partnership.

The 4Cross Love Framework explains how different positions—North, East, South, and West—provide unique strengths and perspectives that, when combined, create balanced and effective partnerships.

Realizing this, you can work with one another more effectively by understanding your partner's perspective and communicating effectively. Perhaps the most powerful thing is realizing that what seemed like shortcomings, weaknesses, or gaps in yourself or your mate are not about weakness or fault. You both can learn to see the cycle, contribute from your position, recognize others, appreciate the game, and play immensely better!

Think of any game you've played. Given your different personal attributes, you are likely good at different aspects of gameplay. You can play the other positions, but you're more likely to have fun and win if you have the right players in the right positions, follow the rules, and play as a team.

One of the biggest things I have gleaned from this discovery is that we are born to play from one of these positions to the best of our ability. *This is your ultimate strength!*

I felt such a relief when I recognized that my innate concern was my contribution and that I didn't have to worry about how weak I was in the other positions. I need to be aware of them, but I don't have to be, and can't be, all of them effectively. I realized how important it is to have a partner, connect with others, acknowledge their contributions with curiosity, and play my position with grace.

The yearning need for connection, I posit, is deeply rooted in our biology. It's like we know intuitively that this compass is guiding us through the intricate landscape of interpersonal relationships. Yet we are not conscious of its instinctual guidance. Our ignorance often leaves us navigating without a clear map, sensing disturbances without understanding their source. It's as though our very nature propels us forward, yet we are oblivious to the undercurrents shaping our reactions because we are unaware of the cycle and our positions, which are hidden in plain sight.

This is why venturing into the realm of love is confusing and frustrating. The potential for joy is matched by the risk of profound heartbreak. Yet imagine the transformation in your journey if you were equipped with a deeper understanding of the intrinsic positions, you and others play in the game of love!

Armed with the 4Cross Love Framework, which reveals the integral roles of the 4Cross positions in the cycle of communication and coordination, you can approach relationships with a heightened awareness and empathy. This knowledge doesn't make the path entirely foolproof, but it significantly clears the fog that often clouds the understanding of love and connection. In essence, while it may not eliminate all risks, it certainly illuminates the path, making your choices more informed, your understanding deeper, and your connections more consciously navigated.

Winning the Game of Love

The key to mastering the game of love lies in understanding your position, recognizing the common moves of others, and strategically navigating the dynamics. Communication is your most powerful tool. Be honest, clear, and empathetic. Respect the positions of others, recognizing their unique perspectives and strengths. Flexibility and adaptability are key as the game evolves. Embrace vulnerability and authenticity, as genuine connections are built on trust and openness.

The more you take accountability for your position and embrace it, the more nuanced you're learning about yourself and others will be.

The key to mastering any game is getting down to the nuances. You see where the ball is going, not where it's at. You learn how to spin the ball, not just hit it. This is truer for your relationships because the satisfaction you get is not just for you but for your mate as well. Love is meant to be a win-win game for the rest of your life. The whole point of life is to love, in my opinion.

Opening Your Eyes

Learning 4Cross is like turning on the lights in a room you've only ever seen in the dark. You'll start recognizing why you gravitate toward certain people and why some relationships feel like you're trying to fit a square peg in a round hole. There is a reason two north poles of a magnet always repel each other. This is your moment of self-awareness, where you start to appreciate the unique spark that makes you who you are.

Have you ever looked at someone and wondered, *what are they thinking?* With the 4Cross Love Framework, you're about to get as close as humanly possible to reading minds. Understanding the positions not only helps you get where others are coming from. It also teaches you the fine art of empathy.

As we dive deep into the nuances of the North, East, South, and West positions it's important to realize that even though you are one position, not every single attribute in your position will necessarily feel like you. Depending on the context, some aspects of another position may resonate with you because you know you do play that role in some way in your life, and want to recognize it. Or you may feel like you would like to be more like that position somehow. You may also want to believe you are more like that position. You also may feel like you have been oppressed and want to be more like another position. It can be really hard to identify your position because in some way you feel like all of them.

We all play the other positions at any given time in life because we must. But when push comes to shove, you operate from your biological position. The primary survival concern of your position propels you in everything you do and how you react. That is what you are looking for. You must drive down and identify what really makes you tick. It's important to be honest and if you really need help, ask your best friends and or family. They will tell you the truth.

Understanding who you are, what you need, what you value, and where you want to go provides a crucial context for understanding your position in the game of love. It's about understanding the why behind the what and finding the patterns in human connections.

Recognizing our survival concern—whether it's for certainty, freedom, stability, or security—shapes the core of how we navigate life and relationships, which in turn drives our need for identity. It's our underlying instinct, our human nature.

For example, if someone's survival concern is stability (South), they may develop an identity around being dependable, hardworking, and grounded because that ensures their emotional and physical safety. If someone's survival concern is certainty (North), they may develop an identity around being decisive, authoritative, and always in control. To feel secure, they need to be seen as the one with the plan, guiding others, and making sure everything is on track. If someone's survival concern is security (West), they may develop an identity around being cautious, thorough, and detail-oriented. They focus on getting things right and avoiding mistakes because that attention to detail makes them feel safe. Their identity often centers on being the one who preserves structure and maintains order. If freedom is the concern (East), their identity revolves around spontaneity, creativity, and resisting restriction, as it protects their need for open possibilities.

Essentially, our survival concern forms the foundation for how we define ourselves, influencing the roles we take on and the way we express ourselves in the world.

In the chapters to come, we'll go into detail about the worldview of North, East, South, and West, discovering how these positions see the world, react to it, and play the game of love. Each position description is designed around how it feels to be around them, their key traits and challenges. How they play their position in relationships and then how they show up in the wilds of life. Then there are the elemental aspects.

Each position has a natural *element* associated with it. These elemental auras are Air, Fire, Earth, and Water.

Each position also has a *season* within the cycle they resonate with: winter, spring, summer, or autumn.

Each position also has a *virtue*. These are emotional qualities that lie within the positions and are what they exude: wisdom, valor, justice, and prudence.

Each position is either on *offense* or *defense*. It's where you play in the game of love. Essentially, it's like any game that has offense and defense. People on offense are trying to create a way to move forward, and people on defense are trying to preserve their lead or place. In some games, like basketball and volleyball, you play both offense and defense. We all do that in love. But in the 4Cross Love Framework, you'll see that two positions are specifically wired for offense and two are on defense.

And last but certainly not least, each position has spirit animals

Learning your position in the game of love is going to open your eyes to the beauty and the challenges we all face based on our position.

Let's go to the positions.

CHAPTER 2

The North Position

"Love is the greatest refreshment in life."

Pablo Picasso

Being around a North is like stepping into a room that suddenly has a clear sense of purpose. They bring this natural focus and drive that can be contagious. When you're with a North, you know things are going to get done. They're often the ones taking charge, making decisions, and leading the way, and they do it with such confidence that it's hard not to trust their vision.

Norths have a way of making you feel like there's a plan, even when things get chaotic. They're calm under pressure, always thinking a few steps ahead, and they tend to inspire others to stay grounded and focused. But don't expect a lot of small talk—they're more about getting to the point and making things happen. There's a decisiveness to them that can be refreshing, especially if you're someone who struggles with indecision or chaos.

At times, they can seem a bit intense, especially if you're more laid-back, but it's usually because they're driven by a strong sense of direction and responsibility. If you're looking for someone to steer the ship, whether in work or relationships, a North is the person you want by your side. Just be ready to keep up with their pace!

Key Traits of a North

Logical and Focused: Norths are like human compasses pointing toward their goals. They approach problems with a logical mindset and are incredibly focused on finding solutions.

Driven and Purposeful: They don't just float through life; they march with purpose. Every step they take is toward a specific goal or vision.

Commanding and Willful: Norths have a presence that demands attention. They can be quite commanding, and their willpower is apparent. This can be both intimidating and incredibly inspiring to others.

Self-Controlled and Independent: Think of the North as the lone wolf. They don't rely on others to get things done and often prefer working alone to ensure things meet their high standards.

Blunt and Assertive: Honesty is their best policy. Norths don't sugarcoat their words. They tell it like it is, which can sometimes come off as blunt, but you'll always know where you stand with them.

Strategic and Innovative: These are the thinkers. Norths love to strategize and come up with innovative solutions with new ideas.

Cavalier: With a boldness born of certainty, the North navigates the landscapes of both heart and mind. Their confidence is an unshakable banner that rallies those around them.

Decisive: Norths make decisions quickly and confidently, relying on their keen sense of judgment and logical thinking.

Resilient: In the face of adversity, Norths stand firm. They are not easily swayed by setbacks and possess a remarkable ability to bounce back from challenges.

Bold: Norths are not afraid to take risks. Their courage and willingness to push boundaries often lead them to success where others might falter.

Challenging Attributes

Domineering: Norths can be overly controlling and assertive, often imposing their will on others and dominating conversations and decisions.

Insensitive: Their blunt and straightforward communication style can come off as harsh and tactless, sometimes hurting others' feelings without intending to.

Stubborn: Norths may be inflexible and unwilling to compromise, insisting on their way even when collaboration would be more beneficial.

Impatient: They often expect quick results and can become easily frustrated when there are delays or others don't keep up with their pace.

Workaholic: Their drive and ambition can lead to workaholism, neglecting personal relationships in favor of professional goals.

Arrogant: Norths can appear arrogant and overconfident, dismissing others' ideas and contributions, which can create tension and resentment in relationships.

Dealing with Stress: A North's drive can sometimes lead to high stress levels. They would benefit from practicing stress management techniques like exercise and hobbies.

Balancing Work and Personal Life: Ambition might lead Norths to prioritize work over personal relationships. To deal with this challenge, they can set boundaries and ensure they're giving enough time and energy to both areas.

Managing Expectations: High expectations can be motivating, but they can also lead to disappointment. Norths need to learn to set realistic goals and be kind to themselves if things don't go as planned.

Avoiding Perfectionism: Striving for perfection can be exhausting. Focusing on doing their best rather than achieving perfection can help them. Progress is more important than perfection.

Handling Criticism: Norths can sometimes take criticism personally. They can learn to take a beat when they feel perturbed. Asking questions with curiosity after criticism can become an opportunity for growth rather than a personal attack.

Overly Independent: Norths can sometimes push people away by insisting on doing everything themselves. Their strong need for control and self-reliance can make it difficult for them to delegate or ask for help, leaving others feeling excluded or undervalued.

Disconnection from Emotions: Focused on logic and strategy, Norths may struggle with emotional intelligence, often overlooking their own or others' emotional needs. This can create a sense of emotional distance in relationships, as they may prioritize results over feelings.

Reluctant to Admit Mistakes: Norths can have a hard time admitting when they're wrong, due to their need for certainty and control. They may dig in their heels and defend their decisions even when it's clear they need to reassess, which can cause conflict and stall progress.

Common Reactions of Norths Under Stress

Under stress, the strengths of a North can become pitfalls:

Dictating: When threatened, Norths may dictate orders with certainty, commanding respect even if unsure themselves.

Controlling: Norths under stress might yell, berate, and force others to follow their directives to maintain control. This can lead to feeling like they must yell, humiliate, berate, rant, abuse, and force people to do exactly what they want or need to get done. Heads will come off when a North is stressed and out of control.

Manipulating: Norths may plot and strategize to manipulate situations and people to achieve their desired outcomes. When under stress, Norths feel like brute force is the only solution. They will strategize in their heads to devise a plan to manipulate the situation or others involved. Norths' ideas are very important to them; they will do what it takes. Norths want to be recognized for being first, having great ideas, and big thinking.

Insisting on Being Right: Norths have a need to feel right and may stubbornly pursue bad ideas rather than admit they are wrong. Sometimes, Norths sacrifice their standards because their idea is more important; they would rather be right and have their way (have their certainty validated). They will compromise a lot to see their ideas work. And if their idea doesn't work, they will accuse others of not doing it right. Norths are masters of rationalizing, reality-bending, and justification. "So, what if you don't like it? MY idea needs to happen!"

Break Down Judgment: Stupid - Norths have disdain for perceived stupidity and may rudely dismiss those who don't understand them. But whatever you do, don't tell a North that they are stupid because those are "fighting words" nearly guaranteed to set a North off.

Confuses Ideas with Accomplishment: Norths often mistake ideation for accomplishment, undervaluing the effort needed to execute their ideas.

Key Struggle for Each Position

Each position struggles with different challenges, but there is one for each position that is persistent and based on their survival concern. This concern manifests in different ways. Seeing how these persistent biological concerns play out for each position can be extremely helpful in gauging how to navigate the game of love.

North individuals often struggle with the need to be right due to their biological concern for certainty.

Control: Norths thrive on certainty and having control over their environment. This need for certainty translates into a strong desire to be right, as being correct affirms their need for control.

Decision-Making: Norths are natural leaders, decisive, and commanding. Their leadership style is often characterized by an impulse to direct action. Admitting they are wrong can feel like a threat to their leadership and decision-making prowess.

Confidence and Assertiveness: Norths project confidence and assertiveness. They approach situations with a strong belief in their ideas and strategies, making it difficult for them to concede to others' viewpoints.

Logical and Rational Thinking: Norths prioritize logic and rationality. They often view their conclusions as the most logical solutions, making it challenging for them to accept alternative perspectives.

Assertive Communication: Norths communicate assertively and directly, which can sometimes come off as confrontational. This communication style is linked to their need to be right, as they strive to ensure their perspectives are understood and accepted.

Impact on Relationships: Norths' need to be right can create tension in their personal and professional relationships. Their assertiveness and confidence in their own logic can come across as domineering or dismissive to others, potentially leading to conflicts.

Resistance to Feedback and Growth: Norths' desire to be right can make them resistant to feedback, which is essential for personal and professional growth. Their focus on maintaining their own correctness can prevent them from acknowledging their mistakes and learning from them.

How the Concern for Certainty Can Manifest in a North's Life

Frequent Arguments: Norths may find themselves frequently arguing with partners, friends, or colleagues because they are unwilling to concede or consider alternative perspectives. This can strain relationships and create an environment where others feel undervalued or unheard.

Difficulty Collaborating: In relationships, Norths' insistence on their own methods and solutions can hinder collaboration. Their partner may become frustrated with their perceived inflexibility, leading to decreased relatability.

Stagnation in Personal Development: By resisting constructive criticism, Norths may miss opportunities for self-improvement. They might continue making the same mistakes, limiting their growth and development.

Stress and Burnout: Constantly striving to be right can be mentally and emotionally exhausting. Norths may experience high levels of anxiety and burnout as they pressure themselves to always have the correct answer or solution.

Isolation: Over time, Norths' need to be right can lead to social isolation. Friends and family might distance themselves to avoid confrontations, leaving Norths feeling lonely and unsupported.

Perfectionism: The need for certainty can drive Norths to perfectionism, where they set unrealistically high standards for themselves and others. This perfectionism can lead to dissatisfaction, as perfection is unattainable.

Understanding the North's biological concern for certainty helps explain why they struggle with the idea of being wrong. It's not just about ego or stubbornness; it's deeply rooted in their biological wiring and the way they interact with the world. By acknowledging these tendencies, Norths can work on improving flexibility and openness in their relationships, balancing their need for certainty with adaptability.

Clues

Here are some clues as to how a North acts that will help you identify a North in your investigations:

Learning: Norths prefer reading and self-study, taking time to fully understand and ensure they feel certain about information.

Assessment vs. Projection: Norths often assess others for their competency, which can sometimes come across as arrogant and judgmental.

Thought vs. Action: Norths typically think before acting, needing to feel certain about their decisions.

Speaking from "Should": Norths instinctively direct others and tell them what they "should" do, focusing on facts and often avoiding small talk.

Communication Style: Norths are very direct, often coming off as abrupt. They prefer to get straight to the point, valuing talking over listening. Norths can struggle to clearly articulate their ideas, often assuming their vision is obvious and becoming impatient when it is not.

Accused Of: Norths are frequently accused of declaring new actions and ideas without providing sufficient evidence.

How North Plays Their Position

North in Relationships

When it comes to relationships, Norths bring the same intensity and focus they use in other areas of their life. Here's how being this position can play out in a North's love life:

Leadership in Love: Norths often take the lead in relationships. They are decisive and usually the ones to make plans and decisions. If you're dating a North, expect them to know the best places to eat, the coolest activities to try, and the most effective ways to tackle challenges together.

Straightforward Communication: With a North, what you see is what you get. They value direct communication and expect the same from their partners. If you appreciate honesty and clarity, a relationship with a North will be refreshingly straightforward.

High Expectations: Norths set high standards for themselves and those around them. This can drive their partners to be their best selves, but it can also create pressure. It's important for Norths to balance their expectations with empathy and understanding.

Passionate and Intense: Norths love deeply and intensely. When they're committed, they're all in. This passion can make for an incredibly dynamic and exciting relationship.

Goal-Oriented: Norths approach relationships with the same goal-oriented mindset they apply to their professional lives. They're often thinking about the future and how to build a successful partnership.

Driven: The North is propelled by an internal engine of ambition and vision, a force that fuels their journey toward uncharted horizons.

Strategic Thinkers: In relationships, Norths plan for the future. They often have a clear vision of where they want the relationship to go and work diligently to make that vision a reality.

In The Wild-

Here are ways that Norths show up in life, what it's like to be around them.

Norths in relationships are all about certainty, control, and making sure things are right. They love to correct their partner when something is off, whether it's the color of a shirt or the details of a story. For a North, truth and precision matter more than anything, and they'll always want to set things straight. It's not that they're trying to be harsh—they just value getting the facts right. You'll notice this when they casually say, "Actually, it was blue," or something similar. They don't like exaggeration and prefer to keep things matter-of-fact.

They can struggle with humor or sarcasm, especially if it's not grounded in reality. Jokes that stretch the truth might fly over their heads, but show them a blooper reel, and they'll be laughing until they cry. It's when the humor is simple and relatable that they really loosen up.

Norths care a lot about how they present themselves in relationships. Their appearance, the way they handle situations—they want it all to look perfect. On most days, things in their world are neat and in order, unless they're feeling off, and then all bets are off. But one thing's for sure: they don't like being told what to do. If you ask them to take the trash out or suggest how something should be done, they may delay it or outright refuse. They want control over how things get done, and they see it as their job to decide.

If you want them to do something, reverse psychology can sometimes work. But don't expect that trick to last long—they'll catch on quickly. Norths can be condescending and cold at times, especially when they feel the need to assert control or when someone challenges them. A mature North, though, will catch themselves and soften their approach, still leading with grace when necessary.

When they're deep in thought, Norths might be quiet for a while, processing everything. And just when you least expect it, they'll suddenly come out with something brilliant. It may take them time to get there, but once they've figured something out, they're all in. They need to make things their own before they'll fully engage, so don't rush them.

They're also slower to pick up on things at times, but when they do, they'll shoot ahead, eager to show their competence. If a North is asking for help, it's a rare occurrence—they don't like admitting they don't know something. But as soon as they get a little bit of information, they'll likely say, "I got it," which is their way of saying they've had enough help and are ready to take control again.

Norths have their own internal clock when it comes to getting things done. If it's time to leave for an event or start something, they may drag their feet to feel like they're in control of the timing. It doesn't matter if it's a two-year-old or a grandparent—Norths will let you know when *they* think it's time to go.

If they suggest an idea, they're often very attached to it. They'll push to get their idea into action, and if you try to tweak it or suggest changes, they'll likely resist. In their mind, the idea was already perfect, and any modification feels like a personal attack on their competence.

Norths don't like to blend in. They prefer to stand out, but in subtle ways—maybe they'll dress sharply but wear quirky socks, just to show their uniqueness. They're always scanning for new trends or ways to stay ahead, and they care a lot about their appearance. If you suggest what they should wear or how to do something, don't be surprised if they do the opposite.

They have endless ideas, sometimes too many. Norths can wear themselves—and their partner—out with constant brainstorming. They're big thinkers, often projecting their thoughts far into the future. But they can struggle with finishing projects because their mind is always onto the next big thing before they've completed the last one.

Despite their high standards, they sometimes let go of enforcing them, not wanting to coach or push their partner into what they feel should be obvious. They often say, "I know," when someone tells them something, even if they didn't know, just to maintain the appearance of certainty.

Norths ignite action. In relationships, they're often the ones to announce, "Let's do this," and get things moving. But they can also become impatient if their partner doesn't understand what seems obvious to them. They'll push forward, even if the situation calls for slowing down and considering the emotional side of things.

When they feel cornered in an argument, Norths are likely to dictate and take control of the situation. They'll yell or shut down the conversation to make sure they "win," and they'll rely on what they see as the truth to back up their stance. Their contribution to relationships is certainty—they bring a sense of direction and confidence, even when they don't have all the answers. And if they don't know something, they'll find out fast.

In relationships, Norths can find it hard to learn from mistakes because they don't want to be seen as not knowing something. They might push forward without considering the consequences, determined to get their way. When they feel strongly about an idea or a course of action, watch out. Their conviction can be fierce, and they won't back down easily.

They are notorious for getting in the last word. Even if a disagreement seems over, they'll poke one more time, just to feel like they've had the final say. Apologies from a North can be tricky—they might say something like, "I'm sorry you feel that way," which feels more like a way to deflect blame than a genuine apology.

Norths want their own space in a relationship—a kind of personal kingdom. Whether it's a physical space or control over certain aspects of the relationship, they need to feel like they're in charge. When two Norths are together, they may butt heads a lot because neither wants to back down or give up control.

Norths can be micromanaging perfectionists, saying things like, "I'll just do it myself so it gets done right." But ironically, they often don't hold themselves to the same standards, rationalizing why their own behavior is an exception.

When balanced, Norths can make their partner feel like they can do anything. They bring a sense of confidence to the relationship, convincing both themselves and their partner that the impossible is possible. They think before they speak because they don't want to look foolish, and when they do speak, it's often with great wisdom.

Norths can be impatient with emotional conversations—they want to get to the point. If they doubt your competence in an argument or discussion, they'll grill you until you second-guess yourself. If a North trusts you, they expect you to just handle things.

When they realize they're wrong, Norths will downplay it, saying, "It's no big deal," to avoid looking foolish. They're great at invalidating whatever they want to be invalidated if it suits their need to be right.

Norths tends to 'talk at' rather than 'talk with,' often dominating conversations to assert their ideas. When unbalanced, they may 'talk over' others to control the dialogue, which can hinder the buy-in needed for their ideas to succeed. Once they've labeled someone (e.g., a liar), they may repeatedly reinforce that judgment."

In relationships, Norths often think far into the future, constantly planning and strategizing. They are independent, strong-willed, and decisive, but they can also become critical when things don't go their way. Their desire for control and immediate results can sometimes make them dismissive of their partner's feelings or concerns.

At their best, Norths are visionary partners. They bring creative ideas and bold plans into the relationship, helping push it forward with confidence and determination. However, they can struggle to share leadership in the relationship, often preferring to be the one in charge. Norths can be argumentative when they feel challenged, but they also rise to any occasion, always striving to make things happen quickly.

 Norths often struggle with idea overload, jumping from one concept to the next without finishing, which can overwhelm others and create chaos, frustration, and hurt feelings as they pursue perfection amid scattered ideas.

If there was a T-shirt for North, it might say:

"Work with me, People!" "My Way or the Highway"

"Let's Skip to the Part Where I'm Right" "I'm Not Bossy, I Just Have Better Ideas"

Lastly, we are going to cover the elemental aspects of North and then their spirit animals.

The Essence of Air

Norths seem to carry this light, airy energy with them. They're the ones who bring clarity and movement, constantly exploring new ideas and connections. They're always looking ahead, imagining what *could* be, instead of just settling for what is.

In the Heart of Winter

Winter is where Norths thrive. Just like winter can bring calm and clarity, Norths shine in chaotic situations. When things get tough, their wisdom and resilience kick in, helping them guide others through the storm with a sense of calm and control.

The Virtue of Wisdom

Wisdom is North's superpower. It's not just about knowing things; it's about knowing how to apply that knowledge in real situations. Their wisdom gives them the ability to navigate life with grace and insight, always seeing the bigger picture.

The Hemisphere of Offense

Norths are on offense, breaking new ground and leading the way. They have a strong need to be seen as reliable and knowledgeable, driving them to seek out certainty in everything they do. This quest shapes how they approach life and relationships.

And for fun, the North spirit animals:

Orca (Killer Whale): Orcas are known for their intelligence, complex social structures, and strategic hunting abilities, mirroring the North's leadership and tactical acumen.

Wolf: Symbolizing leadership, strong social connections, and a deep sense of community, wolves are also known for their strategic thinking and teamwork, resonating with the North's ability to lead and inspire collective action.

Lion: Known as the king of the jungle, the lion represents authority, strength, and courage. Its role as a leader in the animal kingdom echoes the North's natural leadership qualities and commanding presence.

Hawk: Known for their keen vision and perspective, hawks symbolize foresight and strategic thinking, aligning well with the North's visionary qualities.

Panther: Representing power, confidence, and independence, the panther reflects the North's commanding presence and their ability to take decisive action while remaining calm and collected.

As we conclude our exploration of the North position within the 4Cross Framework, we are reminded of the essential strength and leadership that North brings to the fabric of love and human interaction. Their innate ability to provide direction, stability, and wisdom speaks to the core of what makes relationships endure—certainty, trust, and the pursuit of a shared vision. I hope this journey into the North position has been helpful in recognizing their perspective in love and life.

Embracing Your North

If you identify as a North, embrace your strengths. Your drive and determination can take you far in life and love. Just remember to balance your intensity with kindness and understanding. When you do so, you'll create relationships that are not only successful but also deeply fulfilling.

So, whether you're planning the perfect date, leading the charge in your career, or simply being your awesome, confident self, know that North is a powerful position to be in. Use your strengths wisely, stay open to growth, and enjoy the incredible journey of love and life.

CHAPTER 3

The East Position

Being around an East is like being caught up in a whirlwind of energy and excitement. They bring this spontaneous, adventurous vibe wherever they go, and it's hard not to get swept up in their enthusiasm. An East is the life of the party, always ready to try something new, crack a joke, or throw out a crazy idea that somehow sounds perfect in the moment.

Conversations with an East are never boring—they're lively, full of laughter, and can bounce from one topic to another without missing a beat. If you're feeling stuck or in need of some inspiration, being around an East can feel like a breath of fresh air. They have this magnetic charm that makes you feel like anything is possible, and they often come up with creative solutions to problems you didn't even know had options.

However, their energy can sometimes be a bit overwhelming if you're someone who likes structure and plans. They can change direction in a flash, and what was the plan ten minutes ago might not be anymore! But that's part of the fun with an East—you never quite know what adventure you'll end up on. They're always ready to explore, whether it's a new idea, a new place, or a new way of thinking.

In short, being with an East feels exciting, unpredictable, and full of possibilities. If you want to shake things up or add a spark to your life, having an East around will definitely keep things interesting!

Key Traits of an East

Adaptable and Upbeat: Easts are incredibly flexible and can easily adjust to new situations. Their positive attitude and energetic spirit make them a joy to be around.

Charming and Energetic: They have a natural charm that draws people in and an infectious energy that keeps everyone entertained.

Curious and Innovative: Easts are always looking for new ideas and experiences. Their curiosity drives them to explore and innovate in all aspects of life.

Spontaneous and Impulsive: They love spontaneity and often make decisions on the fly. This can lead to exciting adventures and unexpected fun.

Sociable and Engaging: Easts thrive in social settings. They love meeting new people and engaging in lively conversations.

Playful and Fun: They bring a sense of playfulness to everything they do. Life with an East is never dull!

Charismatic: Their natural charisma makes them effective in social and professional environments, often leading by inspiring others.

Energetic: They possess a high level of energy, always ready to take on new adventures and challenges.

Optimistic: Easts have a positive outlook on life, seeing opportunities where others see obstacles.

Engaging: They have a knack for drawing people into their world, making interactions lively and memorable.

Challenging Attributes

Impulsive: Easts can act on a whim without fully considering the consequences, leading to hasty and sometimes regrettable decisions.

Unreliable: Their love for spontaneity and new experiences can make them inconsistent and unreliable in commitments.

Easily Distracted: Easts often struggle with focus, getting sidetracked by new ideas or activities and leaving tasks unfinished.

Superficial: Their tendency to seek excitement and novelty can sometimes result in shallow interactions and a lack of deeper connections.

Attention-Seeking: Easts may constantly crave attention and validation from others, which can come off as needy or self-centered.

Restless: They can become easily bored and restless, always looking for the next thrill, which can make it hard for them to settle down and appreciate stability.

Overly Optimistic: Easts often have an unwavering positive outlook, which can lead them to underestimate challenges or overlook potential risks. This excessive optimism can result in unrealistic expectations and disappointment when things don't go as planned.

Contrary: Easts being contrary often means a reluctance to follow the crowd or agree just for the sake of harmony, they need to contradict is a need to feel like they have a say. Easts enjoy marching to the beat of their own drum, preferring to do things their own way rather than conform to established norms. They tend to resist going along with others' plans, finding more excitement and fulfillment in carving out a unique path or offering an alternative approach.

Resistant to Routine: Easts tend to resist routine and repetitive tasks, finding them monotonous and stifling. This aversion to routine can hinder their ability to maintain consistency in long-term projects or responsibilities, leading to struggles with sustained productivity and discipline.

Dealing with Overcommitment: Their love for new experiences can sometimes lead to overcommitment. Easts need to learn to prioritize and say no when necessary to avoid burnout.

Balancing Work and Play: An adventurous spirit might lead an East to prioritize fun over work. They must set boundaries and ensure they're giving enough time and energy to both areas.

Managing Expectations: High expectations can be motivating, but they can also lead to disappointment. Easts have a tendency to get excited about new possibilities but struggle to narrow things down and stay focused. They need to keep this in mind as they navigate expectations in relationships.

Avoiding Impulsiveness: While spontaneity is a strength, impulsiveness can lead to hasty decisions. Easts benefit when they take time to think things through before making major decisions. It helps to talk to others and know positional tendencies to avoid constant chaos.

Handling Criticism: Easts can take criticism as a personal fault and feel extreme embarrassment that can lead them to defend themselves rather than recognizing and appreciating what is being said about them. Recognizing that different positions say things in different ways is helpful in not getting feelings hurt and spiraling out of control.

Common Reactions of Easts Under Stress

Under stress, the strengths of an East can become pitfalls:

Migrating: The East may move on quickly, preferring to leave rather than confront issues.

Influence: They will try to convince others through their dynamic talking and negotiation skills. They will try to talk you into it. They are great at this. They attract people with their energy, imagination, and ingenuity. They are dynamic talkers and influencers. Easts often excel at negotiation.

Self-Sacrifice: They may take risks to prove themselves, often putting themselves in challenging situations. They may literally jump in front of a bus to convince you or others to do what they think needs to be done. Easts think that they need to be the ones to go first or show others by doing something daring or different. This gets them identity, and it's in their nature to prove to others that Easts are not chickens.

Would Rather Be Free: Easts will go to great lengths for freedom, often seeking an escape route when stressed. Easts will go to the ends of the earth to get their freedom, often despite others and themselves, when their survival concern gets the best of them. They will feel terrible about it later and beat themselves up with conversations running through their heads, then search for another way to escape.

Break Down Judgment: Easts may label others as "chickens" for resisting change and struggling with environments that impede new ideas. East are natural social risk takers. They thrive in environments that bring challenges, new ideas, and different approaches, and they can struggle in situations where others are trying to impede change out of fear of upsetting the status quo.

Confuses with Accomplishment: Making connections with others. Talking and relationships are central, but Easts may struggle to turn talk into action and see things through to completion.

Key Struggle for Each Position

Each position struggles with different challenges, but there is one for each position that is persistent and based on their survival concern. This concern manifests in different ways. Seeing how these persistent biological concerns play out for each position can be extremely helpful in gauging how to navigate the game of love.

East individuals often struggle with doing things the way they are asked due to their survival concern for freedom.

Desire for Freedom and Independence: Easts are driven by a strong desire for freedom and independence. They value their ability to explore, innovate, and try new things. This desire often conflicts with following prescribed methods or directions from others, which can feel restrictive and limiting to them.

Creativity and Spontaneity: Easts are inherently creative and spontaneous. They enjoy thinking outside the box and coming up with unique solutions. Following someone else's way may stifle their creativity and spontaneity, making them feel constrained and less engaged.

Energetic and Enthusiastic Nature: Easts bring a lot of energy and enthusiasm to their endeavors. They thrive in dynamic environments where they can act on impulse and seize opportunities. Structured methods or detailed instructions can dampen their enthusiasm and make tasks feel monotonous.

Openness to New Experiences: Easts are naturally curious and open to new experiences. They enjoy experimenting and discovering different ways of doing things. Rigid adherence to others' ways can feel like a missed opportunity for exploration and learning.

Resistance to Routine: Easts often resist routine and predictability. They prefer variety and excitement in their activities. Being asked to follow a specific way of doing things can feel like falling into a routine, which they typically try to avoid.

Seeking Personal Expression: Easts value personal expression and authenticity. They want their actions to reflect their personality and ideas. Doing things exactly as others ask can feel like a suppression of their true self and creativity.

Lack of Consistency and Follow-Through: Easts' desire to do things their own way often leads them to start new projects or ideas with great enthusiasm but struggle to follow through consistently. Their preference for flexibility and spontaneity can result in a lack of discipline and consistency.

How the Concern for Freedom Can Manifest in an East's Life

Incomplete Projects: Easts may have many unfinished projects or ideas. They often start with high energy but lose interest or move on to something else before completing the initial task.

Difficulty in Career Advancement: In professional settings, their inconsistent follow-through can hinder career advancement. Employers and colleagues may see them as unreliable or lacking commitment to long-term goals.

Strained Relationships: Personal relationships can be affected as friends, family, and partners may feel frustrated with Easts' unpredictability and failure to keep promises or commitments.

Financial Instability: The lack of consistent effort and follow-through can lead to financial instability. Easts might struggle to maintain a steady income or stick to a budget, leading to financial stress.

Health and Wellness: An East's addictive nature can lead to unhealthy habits and behaviors, such as overindulgence in food, alcohol, or risky activities, which can negatively impact their physical and mental well-being.

Difficulty in Long-Term Planning: Easts might struggle with long-term planning and goal setting. Their preference for living in the moment can make it challenging to set and achieve long-term objectives, leading to a sense of aimlessness or lack of direction.

An East's biological concern for freedom helps explain why Easts struggle with direction. Recognizing these manifestations can help us understand Easts and recognize their desire for autonomy and spontaneity in their lives. It's not about being difficult or rebellious; it's a reflection of their natural inclinations and how they engage with the world. By acknowledging these tendencies, Easts can work on finding a balance between their need for freedom and the occasional necessity to adhere to others' guidelines, especially in collaborative or structured environments.

Clues:

Here are some clues that will help you identify an East in your investigations:

Learning: Easts learn by talking, asking questions, and making connections.

Assessment vs. Projection: They project sincerity and care, often seen as persuaders.

Thought vs. Action: Easts tend to act before thinking, thriving on spontaneity.

Speaking from "Could": They see endless possibilities, which can make decision-making difficult.

Communication Style: Easts may exaggerate to entertain or maintain relationships, sometimes creating doubt about authenticity.

Accused Of: Easts may be seen as unpredictable or unreliable due to their comfort with change and variety.

How East Plays Their Position
East in Relationships

When it comes to relationships, Easts bring a sense of fun and adventure. Here's how being this position can play out in an East's love life:

Dynamic and Fun Relationships: Easts bring excitement and spontaneity to their relationships. They love trying new things and keeping the romance alive with fun and adventurous activities.

Engaging Communication: With an East, conversations are always lively and engaging. They love sharing ideas and hearing new perspectives, making every interaction interesting.

Passionate and Enthusiastic: Easts are passionate and enthusiastic lovers. Their zest for life translates into a passionate approach to love and relationships.

Flexible and Open-Minded: They are open to new experiences and willing to adapt to their partner's needs and desires. This flexibility makes them easy to be with and highly supportive.

Innovative Problem Solvers: When challenges arise, Easts approach them with creativity and innovation. They are great at coming up with unique solutions to keep the relationship thriving.

Attention Seekers: Easts love being the center of attention and need a partner who appreciates their vibrant personality and doesn't mind sharing the spotlight.

Empathetic: They are good at understanding their partner's emotions and needs, often providing the support and encouragement needed.

In The Wild-

Here are ways that Easts show up in life, what it's like to be around them.

Easts in relationships bring vibrant energy, spontaneity, and a love for expression. They often speak with a lively, animated style, sometimes exaggerating to make their point or to entertain. When they're trying hard to convince their partner, they can be prone to a bit of dramatics, but it's all part of their charm. You'll often find Easts as the jokester, the one lighting up the room with their humor and playful nature.

Living in the moment is what Easts do best. They don't typically worry about how they're being perceived in real-time, but later, they may replay conversations in their heads and wonder if they "said too much" or overshared. Easts are naturally open and might tell you their life story within minutes of meeting, and in relationships, they'll often give a lot of themselves upfront.

Easts are full of energy, always on the move, talking, and getting things done. They throw themselves into life and relationships with everything they've got, and by the end of the day, they crash—only to wake up and do it all over again. Their energy comes in bursts, cycling between high exertion and deep exhaustion.

When they're interested in something or someone, you won't be able to pull them away. They can seem scattered, but when something captures their attention, they're laser-focused. Their minds are always racing, and they might tell their partner how mentally tired they are from keeping up with their thoughts. Pacing themselves isn't easy for Easts.

Timing is everything with an East. If you interrupt them while they're in the middle of something, they might get frustrated, so it's best to wait for the right moment. And don't try to tell them what to do— Easts are hard-wired for action and freedom. If they feel like they're being restrained, whether by routine, tasks, or expectations, they'll resist it and find a way to break free.

Easts love stories—telling them, hearing them, and living them. They are expressive and colorful, and in relationships, they like to keep things interesting and fun. Boring is not a word you'd use to describe an East. They thrive on being unpredictable, lively, and sometimes a little chaotic, bringing a sense of adventure to their relationships.

Sometimes, Easts can be misunderstood in love. They don't always fit in with traditional expectations because they live life on their own terms. They're free-spirited and sometimes have a hard time in environments that feel too structured or restrictive. If they feel hurt or shut down in a relationship, they may retreat emotionally, but their lively nature usually brings them back quickly.

In social situations, Easts shine. They love meeting new people and engaging in meaningful conversations. However, if they feel like the crowd isn't their type, they'll withdraw or leave, seeking out a space where they feel more connected. They're sensitive, and if their feelings get hurt, they may need time to process before they bounce back.

Drama is a part of an East's life—not necessarily in a negative way, but because they love excitement and storytelling. They create their own movie in their head, living out their relationship as a dynamic narrative. This can make relationships with an East feel like an adventure full of laughter, surprises, and big moments.

East often apologizes, not necessarily because they're at fault, but because they want to ensure the relationship is okay. They'll take the blame if it helps smooth things over, wanting to move forward and maintain harmony.

Easts are also natural negotiators in relationships. They love exploring new directions and finding ways to make things work. They thrive on challenges and will often turn relationship hurdles into opportunities for discovery and growth.

Freedom is essential for an East. They don't want to feel trapped or cornered in a relationship. They'll always look for ways to maintain their independence, whether it's having their own space or ensuring they're not tied down by rigid plans. They need to know they can move freely, both physically and emotionally.

Easts are incredibly empathetic in relationships and are often deeply in tune with what their partner is feeling. However, their sensitivity can sometimes cause them to take things personally, overreacting to situations that weren't even about them. They may dramatize an issue, but once they understand the bigger picture, they're quick to adjust.

Their fear of losing freedom can make commitment difficult at times. They may get bored easily or struggle with routine, but when this fear is harnessed, Easts can push themselves to overcome obstacles and bring a sense of creativity and excitement to the relationship. They may have fewer long-term relationships, but those they do form are deeply meaningful and strong.

Easts can get overstimulated easily in busy environments, so they tend to avoid chaotic places like large stores or restaurants with too much going on. They need quiet and space to recharge, and distractions like a television during dinner can pull their attention away.

Because Easts crave acceptance, they may avoid "closing the deal" in relationships out of fear of upsetting their partner or disrupting the fun. They're eternal optimists, always chasing the next possibility, which can sometimes make them lose sight of the stability needed to keep a relationship grounded.

Talking and relating are East strengths, but these skills can become a curse without restraint and awareness. It's not uncommon for an East to over sell, over explain or over share.

East is a naturally competitive position that loves to entertain others. This inclination can lead them to hog the conversation and leave too little room for others to participate. East needs to focus hard on listening rather than thinking about what they're going to say next.

East can struggle with focus. Easts tends to be looking at what already is and how it could be better. All those better possibilities can distract an East who isn't dead set on a mission.

East excels at flushing out ideas and generating excitement, but at some point, those ideas must be organized into an action plan. East often struggles with this because they LOVE the process of discussing ideas and building relationships, so when it's time to create an action plan, it calls an end to all that fun.

Easts are great at thinking aloud. In relationships, they'll often speak before fully forming their thoughts, leading to spontaneous and often amusing conversations. They're not concerned with being right, but more interested in exploring ideas with their partner.

Rules and routine aren't a good fit for an East in love. They get impatient with anything that feels too structured or limiting, preferring to break free and explore new possibilities. To keep an East engaged, it's best to give them freedom and challenge them to find creative solutions.

Easts are passionate, talkative, and empathic partners. They are outgoing and friendly, often putting the needs of others before their own. However, this can sometimes lead them to overextend themselves, leaving projects or emotional matters unfinished because they've taken on too much.

They love a challenge and will often compete with their partner in a playful, exciting way. They can be dramatic in their approach to love, using big gestures and expressive language to communicate. Recognition and validation from their partner mean a lot to them, and they're drawn to relationships that feel successful and dynamic.

At their best, Easts bring an infectious energy to their relationships, helping their partner see new perspectives and discover new possibilities. They love acting on impulse and creating spontaneous, joyful moments that keep their relationship alive and full of excitement.

If there was a T-shirt for East, it might say:

"Fire, Aim, Ready" "Let's Go" "Chasing Dreams and Butterflies" "Spontaneity is My Superpower" "Let's Make This Fun!"

Lastly, we are going to cover the elemental aspects of East and then their spirit animals.

The Essence of Fire

Easts carry the energy of a flame— bright and always moving. They're on the lookout for the next adventure, driven by curiosity and a love for exploring new ideas and experiences. They're the ones who never seem to slow down, ready for what's around the corner.

In the Embrace of Spring

Spring is where Easts truly thrive. Like the season itself, they bring renewal, growth, and a sense of fresh beginnings. Easts are at their best when they're starting something new, whether it's a project, a relationship, or even just a fun new hobby. They live for the excitement of new possibilities and the thrill of change.

The Virtue of Valor

Easts have this boldness about them—a courageous spirit that pushes them forward, even when things are uncertain. Their bravery is what allows them to take risks, try new things, and face the unknown without hesitation. For them, life is about discovery, and they're always up for a new challenge.

The Hemisphere of Offense

Easts are on the move, engaging with the world around them in the most energetic way. They're innovators and adventurers at heart, driven by a need for freedom and a passion for the unknown. Whether they're planning the next big trip or brainstorming a new idea, Easts are seeking excitement and novelty.

Just for Fun: East's Spirit Animals

Fox: Clever, adaptable, and resourceful, reflecting the East's social skills and charm.

Dolphin: Social, intelligent, and playful, mirroring the East's joy in engaging with others.

Hummingbird: Energetic and agile, much like the East's dynamic spirit.

Parrot: Bright and expressive, embodying the East's adaptability and engaging communication style.

Monkey: Playful, curious, and mischievous, the monkey reflects the East's love for adventure and its ability to think on its feet. Like an East, monkeys are quick-witted and thrive in social settings, always finding creative solutions and having fun while doing it.

As we conclude our exploration of the East position within the 4Cross Love Framework, we are reminded of the essential vibrancy and dynamism that East brings to the fabric of love and human interaction. Their innate ability to adapt, innovate, and inspire speaks to the core of what makes relationships thrive—growth, understanding, and the joy of discovery.

Embracing Your East

If you identify as an East, embrace your vibrant energy. Your charm and enthusiasm can light up any room and create unforgettable experiences. Just remember to balance your spontaneity with consistency and empathy, and you'll build relationships that are not only exciting but also deeply fulfilling.

So, whether you're planning the next big adventure, sparking lively conversations, or simply being your dynamic self, know that East is a fantastic position to be in. Use your strengths wisely, stay open to growth, and enjoy the incredible journey of love and life.

CHAPTER 4

The South Position

"In the game of love, what is important to know is when to

hold on and when to let go."-Anonymous

Being around a South feels like wrapping yourself in a cozy blanket—there's this warmth and calmness that instantly puts you at ease. Souths are the natural caretakers of the group, always making sure everyone feels included, supported, and comfortable. They're the ones who will remember your birthday, check in on you when you're feeling down, and are always there to listen.

If you're having a rough day, a South will be the first to offer a shoulder to lean on or some encouraging words. They bring a sense of stability and emotional security to every situation, which makes it easy to relax and open up around them. They're not flashy or loud, but there's a quiet strength in the way they hold space for others, making them reliable and dependable.

Souths are all about harmony and connection. They want everyone to get along and are often the peacemakers in a group. Their focus on keeping things peaceful and balanced can sometimes make them avoid conflict, but it's because they genuinely care about maintaining a strong emotional bond with the people around them. They make you feel valued, heard, and cared for, and they're often the glue that holds relationships and friendships together.

Spending time with a South feels comforting and safe. They're not about drama or excitement—they're about real connection, support, and making sure everyone feels like they belong. If you need someone to count on, someone who will be there through thick and thin, a South is the person you want by your side.

Key Traits of a South

Supportive and Responsible: Souths are incredibly reliable and always there to support their loved ones. They take their responsibilities seriously and can be counted on in any situation.

Compassionate and Understanding: They have a deep sense of empathy and understanding, making them great listeners and friends.

Loyal and Steady: Souths are the definition of loyal. They stand by their loved ones through thick and thin and provide a steady presence in their lives.

Patient and Tolerant: They exhibit a great deal of patience and tolerance, which helps them maintain harmony in their relationships and environments.

Affectionate and Warm: Souths are naturally warm and affectionate, creating a comforting and welcoming atmosphere wherever they go.

Grounded and Practical: They have a grounded and practical approach to life, making them great at managing everyday tasks and challenges.

Inclusive: Souths are inclusive by nature, ensuring that everyone feels valued and part of the group.

Reliable: Their reliability makes them the rock in any relationship or team.

Diligent: Souths are hardworking and dedicated, often taking on more than their share to ensure everything runs smoothly.

Stabilizing: They provide stability and reassurance, creating a sense of security for those around them.

Challenging Attributes

Overly Dependent: Souths can become too reliant on others for validation and support, potentially neglecting their own needs and autonomy.

Avoidant: They may avoid confrontation and difficult conversations, leading to unresolved issues and suppressed feelings.

Overprotective: Their nurturing nature can sometimes become smothering, inhibiting the independence and growth of those they care about.

Self-Sacrificing: Souths often put others' needs before their own to the point of self-neglect, leading to burnout and resentment.

Stubborn: In their desire to maintain stability, they may resist necessary changes and new ideas, clinging to the status quo even when it's no longer beneficial.

Passive: They can struggle with assertiveness, allowing others to take advantage of their kindness and failing to stand up for themselves when needed.

Conflict-Averse: Souths may go to great lengths to avoid conflict, which can result in them agreeing to things they don't truly support or suppressing their own opinions and desires. This can lead to internal resentment and unresolved issues within relationships.

Overly Sensitive: Souths often have heightened emotional sensitivity, which can lead to them being easily hurt by criticism or negative feedback. This sensitivity can cause them to take things personally and struggle with maintaining emotional balance in stressful situations.

Dealing with Burnout: Their hardworking and giving nature can sometimes lead to exhaustion. Knowing this about their position can give a South permission to stop and take a breath to avoid sickness.

Balancing Work and Personal Life: Their sense of responsibility might lead them to prioritize others over themselves. Being aware of this will allow a South to navigate relationships more effectively, ensuring they're giving enough time and energy to both areas.

Managing Expectations: Having high expectations about getting everything done and making sure everyone is happy can be motivating, but it can also lead to disappointment. Noticing this can help a South realize that it all works out in the end, not at the end of their endless to-do lists.

Avoiding Overcommitment: While their supportive nature is a strength, overcommitting can lead to stress. When a South knows they have a tendency to do too much, it will help them learn to prioritize and say no when necessary.

Handling Criticism: Souths can sometimes take criticism to heart, thinking that they haven't done enough to make others happy. They feel disappointed in themselves. Remembering that the concern behind criticism comes from different perspectives will help a South learn to listen for the intent and not take it so personally.

Common Reactions of Souths Under Stress

Under stress, the strengths of a South can become pitfalls:

Tolerate: Souths will often endure unpleasant situations or people to avoid conflict and maintain harmony.

Power Through: They push themselves to keep going and manage their responsibilities despite feeling overwhelmed or stressed.

Undermine/Gossip: Under stress, they might resort to undermining others or gossiping as a way to indirectly address their frustrations.

Would Rather: Souths prefer to avoid direct confrontation and would rather compromise or give in to keep the peace.

Breaking Down Judgment: When stressed, they may judge others harshly for causing disruption, not working hard enough, or failing to maintain harmony, seeing them as inconsiderate or uncooperative.

Confusing Being Busy with Accomplishment: Souths often equate being busy with productivity, sometimes losing sight of the bigger picture and focusing on tasks that may not be the most important.

Here are some descriptive words that will help you understand the challenges Souths can face in playing the game of love:

Key Struggle for Each Position

Each position struggles with different challenges, but there is one for each position that is persistent and based on their survival concern. This concern manifests in different ways. Seeing how these persistent biological concerns play out for each position can be extremely helpful in gauging how to navigate the game of love.

South individuals often struggle with change due to their survival concern for stability.

Desire for Stability: Souths value stability above all else. They thrive in environments where they feel safe, supported, and consistent. Change often disrupts this stability, making them feel unsettled and anxious.

Emotional Attachment: Souths form strong emotional attachments to people, routines, and places. These attachments provide a sense of comfort and belonging. Change can threaten these attachments, leading to feelings of loss and discomfort.

Routine and Predictability: Souths are comfortable with routines and predictability. They find solace in knowing what to expect and having established patterns. Change introduces uncertainty and unpredictability, which can be challenging for them to navigate.

Dependability and Reliability: Souths pride themselves on being dependable and reliable. They often fear that change might compromise their ability to fulfill these roles effectively. Adapting to new situations can feel like a risk to their reliability and dependability.

Emotional Sensitivity: Souths are empathetic and sensitive to their own and others' emotions. Change can stir up a range of emotions, including fear, sadness, and confusion. This emotional upheaval can be overwhelming for Souths, who prefer emotional equilibrium.

Conflict Avoidance: Souths tend to avoid conflict and seek harmony in their relationships. Change can sometimes bring about disagreements or tensions, which Souths find particularly distressing. They might resist change to maintain peace and avoid potential conflicts.

Need for Consensus: Souths often seek consensus and collective agreement. They may struggle with change if they feel it hasn't been fully endorsed or accepted by their group or community. This need for collective support can make them hesitant to embrace change independently.

How the Concern for Stability Can Manifest in a South's Life

Reluctance to Try New Things: Souths may resist trying new activities or experiences suggested by their partner. This can lead to a feeling of stagnation or boredom in the relationship, as their partner might feel their efforts to introduce variety and excitement are not appreciated.

Difficulty Adjusting to Life Transitions: Major life transitions, such as moving to a new home, changing jobs, or having children, can be particularly challenging for Souths. Their resistance to change can cause stress and strain in their relationship as they struggle to adapt and support their partner during these transitions.

Clinging to Routine: Souths often prefer routines and familiar patterns. While routines can provide stability, an excessive adherence to them can make the relationship feel predictable and inflexible. Their partner might feel frustrated by the lack of spontaneity and flexibility.

Avoidance of Conflict Resolution: In relationships, addressing issues often requires change and adaptation. Souths' resistance to change can lead them to avoid necessary conversations and conflict resolution, causing unresolved issues to fester and grow over time.

Dependency on Comfort Zones: Souths may rely heavily on their comfort zones and avoid stepping out of them. This can limit the growth of the relationship, as their partner might feel constrained by the boundaries of these comfort zones and unable to explore new possibilities together.

Fear of Emotional Vulnerability: Change often involves emotional vulnerability and openness. Souths may resist this vulnerability, making it difficult for them to fully open up to their partner. This can hinder emotional intimacy and connection in the relationship.

Resistance to Personal Growth: Personal growth and self-improvement often require embracing change. Souths' resistance to change can result in stagnation in their personal development, which can affect the relationship's overall health and dynamic. Their partner might feel frustrated by the lack of growth and willingness to improve.

Understanding a South's concern for stability can help explain why they struggle with change. It's not about being inflexible or resistant to progress. Instead, it reflects their natural inclination toward stability, emotional safety, and harmony. By acknowledging these tendencies, Souths can recognize how their resistance to change impacts their relationships. As a result, they can develop strategies to manage change more effectively, such as gradually introducing small changes into their routines, seeking support from their partner, and focusing on the benefits of growth and flexibility in fostering a stronger, more dynamic relationship.

Clues:

Here are some clues to how a South act that will help you identify a South in your investigations.

Learning: Souths learn by doing. They favor hands-on work and tangible results.

Assessment vs. Projection: Souths assess your sincerity and trustworthiness, and they are concerned about stability.

Thought vs. Action: Souths favor action over talking. They might say, "Don't just stand there talking. Get to work!"

Speaking from "Have To": When under pressure, Souths focus on the work at hand and the need to be reliable. They feel that they have to get work done.

Communication Style: They are less direct and can take some time to trust enough to communicate openly.

Accused Of: Souths may resist change, even when it's in their best interest, preferring their certain stability over uncertain new possibilities.

In the wild-

Here are ways that Souths show up in life, what it's like to be around them.

Souths are natural builders in relationships—they thrive on creating stability and working hard to make things last. In a healthy relationship, a balanced South is excellent at forming strong partnerships and putting in the work to make the relationship flourish. They take ideas and emotions from their partner and create a stable foundation for the relationship, making sure it can endure for the long term.

Souths are driven by the need for security and peace. They naturally take on the role of protector in relationships, watching over their partner and ensuring the relationship is stable and safe. They can be wary of outsiders or new influences in the relationship, preferring to keep things familiar and predictable. You may literally see a South cross their arms or keep their distance if they feel threatened by something new or uncomfortable.

Their biggest fear in relationships is feeling excluded or unimportant, and they avoid anything that could disrupt the peace they work so hard to maintain. This fear can make Souths resistant to change, especially when it feels like it could shake up the foundation they've built. When faced with relationship challenges, their first instinct is often action: "What can we do to fix this?" They're quick to jump into problem-solving mode, sometimes confusing busyness with true progress. It's not natural for them to step back and look at the big picture, especially when they're caught up in the day-to-day tasks of keeping the relationship going.

Souths may sometimes tolerate issues in a relationship for longer than they should, out of a desire to keep the peace. They might avoid bringing up problems until they've reached a breaking point, hoping things will improve on their own. In love, Souths often lead by example—they show their love through hard work, dependability, and loyalty, hoping that their partner will follow their lead and match their effort.

When things aren't progressing in the relationship, Souths can become impatient. They don't have much interest in abstract discussions about possibilities or feelings—they want to see action and results. As long as things are moving forward and tasks are being completed, Souths are content. If something new is introduced in the relationship, like a new approach to communication or a change in routine, they may resist it. Souths prefer to stick with what they know works, even if a new way could improve things.

Repetition and predictability make Souths feel secure in love. They're drawn to familiar routines and patterns because it brings them comfort. They don't appreciate surprises or changes unless they can see a clear benefit. They'll stick to the same habits and ways of doing things in the relationship, preferring stability over excitement.

In relationships, Souths are incredibly loyal. They form strong bonds with their partner and expect the same level of commitment in return. They don't want people who are just passing through—they want someone who's in it for the long haul. If they sense that their partner isn't fully committed, they may become distant or emotionally guarded, preferring to protect themselves rather than risk getting hurt.

Souths thrive when they know what to do and can get it done. They value hard work in a relationship and will stay up late to make sure everything is in order, whether it's planning a trip or solving an issue with their partner. They find satisfaction in working hard together and will often boast about how much effort they've put into the relationship. For them, love is a team effort, and nothing makes them happier than knowing they've contributed to the success of the partnership.

Souths crave stability, routine, and predictability, making embracing change a significant challenge for them. In relationships, they often find comfort in familiar patterns and can resist any shifts that disrupt their sense of security. This resistance to change can make it hard for them to adapt when their partner suggests new approaches to problem-solving or wants to try something different.

For a South, being busy often feels synonymous with being successful and accomplished, especially in relationships. They take pride in their hard work and commitment, frequently focusing on getting things done and keeping everything running smoothly. However, this emphasis on busyness can become a pitfall when they measure success solely by how much they're doing rather than whether what they're doing is truly moving the relationship forward.

Confrontation poses a direct challenge to the South's core need for peace and stability. They are deeply uncomfortable with conflict because it feels like it threatens the harmony, they work so hard to maintain. In relationships, this means Souths will often go to great lengths to avoid confrontation, even if it comes at their own detriment. They may suppress their feelings, put their own needs aside, or avoid addressing issues that need to be discussed in order to keep the peace.

Souths can become frustrated when their partner doesn't seem to share their work ethic or when they feel like they're carrying the weight of the relationship. They don't tolerate laziness well and can be quick to point out when their partner isn't pulling their weight. Complaining or excuses won't get far with a South—they believe in doing the work, no matter how hard it is.

In relationships, Souths are slow to trust change. They want to stick with what's familiar and safe, preferring not to rock the boat unless absolutely necessary. They might resist new ways of handling conflict or communicating, even if it could improve the relationship, because they prefer to stick with what has worked in the past. They believe in the motto, "If it ain't broke, don't fix it."

Souths are also incredibly patient in relationships. They're willing to wait things out and tolerate discomfort or hardship if it means keeping the relationship intact. They're steadfast and loyal, and they'll go through a lot to maintain harmony. However, if they feel taken advantage of, they can become resentful, especially if they feel like they're doing all the work without being appreciated.

When faced with conflict in relationships, Souths prefer to avoid drama. They dislike anything that disrupts the peace, and if there's tension, they'll often retreat or shut down to avoid escalating the situation. However, if they're pushed too far, Souths can gossip or vent their frustrations, sometimes creating tension behind the scenes to let their feelings be known.

At their core, Souths are dependable, hardworking, and loyal partners. They thrive on building a stable, predictable relationship where they know what's expected of them and can work toward shared goals. They are patient, generous, and always ready to support their partner through thick and thin, as long as they feel appreciated and included in the process.

However, Souths can struggle when they feel their efforts are taken for granted or when they're stuck in a repetitive cycle without progress. They need to feel that their hard work is valued and that the relationship is moving forward, even if it's at a slow and steady pace. They believe that love is built through consistency and effort, and they'll do whatever it takes to make sure the relationship lasts.

If there was a T-shirt for South, it might say: "Git er done" "Can't we all get along?" "It is what it is" "Suck it up buttercup"

Lastly, we are going to cover the elemental aspects of South and then their spirit animals.

The Essence of Earth

Souths are the ones who keep everything grounded. They bring this calm, reliable energy that makes you feel safe and supported. Whether it's in relationships or just everyday life, Souths are the foundation that holds things together. You'll always feel a sense of stability when they're around.

In the Warmth of Summer

Summer is where Souths truly shine. Just like summer brings warmth and abundance, Souths create that same sense of harmony and growth in their relationships. They're all about making sure everyone feels included, loved, and taken care of, fostering an environment where bonds can grow strong.

The Virtue of Justice

Souths have a deep sense of fairness. They're always looking out for others, making sure everyone's needs are met with kindness and compassion. It's not just about being fair—it's about understanding and supporting people in a way that makes everyone feel valued and heard.

The Hemisphere of Defense

Souths are the protectors and peacekeepers. They focus on keeping things stable and preserving harmony in their relationships. Driven by a need for connection and belonging, they do whatever it takes to maintain that sense of balance and inclusivity in their circle.

Souths are the glue that holds everything together. They're the caregivers, the ones who always make sure everyone is okay, and the peacemakers who step in to smooth things over when needed. If you're the one people come to for comfort, or if you're always making sure everyone feels included and supported, you might just be a South.

Just for Fun: South's Spirit Animals

Elephant: Elephants' strong sense of community and family aligns with the South's support and reliability.

Deer: Deer symbolize gentleness and grace, embodying the South's kind-hearted approach.

Dog: Dogs represent loyalty, protection, and unconditional love, mirroring the South's nature.

Swan: Swans' grace and beauty reflect the South's compassionate character and commitment.

Buffalo: A buffalo makes a great spirit animal for the South position because it embodies —strength, stability, nurturing, and community.

The exploration of the South position within the 4Cross Framework highlights the indispensable role they play in weaving the fabric of love and connection. South's embodiment of nurturing warmth, emotional depth, and unwavering support serves as a reminder of the fundamental human need for belonging and care. Their ability to cultivate harmony, encourage growth, and bridge differences enriches our collective journey, teaching us the value of empathy, patience, and the strength found in unity.

Embracing Your South

If you identify as a South, embrace your nurturing energy. Your compassion and reliability make you a pillar of strength in both your personal and professional lives. If you remember to balance your giving nature with self-care and assertiveness, you'll create relationships that are not only stable but also deeply fulfilling.

So, whether you're organizing a cozy gathering, supporting your friends through tough times, or simply being your warm, caring self, know that South is a beautiful position to be in. Use your strengths wisely and enjoy the incredible journey of love and life.

59

CHAPTER 5

The West Position

Being around a West feels like having everything perfectly in order—there's a sense of calm precision that they naturally bring to any situation. Wests are the detail-oriented thinkers, the ones who notice things others might overlook and make sure everything is running smoothly. They have a quiet, steady energy that helps keep things on track, and you can always count on them to be organized and thorough.

Conversations with a West tend to be thoughtful and deliberate. They're not in a rush to jump to conclusions or make decisions without all the facts. If you're discussing something important, they'll take the time to analyze the details and make sure nothing is missed. This can be incredibly grounding, especially if you're feeling uncertain or overwhelmed—they'll slow things down and give you a clear, logical perspective.

Wests aren't big on surprises or spontaneity; they prefer structure and predictability. They thrive in environments where they can plan, organize, and make sure everything is just right. While this attention to detail can sometimes come across as perfectionism, it also means they're reliable and won't leave anything to chance. You can trust that when a West is involved, the job will be done well.

Being around a West feels stable, thoughtful, and meticulously organized. They bring a sense of calm through their methodical approach, and they're always looking for ways to improve things. If you appreciate having someone who sees the details and ensures that things run smoothly, a West is the perfect person to have in your corner.

Key Traits of a West

Methodical and Precise: Wests are thorough and detail oriented. They approach tasks with a meticulous eye and ensure everything is done correctly.

Organized and Structured: They have a natural ability to create order and structure in their environment.

Analytical and Logical: Wests have strong, analytical minds and rely on logic to solve problems. They excel at breaking down complex issues into manageable parts.

Reliable and Dependable: They can be counted on to follow through on their commitments. Their reliability makes them trusted friends and colleagues.

Practical and Realistic: Wests are grounded in reality and have a practical approach to life. They focus on what is feasible and efficient.

Persistent and Tenacious: They are determined and persistent, often going the extra mile to achieve their goals and ensure high standards.

Prudent: The West's decisions are made with care and consideration, ensuring that long-term consequences are taken into account.

Introspective: The West reflects deeply on their thoughts and actions, striving for a deeper understanding.

Prepared: The West is prepared, considering all eventualities and having a plan in place.

Traditional and Conventional: Wests often value tradition and conventional methods, finding comfort in established norms and procedures.

Challenging Attributes

Overly Critical: Wests can be excessively critical of themselves and others, focusing too much on flaws and imperfections.

Rigid: They may struggle with flexibility, sticking rigidly to rules and plans even when adaptability is needed.

Overbearing: Their meticulous nature can sometimes lead to micromanaging and controlling behavior, making it difficult for others to feel trusted or autonomous.

Perfectionist: Wests can become paralyzed by their pursuit of perfection, leading to procrastination or difficulty in making decisions.

Indecisive: This manifests in several ways. One is an over accumulation of stuff they may or may not need someday.

Overly Cautious: Their careful and methodical approach can sometimes translate into excessive caution, preventing them from taking necessary risks or making timely decisions.

Reluctant to Delegate: Wests often struggle with delegating tasks to others due to their high standards and desire for precision. This can lead to them taking on too much work themselves, resulting in stress and burnout.

Emotionally Detached: Wests can sometimes appear emotionally detached or distant because of their focus on standards and analysis. This detachment can make it hard for them to connect with others on an emotional level, potentially leading to strained relationships and misunderstandings.

Dealing with Perfectionism: Their drive for perfection can sometimes lead to stress. So, Wests need to learn to recognize when good enough is sufficient and avoid overburdening themselves.

Balancing Work and Personal Life: Their sense of accountability might lead them to prioritize work over personal relationships. Recognizing that their position has this propensity will grant them the freedom to ensure they're giving enough time and energy to both areas.

Managing Expectations: Having high expectations of making an impact can be motivating, but it can also lead to never feeling good enough or not having enough time to get it done perfectly. Realizing this about their nature can help Wests take things in stride and appreciate all aspects of the cycle.

Avoiding Rigidity: While their structured nature is a strength, being too rigid can limit a West's flexibility. They can benefit from learning to embrace spontaneity and being open to new experiences.

Handling Criticism: Wests can sometimes take criticism to heart, thinking they can't do anything right. Remembering that there are other views on how things are done can help them see through the actual criticism and glean valuable feedback about how to move forward.

Common Reactions of Wests Under Stress

Under stress, the strengths of a West can become pitfalls:

Hibernate: Under stress, Wests go to their survival comfort zone of thinking and studying, often leading to procrastination and avoidance. When a West is asked to decide or act in an area where they don't feel they can get sufficient certainty from facts and precedent, it's not uncommon for them to "go dark" or avoid you.

Authority: Wests seek authority as a means of effecting change, excelling in established and systematized fields but sometimes hiding behind rules and regulations to avoid responsibility. Technical positions like administration, IT, law, finance, government, law enforcement wand, and research are attractive to West because they are established and systematized. They excel at going deep in their domains and thrive on being asked to share their knowledge. The downside is that they have a tendency to confuse the "letter of the law from the intent of the law." This can cause them to "hide" behind rules and regulations as a means of not taking responsibility for their actions.

Betray and Subordinate: Their indecision can lead to betrayal, as they may support at the last minute the side that appears most secure. What they're doing is biding their time to see which side will prevail, and at the last minute, they'll jump on the secure ship. Their choice can catch you completely off guard, and it feels like a betrayal.

Irreplaceable: Under stress, a West may use system complexity and legacy knowledge to make themselves irreplaceable.

Break Down Judgment: Wests dislike inefficiency and poor craftsmanship, often working to plug every possible failure point—sometimes at the expense of the bigger picture. They believe they are making an impact by constantly trying to plug every possible failure point. The challenge here lies in the saying, "the juice isn't worth the squeeze." Too often West will work in the name of increasing efficiency and security without seeing the bigger picture impact.

Confusing Reflection with Accomplishment: Wests may confuse constant reflection and analysis with accomplishment, needing to use their knowledge productively.

Key Struggle for Each Position

Each position struggles with different challenges, but there is one for each position that is persistent and based on their survival concern. This concern manifests in different ways. Seeing how these persistent biological concerns play out for each position can be extremely helpful in gauging how to navigate the game of love.

West individuals often struggle with decision-making due to their survival concern for security.

Need for Accuracy: Wests value accuracy in what they do. They often feel the need to gather all possible information and analyze every detail before making a decision. This can lead to paralysis by analysis, in which they become so caught up in the details that they struggle to make a final choice.

Fear of Making Mistakes: Wests are detail oriented and methodical, which makes them keenly aware of the potential consequences of their decisions. This awareness can make them overly cautious, as they fear making mistakes and prefer to avoid risks.

Desire for Thoroughness: Wests strive for thoroughness and completeness in their decision-making process. They often want to consider every possible angle and outcome, which can delay decision-making as they seek to cover all bases.

High Standards: Wests often have high standards and detailed mindsets. They want to ensure that their decisions are the best possible ones, which can lead to overthinking and difficulty in settling on a choice.

Analytical and Logical Thinking: Wests approach decisions analytically and logically. While this is a strength, it can also be a hindrance when decisions require intuition or there is no clear, logical answer. They may struggle to make decisions in ambiguous or uncertain situations.

Tendency to Overthink: Wests are prone to overthinking, continuously weighing the pros and cons and considering various scenarios. This can make it difficult for them to get rid of things they may or may not need someday, leading to overaccumulation of junk. This overthinking can lead to indecision, as they get stuck in an endless loop of consideration.

Reluctance to Delegate: Wests may struggle with delegating decisions to others because they trust their own thoroughness and attention to detail. This can lead to them taking on too much responsibility and further complicating their decision-making process.

How the Concern for Security Can Manifest in a West's Life

Delayed Decisions: Wests often take longer to make a decision, whether about career moves, personal relationships, or daily choices. This delay can sometimes result in missed opportunities.

Second-Guessing: After making a decision, Wests may frequently second-guess themselves, revisiting their choice and questioning if it was the right one. This can lead to stress and anxiety.

Difficulty in Choosing Between Options: When presented with multiple options, Wests may struggle to choose one. They may spend a lot of time comparing the options, trying to find the perfect solution, which can be exhausting and time-consuming.

Avoidance of Decision-Making: In some cases, Wests might avoid making decisions altogether, hoping that more information will become available or that circumstances will change to make the decision clearer.

Reliance on Rules and Guidelines: To cope with their decision-making struggles, Wests may rely heavily on rules, guidelines, or advice from trusted sources. While this can be helpful, it can also limit their ability to make independent decisions.

Stress and Frustration: The pressure to make the right decision and the fear of making mistakes can lead to significant stress and frustration for Wests. This stress can affect their overall well-being and productivity.

Impact on Relationships: Wests' decision-making struggles can impact their relationships, as partners or colleagues may become impatient with their indecisiveness. This can lead to tension and misunderstandings.

Understanding a West's need for security can explain why they struggle with making decisions. It's not about being indecisive or hesitant; it's a reflection of their natural inclination toward thoroughness, precision, and a desire for order. By acknowledging these tendencies, Wests can work on developing strategies to make decisions more effectively, such as setting deadlines for decision-making, prioritizing key factors, and learning to trust their instincts when appropriate.

Clues:

Here are some clues that will help you identify a West in your investigations:

Learning: Wests look to data and precedents for decision-making, excelling in traditional education.

Assessment vs. Projection: Wests project their competence. They want to be seen as competent, often convincing others of their indispensability.

Thought vs. Action: Wests think before speaking, especially about topics they know well.

Speaking from "We Ought to Have": Wests speak based on gathered information, focusing on past evidence.

Communication Style: They wait, concealing their true feelings until they feel secure enough to tell you their well-thought-out opinion about how to do things correctly.

Accused Of: Impeding progress and pointing out what's wrong. Wests may slow progress by focusing on potential pitfalls and security.

How West Plays Their Position

West in Relationships

When it comes to relationships, Wests bring a sense of order and reliability. Here's how being in this position can play out in a West's love life:

Pensive: The West is frequently pensive, lost in thought as they ponder the various facets of a problem and consider all angles before coming to a decision.

Thoughtful and Considerate: Wests think things through before acting, making them considerate and thoughtful partners who take their loved ones' feelings into account.

Detail-Oriented Planners: They are great at planning and organizing, which makes them good at arranging thoughtful dates and memorable experiences.

Logical Problem Solvers: Wests approach relationship challenges with logic and practicality, often finding effective solutions to problems.

Value Consistency: They appreciate routine and consistency in their relationships, which helps create a stable and secure environment.

Persistent Support: Their determination ensures they support their partners through all challenges, fostering a reliable and stable relationship.

Emotionally Steady: Wests maintain emotional steadiness, providing a calming influence in the relationship.

In The Wild

Wests in relationships thrive on analysis and careful thought. They are the partners who will notice small details, pick up on subtle shifts in tone, and remember everything you've said from previous conversations. They're naturally inclined to spot problems or inconsistencies, and they take pride in being the one who ensures things are done the "right" way. However, their greatest challenge in relationships is decision-making, as they often get caught up in weighing every possible consequence before moving forward. Wests excel in gathering information and reflecting on outcomes but tend to hesitate when it's time to choose a direction.

In relationships, Wests can be your biggest support, always keeping an eye on potential risks or issues while you focus on other aspects. They'll point out possible pitfalls and are naturally protective, ensuring the relationship stays secure. However, this focus on avoiding mistakes can sometimes slow things down. Wests tend to want more data, more time, and more certainty before moving forward in a relationship decision.

Wests often come off as cautious and reserved. They don't like being the one to make big relationship choices, preferring instead to advise on the possible outcomes and consequences. They'll focus on keeping things organized, structured, and efficient within the relationship, whether it's planning future events, managing day-to-day tasks, or remembering important milestones. But their need for structure can sometimes make them feel overwhelmed by spontaneity or uncertainty.

Because they are natural protectors of information and memories, Wests hold onto the past and can be very nostalgic in relationships. They might remember the smallest details of your first date or cherish keepsakes that reflect shared experiences. They're the ones who remember anniversaries, old conversations, and the little things that matter, making them incredibly thoughtful partners.

Wests are highly sensitive to inefficiency in relationships. They can get frustrated when things seem disorganized or chaotic and may struggle when their partner isn't as detail-oriented as they are. Their drive for efficiency can sometimes come across as nitpicking, but it's because they genuinely want things to run smoothly. They'll often offer suggestions like, "Here's the best way to do this," or "Why don't we try it like this?" because they are focused on ensuring everything is done as perfectly as possible.

One of the strengths Wests bring to relationships is their deep listening ability. They're attentive to their partner's needs and feelings, picking up on things that others might miss. They can recall important details from conversations, often remembering what was said and reflecting on it later. This makes them excellent at providing thoughtful advice or feedback when needed.

In love, Wests are often the tradition keepers. They enjoy creating routines and rituals that bring stability and meaning to the relationship. Whether it's celebrating anniversaries in a particular way or maintaining a weekly date night, Wests thrive on consistency and order. They love the comfort of knowing what to expect and can struggle with sudden changes that disrupt their carefully constructed routines.

When Wests feel unprepared or uncertain, they can get stuck in their heads, overthinking and analyzing every little thing, which can make it hard for them to take action.

In terms of decision-making, Wests in relationships can find it difficult to move forward because they are always thinking about the potential consequences of their actions. They want to be sure that they're making the best possible choice, but the fear of making the wrong decision can paralyze them. They may prefer to research and gather facts in private before discussing their thoughts with their partner, rather than making decisions on the spot.

Change can be especially challenging for Wests. They often feel secure in routines and patterns that have worked in the past, so introducing something new into the relationship can feel like a risk. They worry about investing time and energy into something only to realize later that it wasn't the best choice. This makes them more likely to stick with what they know, even if it's not the most exciting option.

Wests are often seen as the problem-solvers in relationships. They love discussing challenges and finding ways to fix them, but this focus on problem-solving can sometimes slow things down. They'll think through every possible scenario before acting, which can keep them from being spontaneous or adventurous.

Wests are very rational and logical when it comes to love. They focus on protecting the relationship and making sure everything is organized, from future plans to daily responsibilities. Their attention to detail and deep thinking makes them great at seeing potential issues before they become problems, but it can also make them hesitant to take risks.

Wests often feel embarrassment in relationships when they don't know the right answer or when they feel unprepared. They strive for perfection, and when things feel uncertain, they may retreat into their thoughts, searching for clarity. This can sometimes lead to a cycle of overthinking, where they get stuck analyzing the relationship instead of enjoying it.

When it comes to commitment, Wests are cautious. They don't jump into relationships lightly and need time to feel secure. They want to be sure they've considered all the consequences before making big decisions, whether it's moving in together, getting married, or taking a significant step forward. This need for certainty can sometimes cause delays in moving the relationship forward.

Wests value efficiency and dislike waste in relationships. They don't like seeing time, energy, or emotions misused, and they'll work hard to ensure things are done in the most efficient way. However, this desire for perfection can sometimes prevent them from seeing the bigger picture, as they get caught up in the details.

At their best, Wests bring stability, order, and deep thoughtfulness to a relationship. They're reliable, attentive, and protective, ensuring that everything is running smoothly. They thrive on preserving what's important, whether it's the relationship itself or the memories and traditions that come with it.

West immediately thinks of consequences to ideas being presented more than contributing truly new ideas for growth. Because West has a hard time seeing the possibility of something new, they will try to stop it or ignore it. If something new is declared, they may be left out.

It's hard for the West to move to the North because it's the unknown. It's the conception of perhaps a completely new idea. And why would you want to do that if we already know what works? What it the new idea puts what we have at risk? These situations go against their survival concern for security if they haven't seen it before.

Over accumulation - "Why would someone throw that away? I could refurbish it." Or "that's a bargain, I should get it while it's cheap as it may come in handy someday." Or "you're giving that away? I'll take it" In the extreme this mindset can lead to hoarding and what can look to others as a pile of junk. If there is any position that is likely to have a bunch of what looks like junk piled everywhere to be used some day, it's a West. So, although they have a propensity for order their concern for not wasting can lead to a junkyard.

If there was a T-shirt for West, it might say:

"It Depends" "I'm silently telling you how to do it right"

"Hold on, Let Me Fact-Check That" "Efficiency is My Love Language"

Lastly, we are going to cover the elemental aspects of West and then their spirit animals.

The Essence of Water

Wests are deep thinkers. They have this reflective, adaptable energy, always ready to dive into the details and analyze a situation from every angle. When you're around them, you'll feel their calm, thoughtful presence. They take their time to get to the heart of things, making sure every decision is well-considered.

In the Tranquility of Autumn

Autumn is when Wests are at their best. Just like the season, they're all about careful planning and reflection, looking back at what's been done and preparing for what's next. They thrive on honoring past efforts while making sure everything is in place for future success.

The Virtue of Prudence

Wests are naturally prudent. They're levelheaded and know how to handle uncertain situations with care. They balance the need for security with their love of order, always making decisions based on wisdom and understanding. Their actions are measured, driven by the lessons they've learned and a desire for precision.

The Hemisphere of Defense

Wests are the protectors, always focused on preserving what matters. They're the ones who carefully weigh every option before acting, making sure it's the right move. They love structure and efficiency, and their cautious approach ensures that nothing is wasted, and everything is in its proper place. They're motivated by a need for certainty and a desire to create order in the world around them.

Wests are the go-to person when something needs to be done right. They're organized, detail-oriented, and always prepared. That's the essence of a West. They're the ones who scrutinize every detail, making sure everything runs smoothly. If you're someone who loves efficiency, gets frustrated by waste, or always ensures things are perfectly in order, you're probably a West.

Just for Fun: West's Spirit Animals

Bear: Symbolizing introspection and strategic preparation, bears align with the West's planning abilities.

Hedgehog: Representing efficiency and resource management, hedgehogs mirror the West's protective instincts.

Owl: Owls embody wisdom and keen observation, reflecting the West's analytical skills.

Badger: Badgers' determination and resourcefulness align with the West's attention to detail and structured methods.

Tortoise: Symbolizing patience, steadiness, and long-term thinking, the tortoise reflects the West's careful, methodical approach to life and relationships. Its slow yet deliberate pace mirrors the West's tendency to take their time before making decisions, ensuring every detail is considered.

The exploration of the West position within the 4Cross Framework highlights the indispensable role they play in weaving the fabric of love and understanding. West's embodiment of thoughtful analysis, meticulous planning, and careful evaluation serves as a reminder of the fundamental human need for reflection and structure. Their ability to bring clarity, ensure precision, and uphold fairness enriches our collective journey, teaching us the value of patience, discernment, and the strength found in deliberate, well-considered action.

Embracing Your West

If you identify as a West, embrace your meticulous energy. Your organizational skills and reliability make you a pillar of strength in both your personal and professional life. Just remember to balance your structured nature with flexibility and empathy, and you'll create relationships that are not only stable but also deeply fulfilling.

So, whether you're planning the next big project, organizing an event, or simply being your reliable, detailed self, know that West is a powerful position to be in. Use your strengths wisely, stay open to growth, and enjoy the incredible journey of love and life.

CHAPTER 6

It's All About You

This chapter will help you identify your position. You are going to think about what makes you tick, why you are the way you are, and how you relate to others. Being self-aware is the most important thing you can do to not only identify your position on the love compass but embrace it, own it, and love it!

Self-awareness and knowing your position in the 4Cross Love Framework are the most critical aspects of personal growth and development. By achieving self-awareness through understanding your position, you can navigate your personal life more effectively, fostering better relationships and achieving greater success.

The ancient Greek philosopher Socrates famously championed the maxim "Know thyself," a tenet that continues to be profoundly relevant today. This call for self-awareness is pivotal, serving as an essential foundation for personal growth. Utilizing the 4Cross Love Framework will serve as a practical method to achieve the self-knowledge Socrates emphasized.

The pursuit of self-awareness can facilitate a more structured and deeper exploration of yourself. For instance, by identifying and articulating your core identity ("Who am I?"), understanding intrinsic and extrinsic needs ("What do I need?"), clarifying personal and societal values ("What do I value?"), and envisioning a future that aligns with your true self ("Where do I want to go?"), you can make decisions that are wise and aligned with your deeper goals and principles. This alignment fosters a life of authenticity and integrity, giving you a much better chance to find true love.

Knowing yourself deeply can foster greater empathy and understanding toward others. Recognizing your own challenges and strengths through this self-exploration can lead to a greater appreciation of others' qualities. This deepened awareness also supports the Socratic method of questioning and dialogue, which seeks to uncover and scrutinize underlying beliefs and assumptions. By rigorously examining yourself using a structured framework, you can effectively challenge personal biases and prejudices, leading to an enlightened, more joyful, and loving life.

Identifying your position within the 4Cross Love Framework can be challenging because each position—North, East, South, and West—is rooted deeply in our biological concerns, which can subtly influence us in ways we may not immediately recognize.

Here's why finding your true position can be complex:

1. Overlap in Behavioral Traits: Each position shares some surface traits with the others, such as ambition, empathy, or curiosity, depending on the context. For example, both North and West can be detail-oriented, but for entirely different reasons: Norths for control and strategic clarity, Wests for security and precision. This overlap can make it hard to differentiate which underlying motivation drives these behaviors.

2. Influence of Social Conditioning: Society, family expectations, and cultural norms shape us from a young age, sometimes leading us to behave in ways that don't necessarily align with our core biological concerns. For instance, if a South grows up in a family that values high achievement, they may adopt North-like traits of goal-setting and drive, even though their core concern remains stability and connection.

3. Adaptive Behaviors: Over time, we adapt to our environments to fit into specific roles, especially in relationships and work. A South might adopt East-like traits, such as spontaneity, to keep up with a partner or workplace culture that values flexibility and creativity. These adaptive behaviors can obscure our true position, making it seem as if we operate from multiple positions.

4. Emotional Blind Spots: Our core concerns (control, freedom, stability, and security) are often rooted in emotional needs that can feel vulnerable or uncomfortable to explore. Admitting, for instance, that you seek control because uncertainty makes you feel insecure can be challenging. This discomfort can make it easier to overlook or dismiss traits linked to our true position, making it harder to identify it accurately.

5. Misinterpretation of Personality Traits: We often confuse personality traits, such as introversion or extroversion, with positional traits. For example, an extroverted South may seem outgoing like an East, but their need for social interaction is driven by a desire for stability and belonging rather than freedom and excitement. This confusion can make identifying one's position more difficult.

6. Projection of Ideal Self: Many of us have an idealized version of ourselves that we aspire to be. For instance, you may see yourself as a leader (North), valuing control and strategic thinking, because society often rewards those traits. However, your true core concern might be stability (South), and your leadership style may be more about fostering harmony than taking charge. This projection of an ideal self can cloud recognition of one's authentic position.

7. Complexity of Position in Different Roles: We often play different roles in life—partner, friend, parent, or professional—and these roles can bring out varied aspects of our personality. In work, you may adopt North-like decisiveness, while in friendships, you show South-like loyalty. This variation can make it difficult to pinpoint a single, consistent position, especially if you lean into different concerns depending on the context.

8. Difficulty in Self-Reflection: Identifying one's position requires honest self-reflection, which isn't always easy. We may unconsciously resist certain truths or shy away from deeper introspection due to discomfort or fear of judgment. Recognizing core concerns and inherent tendencies involves accepting parts of ourselves that we may have spent years trying to change or hide.

9. Influence of Stress and Conflict: Stress and conflict often reveal our true positional concerns. However, because stress responses can be intense, we might misinterpret these reactions as temporary rather than seeing them as indications of our core position. For example, a North might become controlling under stress, but they might attribute it to situational pressure rather than acknowledging it as part of their core need for control.

In Summary:

Recognizing your position within the 4Cross Love Framework can be challenging due to overlapping traits, social conditioning, adaptive behaviors, and emotional blind spots. It requires honest self-reflection and a willingness to explore motivations that may feel vulnerable or surprising. By identifying and accepting your true position, you gain greater clarity, self-acceptance, and the ability to create fulfilling relationships based on genuine understanding and respect. It is very helpful to explore some of these questions and exercise with someone who is close to you where you can both be honest, sincere, and considerate while also being forthright. The ones closest to us are that way for a reason, they know us well, even if we don't want to admit it. Of course, their positional awareness is a huge factor, but even without that, they will likely be able to point out some of the things you may not see in yourself.

Let's move on to the exercises and questions.

You are going to dive deep into your true self by answering some questions and then asking why, when appropriate, until the why is apparent. Within the why are your clues. This is the ultimate investigation of self. You do not have to answer all the questions. If one is tripping you up or tripping you out, move on. The whole point is to be honest about who you are, what you want, what you value, and where you want to go. This will give you the best chance at not only identifying your position but truly winning the game of love and living your dreams.

These questions aim to help you reflect on your decision-making process, responses to challenges and criticism, relationship dynamics, personal growth, and overall understanding of yourself. It helps to journal as you reflect and start to decode how you show up in your relationships.

Here is an organized list of questions for evaluating values, self-awareness, and relationship dynamics:

Self-Reflection on Values and Priorities

1. What values are most important to you in life and why?

2. Write down what is most important to you in areas like career, relationships, personal growth, and leisure. Rank these values in order of importance.

3. Use a list of common values to select your top ten and then narrow down to your top three. Reflect on how these core values influence your decisions.

4. Imagine you are at the end of your life. What do you want to be remembered for, and how does this align with your current values?

5. Reflect on your daily activities and assess how well they align with your core values. Identify any discrepancies and how you might address them.

Understanding Strengths and Growth Areas

1. List your top strengths. Think about compliments you've received or tasks you excel at, and validate this by asking close friends or colleagues.

2. Write about three times you felt successful. Identify the strengths you used in each situation.

3. Keep a log of creative ideas and solutions you've come up with. Reflect on the strengths you used in these instances.

4. List projects or activities you are passionate about and identify the strengths these passions highlight.

5. Identify situations where you acted with wisdom or prudence. What values guided your actions?

6. Write about traditions that are important to you and reflect on the values these traditions represent and how they shape your life.

Self-Awareness in Relationships and Communication

1. Describe a relationship that was immensely satisfying. Why was it so good, and what happened to it?

2. How do relationships typically go for you? Are you in control, or do you expect someone else to take the lead?

3. Do you feel like it's important to make changes for the other person in a relationship, or should they accept you as you are? Do you expect others to change for you?

4. What is a successful relationship to you? Have you ever had one, and what made it successful?

5. When you get into an argument with someone you care about, how does it affect you? What do you do, and how do you feel later?

6. How do you prefer to communicate with others? Are you more direct or indirect?

7. What do you find most challenging about communicating with others?

8. How do you typically handle feedback from others?

Reflecting on Challenges, Stress, and Emotional Needs

1. List things that challenge you and situations that make you feel threatened.

2. Identify situations that evoke strong emotions. Reflect on the unmet needs that might be triggering these responses.

3. Describe a recent stressful situation and how you handled it.

4. What strategies do you use to manage stress?

5. When it comes to challenging decisions, what are you likely to do? Has this kept you from adventure or gotten you into trouble?

6. How do you respond to criticism, and how has this shown up in your love life?

7. How have you handled failure in the past, especially in relationships? Did it help you grow or leave you feeling stuck?

Self-Development and Personal Growth

1. Establish a regular feedback loop with a mentor or coach to discuss areas where you might need improvement.

2. What areas do you focus on for personal growth and improvement?

3. Track moments when you feel scattered or distracted. Identify common themes and consider how these challenges impact your effectiveness.

4. Set aside regular time for introspection. Reflect on your emotional needs and how they influence your behavior and decisions.

5. List your emotional needs (e.g., recognition, independence, control) and assess how well these needs are being met in your current life.

Decision-Making and Self-Management

1. How do you prioritize your daily tasks and responsibilities?

2. Reflect on times when you struggled to make decisions. Identify the weaknesses that contributed to these struggles.

3. Track instances of perfectionism, reflecting on how it impacts your productivity, and consider strategies to manage this trait.

Exploring Passions and Social Connections

1. Reflect on times when you felt most alive and engaged. What values were being honored in these moments?

2. Reflect on your need for new experiences and excitement. Write about ways to incorporate more adventure into your daily life.

3. Reflect on your need for belonging and community. Write about how well these needs are being met and ways to enhance them.

Create a map of your social connections. Identify the emotional needs each connection fulfills and areas where you might need more support.

This set of questions provides a structured approach to explore your values, strengths, emotional needs, relationship patterns, and personal growth, helping you better understand and navigate your life and relationships.

This exercise isn't easy. Getting down to who you really are, what you need, what you value, and where you want to go isn't always clear. So many influences can thwart your efforts to be yourself. I have been through this myself, and I know how hard it is to get to what's driving you. But you can do it!

After this exercise, you should have a good idea of your position. As I say that, I recognize that I have the curse of knowledge and many years of observation and experience. But there is no time like the present to learn something new, especially how to win the game of love.

If you would like some help investigating, my appointment calendar is on my website <u>4Crosslove.com/appointment</u> . I would love to help you dig deeper and get some answers with you.

Let's continue with a couple more exercises and questions to determine your position. I have written them from a perspective of how to get the best answers from each position. If you are close to identifying or narrowing down your position, this approach will help. But all the questions are helpful in learning more about yourself and your positional perspective.

Here are two ongoing exercises that will give you real-time information about your place in the 4Cross Love Framework.

Observation Journal: Keep a journal where you take note of your own behaviors, reactions, and communication style. Look for patterns that align with the characteristics of each position.

Situational Analysis: Observe how you react in different situations, such as stress, joy, conflict, and teamwork. Different positions tend to exhibit distinctive behaviors under various circumstances.

One key lesson I've learned through this process is that it's nearly impossible to create a definitive quiz, test, or assessment because almost everyone struggles to see their true self as discussed earlier. This is also why personality tests often feel inconclusive and confusing. We might think we are one way, but in reality, we are quite different. Just ask your siblings, best friend, or parents.

As I said before, if you trust someone to be honest with you and can take their feedback constructively, the next section will be very enlightening if you do it with someone close to you. Keep in mind the positions of the people you invite to do this with you, as they will have different perspectives based on their own positions. Take their insights with this understanding in mind.

Let's consider how you have handled yourself with others in the past:

North Position

1. Reflect on a time when your desire for certainty led you to take charge of a situation. How did your actions impact those around you, and would you approach it differently now?

2. Consider a moment when you had a bold idea or vision. How did you communicate this to others, and was your method effective in rallying their support?

3. Think about a situation where you felt your value or competence was questioned. How did you respond, and what does that reveal about your need for certainty?

4. Recall an instance when your directness or desire to be right might have led to a misunderstanding or conflict. How can you balance your natural assertiveness with sensitivity to others' perspectives in the future?

East Position

1. Reflect on a time when your energetic and engaging personality opened up new possibilities in your relationships. How did this affect your interactions and the outcome of the situation?

2. Think about a situation where your spontaneity and desire for excitement led you to make a rash decision. What did you learn from this experience about balancing spontaneity with consideration?

3. Consider a moment when you used your charisma to influence or persuade others. Did you consider their needs and viewpoints, and how could you ensure a win-win outcome in future situations?

4. Recall an instance when your competitive nature came into play in a relationship. How did it affect the dynamic, and how can you use your competitiveness positively without overshadowing cooperation?

South Position

1. Reflect on a time when your supportive and empathetic nature significantly impacted someone's life. How did this strengthen your relationship, and what does it teach you about the power of empathy?

2. Think about a moment when your desire for harmony led you to compromise more than you should have. What did this experience teach you about setting boundaries and advocating for your needs?

3. Consider a situation where your reliability and loyalty were put to the test. How did you handle it, and what did it reveal about your values and commitment to others?

4. Recall an instance when you might have avoided confrontation to maintain peace. How could addressing issues directly, despite the discomfort, benefit your relationships in the long run?

West Position

1. Reflect on a time when your methodical and analytical approach helped solve a complex problem in a relationship. How did this affect the outcome, and what did it teach you about the value of thoroughness?

2. Think about a situation where your preference for detail and precision might have caused impatience or frustration for others. How can you communicate your needs for accuracy without compromising the relationship's harmony?

3. Consider a moment when your cautious and reflective nature allowed you to give valuable advice to someone. How does this ability strengthen your relationships, and how can you continue to offer your insights effectively?

4. Recall an instance when your need for organization and structure clashed with someone's spontaneity. How can you find a balance between meeting your need for order and accommodating others' flexibility?

On my website 4Crosslove.com in the resources tab is a grand list of questions if you would like to delve deeper and or have a resource for asking questions of others. There are also more exercises and activities at the end of the book. In the next part, we are going to go through each section of the 4Cross Love Checklist so you can precisely navigate and check off everything you need to successfully play the game of love, find your best mate, or love the one you're with.

Part 2

CHAPTER 7

The 4Cross Love Checklist

"Love is an irresistible desire to be irresistibly desired." -
Robert Frost

The 4Cross Love Checklist is a valuable tool for navigating relationships by fostering awareness, attraction, shared interests, values, communication, and informed decision-making. Here's the checklist and an explanation of how each aspect of the checklist relates to understanding yourself and your partner while ensuring a strong, compatible relationship. On my website 4crosslove.com/resources is a free checkable, downloadable, PDF of the checklist.

The 4Cross Love Checklist covers various aspects of a relationship that are crucial for understanding and compatibility. This holistic approach ensures that both partners are aware of their own and each other's needs while also recognizing the need for a more systematic approach to relationships that can increase harmony and long-term satisfaction.

This is the checklist strategy you need to win the game of love.

You will realize that you have far more options for a great match than you probably imagined, considering there are only four positions in the game of love. There isn't just "the one," but many potential matches. Understanding your position in the game of love is crucial for recognizing these possibilities. With this tool and knowledge, you can play like a champion in the game of love, find a great match or love the one you're with, and live happily ever after.

88

In the following 6 chapters we will go into each checklist point in detail.

The 4Cross Love Checklist

1. Awareness:

☐ **Self-awareness**: You have done the work to truly understand your own values, strengths, weaknesses, and emotional needs. You know who you are, what you need, what you value, and where you want to go.

☐ **Positional awareness**: Recognizing your own position within the 4Cross Framework and understanding its implications. You have identified your position and have identified and embraced your potential partner's position.

2. Attraction:

☐ **Physical**: Reflecting on physical attraction and chemistry. You love being in the presence of your potential mate, and it's clear they enjoy your physical attributes as well.

☐ **Emotional**: Considering the depth of emotional connection and support. You feel like you are listened to and respected, and you feel good about yourself around your potential mate and vice versa.

☐ **Intellectual**: Assessing the intellectual stimulation and engagement in the relationship. Your potential mate is interesting to you. They present a challenge and have a mutual respect for your points of view.

☐ **Positional**: Evaluating positional attraction and how well the partner's position aligns with or complements your own.

3. Interests:

☐ Reviewing shared interests and activities to ensure companionship and mutual enjoyment. You have many of the same interests, not all, but you share some interests in several areas of exploration, hobbies etc.

4. Values:

☐ Ensuring alignment of core values and long-term goals, such as ethics, lifestyle, family planning, and career ambitions. You have talked about what you need, who you are and what matters to you going forward in regards to several values and ambitions.

5. Effective Communication:

☐ Evaluating how clear, empathetic, and respectful dialogue is to resolve conflicts, express needs, and deepen connections. You feel like you can talk to your potential mate, and they listen. You feel safe to be yourself. And they have expressed the same to you.

6. Choice:

☐ Making an informed decision by synthesizing all the information gathered through the previous steps, considering pros and cons, having deep and honest conversations, and trusting instincts.

We are now going to go into each part of the checklist in detail so you can get a holistic view of how to effectively navigate your relationships and win the game of love!

CHAPTER 8

Checklist Point #1 Awareness

"Love is a wild game that neither the timid nor the bold play well."-Mignon McLaughlin

Self-Awareness

Self-awareness is the conscious knowledge of your own character, feelings, motives, and desires. It involves recognizing your strengths and weaknesses, understanding your emotions, and being aware of the impact of your behavior on others.

The value of self-awareness and knowing your position in the 4Cross Love Framework is the most critical aspect of personal growth and development. By achieving self-awareness through understanding your position, you can navigate your personal life more effectively, fostering better relationships and achieving greater success.

Self-Awareness Is Crucial for Fostering Several Things

Improved Decision-Making: This is one of the primary benefits of self-awareness, as it helps you understand your motivations and how your emotions influence your choices.

Enhanced Relationships: Recognizing your behavior and its effects allows you to better navigate social interactions, which leads to healthier and more meaningful connections.

Personal Growth: By being able to identify areas for improvement and take proactive steps toward self-improvement, you experience personal growth. Additionally, emotional regulation is enhanced through self-awareness, helping you manage and control emotions, which contributes to better stress management and overall well-being.

Knowing your position in the 4Cross Love Framework is paramount because it provides insight into your self-awareness in several ways. It gives you a structured understanding of your innate characteristics, strengths, and areas for improvement.

For those in the North position, self-awareness means recognizing your need for certainty and how it influences your relationship behavior. Understanding your position allows you to leverage your strengths in leadership, direction, and strategic thinking. To enhance your effectiveness as a partner, you should work on improving flexibility and communication, balancing your need for certainty with adaptability in relationships.

For those in the East position, self-awareness means understanding your desire for freedom and how it influences your relationship choices. Recognizing your position allows you to channel your creativity and social skills effectively. While your strengths lie in innovation and charm, you may need to improve consistency and focus to sustain meaningful relationships. By balancing freedom with responsibility, you can use your strengths to build lasting and fulfilling connections.

For those in the South position, self-awareness means recognizing your role as a stabilizer and supporter. Understanding your position helps you leverage your emotional intelligence to build harmonious relationships. Your strengths include providing emotional support and reliability, but you may need to work on assertiveness and adaptability. By enhancing your emotional intelligence and balancing stability with adaptability, you can create supportive environments while also embracing growth and change in relationships.

For those in the West position, self-awareness involves understanding your meticulous nature and how it contributes to your effectiveness in relationships. Recognizing your position helps you maintain high standards without becoming overly rigid. Your strengths include attention to detail and organizational skills, but you may need to work on flexibility and interpersonal skills. By balancing your need for precision with flexibility, you can achieve high standards while also adapting to changing circumstances and fostering better relationships.

The 4Cross Love positions give you inside knowledge about yourself like no other. Knowing your position within the 4Cross Love Framework helps you see yourself more clearly by providing a structured understanding of your innate characteristics, strengths, and areas for improvement. This self-awareness allows you to recognize how your natural tendencies influence your behavior, decisions, and interactions with others. By identifying your position, you can:

Understand Your Motivations: Gain insight into what drives you, helping you make decisions that align with your true values and goals.

Recognize Strengths: Identify and leverage your inherent strengths, boosting confidence and effectiveness in various areas of life.

Address Weaknesses: Pinpoint areas for improvement, enabling targeted personal growth and development.

Improve Emotional Intelligence: Better understand your own emotions and how they affect your actions, leading to improved emotional regulation and well-being.

Enhance Relationships: See how your behavior impacts others, fostering empathy and more meaningful connections.

Boost Self-Confidence: Develop a clearer sense of identity and purpose, leading to greater self-acceptance and confidence.

Knowing your position in the 4Cross Love Framework provides a mirror for self-reflection, offering valuable insights that promote personal growth and a deeper understanding of yourself.

Positional Awareness

Understanding and identifying the positions within the 4Cross Love Framework is a powerful tool for enhancing personal relationships, improving communication, and fostering collaboration. By recognizing these positions and strategizing accordingly, you can navigate social dynamics more effectively, leading to more harmonious and productive interactions.

Recognizing positions can significantly enhance relationship-building efforts. Each position has different needs and ways of connecting with others, and understanding these can help foster deeper and more meaningful relationships:

Norths value relationships that respect their leadership and strategic thinking. Engaging in activities that allow them to demonstrate their strengths and offering support in their endeavors creates mutual respect and admiration.

Easts thrive in dynamic and fun relationships, where creativity and spontaneity are encouraged. Building a relationship with an East involves being flexible and embracing new experiences together.

Souths value emotional support and stability, appreciating reliable and empathetic friends or partners. Engaging in activities that promote togetherness and emotional bonding builds trust and a strong emotional connection.

Wests appreciate order and predictability in relationships, valuing punctuality and organization. Engaging in activities that involve planning and attention to detail fosters mutual respect and dependability.

Effective communication is fundamental to any successful relationship. Understanding others' positions in the 4Cross Love Framework allows for tailored communication strategies that resonate more deeply with the individuals involved:

Norths, characterized by their logical and strategic thinking, respond well to clear, concise, and data-driven communication. They appreciate logical arguments and evidence to support points.

Easts, who are adaptable and energetic, prefer enthusiastic and engaging communication, encouraging brainstorming and open-ended ideas.

Souths, known for their emotional intelligence and reliability, value empathy and emotional connections in communication. A warm and inclusive tone that fosters harmony and stability works best for them.

Wests, being methodical and detail oriented, appreciate structured and thorough communication with clear, step-by-step information.

Conflict is inevitable in any relationship, but understanding others' positions can help in resolving conflicts more effectively by tailoring strategies to address the concerns and motivations of each position:

Norths prefer direct and logical approaches to conflict resolution, using clear, fact-based arguments and practical solutions.

Easts respond well to open and flexible strategies, exploring multiple solutions and creative compromises.

Souths prefer empathetic and harmonious approaches, focusing on understanding feelings and maintaining harmony.

Wests appreciate structured and thorough approaches, providing detailed analyses and step-by-step solutions to address all aspects of the conflict.

Being positionally aware involves being mindful of how your position—North, East, South, or West—shapes your actions, reactions, and communication in relationships.

Here's how you can develop positional awareness and what you can do to enhance it:

1. Understand Your Own Position

- **Self-Reflection**: Begin by reflecting on your core tendencies. What drives your behavior in relationships? Are you someone who needs control and certainty (North), freedom and excitement (East), stability and support (South), or security and structure (West)? Take the time to examine how your position influences your everyday actions and decisions.

- **Identify Your Core Concern**: Each position has a core concern. For example, North is driven by the need for control and certainty, East by freedom, South by stability, and West by security. Recognize what you're most concerned about and how that drives your approach to relationships.

- **Evaluate Your Strengths and Weaknesses**: Acknowledge your strengths, such as leadership for North or empathy for South, and your challenges, such as impatience (North) or avoidance of conflict (South). This helps you be more mindful of how your position shows up in interactions.

2. Observe Your Reactions in Conflict

- **Notice Patterns**: Pay attention to how you react during disagreements or stressful situations. Do you tend to take control (North), avoid the issue (South), lighten the mood with humor (East), or withdraw to analyze the situation (West)? Becoming aware of your automatic reactions helps you adjust your behavior in ways that promote better communication.

- **Understand What Triggers You**: Recognize the situations that tend to trigger your survival concern. For example, a North might feel triggered when things are chaotic or uncertain, whereas a West might feel uneasy when there's a lack of structure. Being aware of your triggers allows you to take a step back and respond mindfully.

3. Understand and Respect Others' Positions.

- **Ask Yourself How Others Operate**: Reflect on your partner's or friend's core concern. What drives their behavior? Do they prioritize freedom, stability, security, or control? Recognizing their position helps you empathize with their perspective and understand their actions.

- **Adjust Your Expectations**: Based on their position, adjust your expectations. If you're a North with an East partner, understand that they may not always follow rigid plans. Instead, appreciate their spontaneity and adapt when possible.

- **Acknowledge Their Strengths and Challenges**: Just as you've acknowledged your own strengths and weaknesses, do the same for others. If you're dealing with a South, appreciate their nurturing nature but also recognize they may avoid conflict. If you're with a West, value their precision while being aware they might overanalyze things.

4. Improve Communication by Position

- **Adapt Your Communication Style**: Each position has different communication preferences. Norths are direct, Easts prefer flexibility, Souths value harmony, and Wests need clarity and details. Tailor your communication style to match the needs of the person you're interacting with. For example, with a South, focus on creating emotional safety, whereas with a North, be clear and to the point.

- **Use Positional Language**: Frame your conversations in ways that respect the other person's position. For a West, emphasize the structure and long-term benefits of your plans. For an East, talk about the freedom and creativity the plan allows. Aligning your language with their concerns fosters mutual understanding.

5. Balance Your Core Concern

- **Be Aware of Over-Reliance on Your Position**: Sometimes, you may lean too heavily on your core concern, such as always needing control (North) or constantly avoiding conflict (South). Practice balancing these tendencies by exploring other aspects of yourself. For example, if you're a North, try relinquishing control in certain situations to see how it affects your relationships.

- **Practice Flexibility**: While you can't change your position, you can develop flexibility. If you're a West, practice being more spontaneous and less detail-oriented in low-risk situations. If you're an East, work on sticking to plans when they matter. Flexibility helps you grow within your position without denying your core nature.

6. Practice Empathy and Understanding

- **Put Yourself in Others' Shoes**: Actively practice empathy by putting yourself in the mindset of someone from a different position. Imagine how a South might feel during a tense situation where stability is threatened, or how an East feels when restricted by too many rules. This helps you see beyond your own concerns and better understand others' behavior.

- **Don't Take It Personally**: Understand that people act based on their positional concerns, not necessarily to challenge or upset you. For example, a North's controlling behavior might stem from their need for certainty, not from a desire to dominate you. This awareness helps you respond with patience and perspective.

7. Foster Positional Compatibility

- **Assess Compatibility in Relationships**: Be mindful of how your position interacts with others in relationships. For example, a North-East relationship may require finding a balance between structure (North) and spontaneity (East). Knowing where potential friction might arise can help you proactively address and navigate those differences.

- **Collaborate Effectively**: Work together with others by allowing each person to operate from their position of strength. If you're a North, you can lead and plan, while encouraging an East partner to contribute their creativity. If you're a South, support a West's need for thorough analysis, while also helping them see when to move forward.

8. Use Positional Awareness for Growth

- **Set Personal Goals**: Use your positional awareness as a tool for personal growth. If you're a South, challenge yourself to express your needs more clearly rather than avoiding conflict. If you're a North, practice relaxing control and trusting others to take the lead. This awareness helps you expand within your position and develop new strengths.

- **Learn from Different Positions**: Each position has valuable traits that you can learn from. For example, a North can learn adaptability from an East, while an East can learn patience from a South. Being aware of these differences helps you integrate aspects of other positions into your life for a more balanced approach.

9. Reflect Regularly

- **Check-In with Yourself**: Regularly reflect on how your positional tendencies are showing up in your relationships and life. Are you falling into habits that might cause tension? Are you embracing the strengths of your position? Regular self-awareness ensures that you stay mindful of how your position influences your interactions.

- **Journal Your Observations**: Writing down how you respond in different situations can help clarify patterns in your behavior that are tied to your position. Journaling can help you track moments where your core concern—such as control for North or security for West—plays a significant role in your decision-making.

10. Seek Feedback from Others

- **Ask for Feedback**: Ask friends, family, or your partner how they perceive your actions and behaviors. This can offer valuable insight into whether you're over-relying on certain aspects of your position or where you can improve.

- **Be Open to Criticism**: Positional awareness involves growth. Be willing to hear where your natural tendencies might be hindering communication or harmony in your relationships, and use that feedback to become more mindful and adaptive.

In Summary:

Being positionally aware involves understanding your core drivers in the 4Cross Love Framework and recognizing how they influence your interactions with others. By becoming aware of your strengths, challenges, and tendencies, you can improve communication, foster stronger relationships, and develop greater empathy. Positional awareness allows you to balance your own needs with those of others, resulting in more harmonious and fulfilling connections.

Positional Awareness Beyond Romantic Relationships

Identifying others' positions also contributes to personal growth and development. It allows you to understand different perspectives and adapt your behavior to interact more effectively with people of all positions.

Understanding others' positions fosters empathy, promoting a more inclusive and understanding mindset. It also improves adaptability, enabling you to adjust your communication and interaction styles to better suit different positions.

Additionally, being able to identify others' positions aids in conflict management, allowing you to tailor your conflict resolution strategies to address the specific concerns and motivations of each position, reducing misunderstandings and promoting quicker and more effective resolutions.

Understanding family members' positions can improve family dynamics, such as planning activities and decisions that align with a North's need for structure and direction, or enhancing familial support and harmony by recognizing a South's need for emotional connection.

In friendships, recognizing friends' positions can enhance the quality of interactions, allowing you to tailor activities to suit each friend's preferences and strengthen the bond.

In educational settings, understanding students' positions can make teaching and mentoring more effective by adapting teaching methods to suit each student's position. Recognizing peers' positions can improve interactions and collaboration, promoting positive relationships and a more cohesive educational experience.

Knowing others' positions in the 4Cross Love Framework helps you understand and interact with those around you more effectively by providing insight into their innate characteristics, strengths, and areas for improvement. This awareness allows you to:

Improve Communication: Tailor your communication style to resonate more deeply with others, leading to clearer and more effective interactions.

Enhance Empathy: Understand others' motivations and emotions, fostering greater empathy and emotional connection.

Resolve Conflicts: Address conflicts with strategies that consider the unique concerns and perspectives of each position, leading to more effective and amicable resolutions.

Build Stronger Relationships: Recognize and appreciate other's strengths and contributions, creating more supportive and harmonious relationships.

Foster Collaboration: Leverage the diverse strengths of different positions to enhance teamwork and collaboration, achieving better collective outcomes.

Support Personal Growth: Help others identify their strengths and areas for improvement, encouraging mutual growth and development.

Overall, knowing others' positions in the 4Cross Love Framework equips you with the tools you need to navigate social dynamics more effectively, fostering deeper connections and more productive interactions.

In conclusion, being self-aware and positionally aware is a game-changer for communication, relationships, collaboration, and conflict management. It promotes personal growth by boosting empathy, adaptability, and leadership skills. In the dating game, this framework turns you into a relationship ninja, fostering self-awareness and mutual understanding. Recognizing your strengths and areas for improvement leads to better communication and deeper emotional connections. It helps tailor your interactions to vibe perfectly with your partner, making conflicts easier to resolve. By understanding each other's quirks and motivations, you can build a stronger, more harmonious relationship. Ultimately, this knowledge lays the groundwork for deeper bonds and a partnership that's not just fulfilling but also fun.

We're going to cover attraction next. Are you attractive in four ways?

CHAPTER 9

Checklist Point #2
The Four Attraction

> *"The greatest thing you'll ever learn is to love and be loved in return."-Moulin Rouge!*

In this chapter, we will explore each type of attraction in detail, providing insights into how they manifest and influence our relationships. By understanding these four attractions, we can better appreciate the different dimensions of love and build stronger, more fulfilling connections.

Attraction is about you being attracted to someone and them being attracted to you. It is a multifaceted concept that goes beyond just the physical. In relationships, four main types of attraction play crucial roles: physical, emotional, intellectual, and positional. Understanding these attractions helps us navigate the complex dynamics of love and connection more effectively.

Physical Attraction

We all know physical attraction is a part of the love equation. There is no denying it. Biologically, we are trying to find the most attractive mate. From an evolutionary standpoint, physical attraction is deeply rooted in the survival and reproduction of the human species. Physical attraction has profound psychological effects, influencing self-esteem, social interactions, and overall well-being.

Physical attraction goes beyond just liking how someone looks. It encompasses various other elements that contribute to a deeper, more holistic attraction to someone's physical presence. Here are some additional aspects of physical attraction:

1. **Body Language and Gestures**: The way a person carries themselves, their posture, and how they use gestures can be incredibly attractive. Confident, open body language signals approachability and can enhance attraction. Eye contact, the way they move, or how they use their hands while speaking can all add to physical attraction.

2. **Scent**: Natural body scent, combined with personal hygiene or chosen fragrances like perfume or cologne, can play a significant role in physical attraction. Pheromones, though subtle, influence attraction on a biological level.

3. **Touch and Tactile Connection**: Physical touch, such as hand-holding, hugging, or even the warmth of a person's touch, can deepen physical attraction. The feeling of comfort and connection when in physical proximity to someone can be a powerful part of attraction.

4. **Voice and Tone**: A person's voice can be very attractive, whether it's the sound, tone, or how they articulate words. A soothing or charismatic voice, or even the way they laugh, can enhance physical attraction.

5. **Facial Expressions**: The subtleties in a person's expressions, such as their smile, the way they laugh, or how their eyes light up, can amplify physical attraction. Genuine warmth and emotion displayed through facial expressions can create a stronger connection.

6. **Health and Vitality**: A person's overall energy and vitality, reflected through their level of fitness, stamina, or general health, can be appealing. This often includes glowing skin, vibrant eyes, and an overall sense of wellness.

7. **Style and Grooming**: How someone presents themselves in terms of clothing, grooming, and personal style can also contribute to physical attraction. The way someone dresses, their hairstyle, and how they take care of themselves can communicate confidence and individual personality.

8. **Confidence and Presence**: Confidence is often a key factor in physical attraction. A person who exudes self-assurance and carries themselves with ease tends to be more physically appealing. This is often reflected in the way they walk, stand, or engage with others.

All of these aspects work together to create a multifaceted sense of physical attraction that goes beyond just appearance, contributing to a deeper and more meaningful connection.

Emotional Attractiveness

It's also quite obvious that we're attracted to more than physical qualities. Emotional attraction is equally important.

Emotional attraction is essential for creating a deep and lasting bond in a relationship. It goes beyond physical chemistry and involves feeling connected, understood, and supported on an emotional level. Here are the key aspects of emotional attraction that need to be considered in a relationship:

1. Emotional Support and Care: Feeling cared for and supported is crucial for emotional attraction. Both partners should be there for each other in times of need, offering comfort, encouragement, and understanding. A strong emotional connection means you can rely on your partner during challenges and share in each other's successes and struggles.

2. Empathy and Understanding: Empathy is the ability to understand and share your partner's feelings. Partners should feel heard, validated, and understood, which fosters emotional intimacy. The ability to "put yourself in their shoes" strengthens emotional bonds and creates a safe space for vulnerability.

3. Emotional Availability: Both partners need to be emotionally available and willing to invest in the relationship. This means being open to sharing emotions, being honest about feelings, and being willing to address emotional needs. A partner who is emotionally unavailable can lead to frustration and emotional distance in the relationship.

4. Trust and Security: Trust is a foundational element of emotional attraction. Feeling secure in the relationship, knowing your partner is reliable, honest, and faithful, fosters a sense of emotional safety. Emotional attraction deepens when partners feel they can trust each other without fear of betrayal or dishonesty.

5. Vulnerability and Openness: Being able to share your true self without fear of judgment is a critical aspect of emotional attraction. When both partners are open and vulnerable, it creates a space for authentic connection. Vulnerability allows both people to feel seen and accepted for who they are.

6. Shared Values and Goals: A strong emotional connection often comes from shared values, beliefs, and life goals. Aligning on important life decisions—such as family, career, or lifestyle choices—creates emotional harmony. This connection allows partners to feel like they are on the same page and working toward a common future.

7. Emotional Consistency and Stability: Emotional consistency is key in a relationship. Partners should feel that they can rely on each other emotionally, without unpredictability or emotional swings. Consistent emotional behavior builds trust and stability in the relationship, allowing both people to feel grounded.

8. Affection and Appreciation: Regular expressions of affection and appreciation help to sustain emotional attraction. Small gestures of love, care, and gratitude, such as compliments, acts of kindness, or simply saying "I appreciate you," can maintain emotional connection and reaffirm the bond.

9. Emotional Growth: Both partners should support each other's emotional growth and self-improvement. Emotional attraction deepens when partners challenge and inspire each other to grow, both individually and together, in ways that enhance emotional intelligence and relationship health.

10. Sense of Belonging and Connection: Feeling like you "belong" with your partner, that you are a team, and that you truly "get" each other, is a fundamental aspect of emotional attraction. This sense of connection makes both partners feel valued and appreciated in the relationship.

In summary, emotional attraction is about more than just feeling good together—it's about building a relationship where both partners feel safe, supported, and deeply connected. These aspects ensure that the relationship is emotionally fulfilling and has the potential to grow over time, leading to a more stable, satisfying connection.

Intellectual Attractiveness

Maybe the least obvious attraction is intellectual attraction, but it does play an interesting role in a relationship, as it fosters a deep and meaningful connection beyond physical or emotional appeal.

Intellectual attraction is the draw you feel toward someone based on their thoughts, ideas, and ability to engage in stimulating conversation. It goes beyond just physical or emotional chemistry and centers around the mental and intellectual connection you share with a partner. Here's how intellectual attraction plays out and why it's important in a relationship:

1. Engaging Conversations: One of the most immediate signs of intellectual attraction is the ability to have deep, engaging conversations with someone. This means not only discussing surface-level topics but diving into complex subjects, whether it's philosophy, current events, science, art, or personal passions. Partners who are intellectually attracted to each other enjoy conversations that challenge their thinking, broaden their perspectives, and offer opportunities to learn from one another.

2. Shared Curiosity and Learning: Intellectual attraction often involves a mutual curiosity about the world. Both partners are open to new ideas, eager to explore and learn, and share an enthusiasm for acquiring knowledge. This shared intellectual curiosity fosters growth in the relationship as you explore new topics, read books together, debate ideas, or take on new learning experiences like traveling, attending seminars, or simply discovering new hobbies and interests together.

3. Stimulating Challenges: In a relationship marked by intellectual attraction, partners often challenge each other in ways that lead to personal and intellectual growth. They inspire one another to think more critically, question assumptions, and push beyond intellectual comfort zones. This can manifest in healthy debates or discussions where each person's viewpoint is respected, even if you don't always agree. The challenge isn't about competition but about sharpening each other's thinking and expanding horizons.

4. Mutual Respect for Intelligence: Intellectual attraction thrives on respect for each other's intellect. It's not just about one person teaching the other but about mutual admiration for how your partner thinks, processes information, and approaches the world. Whether it's through problem-solving, creative thinking, or analyzing complex ideas, you admire the way their mind works and how they see things differently.

5. Growth Through Shared Exploration: Intellectual attraction drives shared exploration—whether it's taking on new challenges together, diving into shared hobbies, or engaging in thought-provoking experiences like attending lectures, reading books, or traveling to new places. This intellectual companionship helps the relationship grow in a dynamic way, where both partners feel like they are learning and evolving together, building a deeper connection through the expansion of their minds.

6. Debate and Respectful Disagreement: Intellectual attraction also involves healthy debate and respectful disagreement. Partners with strong intellectual connections don't shy away from differing opinions but see them as opportunities to learn and grow. They engage in thought-provoking discussions where different viewpoints are shared without hostility, fostering a relationship where curiosity and mutual respect guide intellectual exchanges.

7. Building a Strong Mental Connection: Over time, intellectual attraction creates a strong mental connection that becomes a core part of the relationship. This connection forms the basis of shared conversations, debates, inside jokes, and problem-solving together. It also ensures that even as the relationship evolves, there's always a rich mental foundation that keeps things stimulating and engaging, allowing both partners to feel valued for their thoughts and intellect.

Why It's Important in a Relationship:

- **Long-Term Fulfillment:** While physical attraction may initially draw you together, intellectual attraction often plays a key role in long-term relationship satisfaction. It creates a bond that goes beyond surface-level attraction, ensuring that you can continue to connect on deeper levels as the relationship matures.

- **Mental Stimulation:** Intellectual attraction ensures that you keep each other mentally engaged, preventing boredom and fostering continued growth within the relationship. This mental stimulation is crucial for relationships to thrive over time.

- **Building Deeper Bonds:** When intellectual attraction is present, partners are able to discuss their hopes, dreams, and ideas, which strengthens emotional intimacy. It provides a sense of shared purpose and intellectual companionship, creating a deeper connection.

In conclusion, intellectual attraction isn't just about agreeing on every idea or having the same interests—it's about being **stimulated and challenged** by your partner's mind. It ensures that the relationship remains mentally engaging, fulfilling, and dynamic, fostering a deep connection that complements emotional and physical attraction.

Positional Attractiveness

The one attraction we have not been aware of until now is positional attractiveness. And, I dare say, it is the most important of all because no matter how physically, emotionally, or intellectually appealing someone is, it makes no difference in a romantic relationship if you are positionally the same. Two Norths will deflect each other like the same polarities of a magnet. There is no amount of intelligence or beauty that will have two Easts not drive each other crazy. There is no force of nature that can direct two Souths out of their comfort zones, and there is definitely no way two Wests can decide to do anything together without driving one over the edge of indecision.

When I realized this myself, I finally understood why I was attracted to some of the attributes of a North (myself), but it was clearly a positional impossibility. It is the very reason why opposites attract. It provides balance, fulfills complementary needs, and brings new dynamics into each other's lives. It's in our human nature to know that we need someone to survive. We need others to survive. Yet, because we are unaware of this dynamic, we misinterpret, misunderstand, and confuse the reasons behind it.

It fascinates me how these attributes of attractiveness play out so naturally in life, acting as an underlying elemental force driving the energy of connection.

Positional attraction refers to the compatibility of two individuals based on their positions within the 4Cross Love Framework, which highlights distinct biological concerns that drive each person's worldview and behavior in relationships. Each position—North, East, South, and West—has unique traits and motivations, and positional attraction examines how well these traits complement or challenge each other in a relationship. Understanding positional attraction helps partners navigate their inherent differences, fostering compatibility and reducing potential conflicts by aligning their core motivations and concerns.

Here's a deeper look at how positional attraction works and its importance:

1. Alignment of Core Concerns

- Each position in the 4Cross Love Framework is driven by a fundamental concern that shapes how a person approaches relationships and life. Positional attraction occurs when these core concerns either complement each other or are balanced in a way that creates harmony, rather than friction, within the relationship.

- **Complementary Concerns**: For instance, a South's desire for stability may align well with a North's need for control, creating a dynamic where the North leads with direction, and the South offers steady support. Both partners feel secure in their roles.

- **Balancing Differences**: In other cases, opposites can attract and balance each other. For example, an East's love for spontaneity may balance a West's cautious and methodical approach, bringing excitement and energy to the relationship while still maintaining some structure.

2. Shared Approach to Conflict Resolution

- Positional attraction helps reduce conflicts because partners understand and respect each other's natural ways of resolving disagreements. Each position approaches conflict differently:

- **Norths** tend to be direct and decisive, seeking resolution through leadership and clarity.

- **Easts** may avoid rigid conflict structures, preferring to keep things light and flexible.

- **Souths** will seek to maintain peace and harmony, often avoiding confrontation to preserve stability.

- **Wests** will focus on analyzing the details and finding the most thought-out solution.

- When partners are aware of each other's positional tendencies, they can adjust their approach, ensuring smoother conflict resolution and avoiding misunderstandings. For example, if a South understands that a North values direct communication, they may feel less anxious about having a difficult conversation. Likewise, a North may learn to soften their approach to avoid overwhelming a more sensitive partner like a South.

3. Natural Compatibility in Roles

- Positional attraction can ensure that partners naturally fall into roles that feel comfortable for them. Each position thrives in different areas of life:

- **Norths** excel at leadership and decision-making.

- **Easts** bring creativity and spontaneity.

- **Souths** offer nurturing and emotional support.

- **Wests** focus on careful planning and ensuring precision.

- When positional attraction is strong, partners complement each other in these roles, allowing each to contribute their strengths to the relationship without feeling like they're competing or trying to change each other. For example, a North might take charge in organizing and planning a vacation, while an East adds excitement and creativity, making the experience enjoyable for both without stepping on each other's toes.

4. Reducing Miscommunication

- A major benefit of positional attraction is that it reduces miscommunication. When partners understand each other's positional motivations, they are less likely to take things personally or misinterpret each other's actions.

- A **West's** attention to detail and cautious approach won't be seen as overthinking by an **East** who values spontaneity. Instead, the East can appreciate how the West's planning helps prevent future issues.

- Similarly, a **South** won't take a **North's** need for control as a personal attack, understanding that it's part of the North's natural way of operating in the relationship.

- This understanding allows partners to communicate more effectively, knowing that their motivations are different but complementary.

5. Long-Term Compatibility

- Positional attraction provides a foundation for long-term compatibility by ensuring that partners' fundamental ways of interacting with the world align. While initial physical, emotional, or intellectual attraction might bring people together, it's positional compatibility that helps relationships last. Partners with strong positional attraction are better equipped to handle challenges, navigate life's changes, and grow together, because their core needs are met and respected.

- For example, if a **South** and a **West** are in a relationship, the South's desire for stability complements the West's need for security, providing a relationship that feels safe and reliable for both.

6. Managing Differences Through Awareness

- Even when positional attraction involves differences, these differences can be managed through awareness. Knowing the strengths and challenges of your partner's position allows for better understanding and empathy. For example, a North-East relationship might involve the North's need for control clashing with the East's desire for freedom, but if both are aware of these tendencies, they can make conscious efforts to compromise and respect each other's boundaries. The North may learn to loosen the reins a bit, while the East may recognize when it's important to follow the plan.

7. Balanced Dynamics in Decision-Making

- Positional attraction ensures that the decision-making process in a relationship feels balanced. Different positions contribute distinct perspectives:

- A **North** may initiate decisions with confidence.

- An **East** brings in creative possibilities.

- A **South** considers how the decision affects emotional stability.

- A **West** ensures that all details are accounted for.

- When positional attraction is strong, the balance between these approaches creates a more holistic decision-making process where everyone feels heard and valued.

Why Positional Attraction Matters in Relationships:

- **Understanding and Respect**: Positional attraction fosters greater understanding and respect between partners by acknowledging the biological and psychological drivers behind each person's actions.

- **Harmony in Differences**: It helps navigate and balance differences that might otherwise create friction, leading to more harmonious interactions.

- **Long-Lasting Compatibility**: Positional attraction helps ensure that relationships are based on a deeper level of compatibility that stands the test of time.

In conclusion, positional attraction within the 4Cross Love Framework provides a vital layer of compatibility that goes beyond surface-level traits. It ensures that your partner's inherent motivations align with or complement your own, helping to create a relationship where both individuals feel understood, supported, and able to thrive. By embracing positional attraction, you reduce potential conflicts, improve communication, and foster a stronger, more resilient connection.

Understanding the four types of attraction—physical, emotional, intellectual, and positional—gives us a comprehensive view of what draws people together and sustains relationships. Physical attraction might spark the initial interest, but it is the deeper connections that truly bind us.

Physical attraction is the first step, engaging our senses and creating that initial spark. However, as relationships progress, the importance of emotional and intellectual connections becomes apparent.

Emotional attraction builds trust and intimacy, creating a safe space for vulnerability and growth. It is the foundation of a supportive and nurturing relationship where both partners feel understood and valued.

Intellectual attraction stimulates our minds and fosters a deep sense of respect and admiration. Engaging in meaningful conversations and sharing ideas enriches the relationship, making it more dynamic and fulfilling.

Positional attraction, unique to the 4Cross Love Framework, highlights the importance of compatibility in our innate qualities. Understanding how different positions complement each other helps us appreciate the balance and harmony in our relationships. It explains why opposites often attract and how these dynamics contribute to a well-rounded and stable partnership.

By recognizing and valuing all four types of attraction, we can cultivate more holistic and enduring relationships. Each type of attraction plays a vital role in different stages of a relationship. Together, they create a powerful synergy that enhances our connections.

Next is interests. Are *you* interesting?

CHAPTER 10

Checklist Point #3 Interests

"There is no remedy for love but to love more." - Henry David Thoreau

---

Is it nice to have some interests in common?

Yes, but these things don't make you similar or necessarily compatible. If there is one mistake that is continually made in all the land, it is thinking that just because you have similar interests, you're a good match.

Having similar interests is important and nice, but based on your position, you will look at them differently. It's important to realize that the underlying motivations and ways of interacting with the world can differ significantly based on position. The great thing about knowing your position and realizing you have similar interests, like pottery, is that it can accentuate your reasons for liking something! Each of you can bring an entirely different perspective to pottery and appreciate not only pottery but each other!

Let's talk about the different ways each position looks at interests.

Interests vs. Underlying Motivation

The North position tends to be interested in leadership roles, strategic games, or innovative projects. This reflects their underlying motivation to provide certainty and direction. Norths engage in activities to assert their knowledge and vision. They thrive on being seen as leaders and innovators and are driven by a deep need to know and be seen as competent.

The East position tends to show an interest in social events, adventure sports, or creative endeavors, which aligns with their underlying motivation for freedom and exploration. Easts engage in activities to experience excitement and connect with others, bringing energy and spontaneity to their interests. They are motivated by a desire to explore new possibilities and maintain their sense of freedom.

The South position tends to demonstrate an interest in community service, team sports, or family gatherings. This reflects their underlying motivation for stability and harmony. Souths participate in activities driven by a desire to support and connect with others, fostering a sense of belonging and emotional security that's motivated by the need to create and maintain supportive, harmonious environments.

The West position tends to have interests in analytical puzzles, detailed crafts, or systematic research, which correlates with their underlying motivation for thoroughness and precision. Wests engage in activities that allow them to plan meticulously and ensure everything is well organized and efficient. They are motivated by a desire for order and mastery of their chosen tasks.

Similar Interests, Different Dynamics

People from different positions might share an interest, but their approaches and interactions, as well as the satisfaction they derive from that interest, will vary.

For example, in team sports, Norths take on leadership roles, strategize the game, and motivate the team. Easts bring enthusiasm, keep the energy high, and enjoy the social aspect. Souths focus on team cohesion, support teammates, and ensure everyone feels included. Meanwhile, Wests analyze the rules and strategies, work on improving techniques, and ensure the team is well-prepared and safe.

Let's go through some examples to demonstrate what I mean.

Example: Cooking

An interest in cooking can differ significantly for each position within the 4Cross Love Framework, reflecting unique perspectives, motivations, and values. Here's how each position might approach and engage with cooking:

Norths see cooking as a project to be mastered and a way to demonstrate their skills and innovation. They approach it with a goal-oriented mindset, focusing on precision and excellence. Enjoying experimentation, they aim to create unique and impressive dishes, often involving a lot of planning to perfect their culinary skills. Cooking provides an opportunity for Norths to showcase their knowledge and ingenuity, combining unusual approaches to create something distinctive, though not always successful.

Easts view cooking as a fun, social activity that brings people together and creates enjoyable experiences. They embrace the creative and spontaneous aspects, often improvising rather than strictly following recipes. For Easts, cooking is a way to engage socially, whether through cooking together or hosting gatherings. They enjoy trying new foods and experimenting with flavors, valuing the process as much as the end result.

Souths see cooking as a way to nurture and provide for loved ones, express care, and create a sense of home and community. They often prefer traditional recipes and comfort foods that offer reliability and emotional warmth. Cooking allows Souths to connect emotionally with others, showing love and care through food, and they value the stability and comfort that traditional meals bring to their household.

Wests view cooking as a precise and methodical activity, and they closely follow recipes to ensure accuracy and consistency. They pay attention to details, ensuring measurements and techniques are executed perfectly. For Wests, cooking provides a sense of order and control, allowing them to apply their meticulous nature productively. They take pride in mastering cooking techniques and producing high-quality dishes that meet their exacting standards.

By understanding these different perspectives and motivations, we can appreciate how the same interests, such as cooking, can be experienced and valued in diverse ways based on an individual's position within the 4Cross Love Framework.

Example: Fitness

Let's explore how the interest in fitness differs for each position within the 4Cross Framework, reflecting their unique perspectives, motivations, and values.

Norths often see fitness as a goal-oriented activity. They approach it with a strategic mindset, setting clear objectives to build strength, improve endurance, or excel in a particular sport. They enjoy trying new fitness technologies or methods and are always looking for the exact way to achieve their goals. Fitness is a way for a North to demonstrate discipline, strength, and competence, and they take pride in reaching their fitness milestones. Additionally, they may enjoy leading fitness groups or teams, using their knowledge to guide others.

Easts can view fitness as a social and fun activity, but not always. They thrive on variety and spontaneity, enjoying group activities like team sports, fitness classes, or outdoor adventures. For Easts, fitness is a platform for socializing and building relationships, and they are motivated by the enjoyment and exhilaration that come from engaging in diverse physical activities.

Souths see fitness as a means to well-being, focusing on maintaining overall health and balance. They often prefer activities that promote relaxation and well-being, like yoga or walking, and they enjoy consistent routines, often participating with family or close friends. Fitness is crucial for their physical and emotional well-being, and they value activities that contribute to their long-term health and provide opportunities to support and be supported by others.

Wests view fitness as a systematic and methodical activity. They approach it with precision, following detailed plans and tracking their progress meticulously. Interested in the science behind fitness, they focus on optimizing their workouts through careful analysis and technique improvement. Fitness allows Wests to apply their methodical nature, providing a sense of control and accomplishment. They take pride in mastering specific techniques and understanding the detailed mechanics of fitness and exercise.

Shared interests provide a foundation for activities and experiences that you can enjoy together. They help build a sense of companionship and partnership. Having shared interests ensures that you can spend quality time together doing things you both enjoy, strengthening your bond. Finding common ground through shared interests can significantly enhance your connections with others. Recognizing that you and your mate may see and experience these interests differently makes it that much more exciting to share.

Ask about hobbies, passions, and activities a potential mate enjoys to determine whether you share common interests. This exploration helps you gauge whether you can build a life together based on mutual enjoyment.

It's important to ask questions in a way that doesn't make them feel trapped by using the term *favorite*. It's better to leave a question open for many possible answers to keep the conversation flowing and open.

Here are some questions to help you discover if you and someone else share hobbies, passions, or activities.

1. "What are some things you enjoy doing in your free time?"

2. "Do you have any hobbies or activities that you're passionate about?"

3. "Are there some things you're passionate about?"

4. "What are some topics or activities that make you feel most alive and engaged?"

5. "Is there a fun activity you have done recently?"

6. "Have you tried any new hobbies or activities recently?"

7. "Do you play any sports or have a fitness routine?"

8. "Are there some things you like to do to stay active?"

9. "Are you into any creative activities, like painting, drawing, or crafting?"

10. "Have you made anything recently that you're proud of?"

11. "Do you play any musical instruments or sing?"

12. "Have you been to any good concerts or performances lately?"

13. "What kind of books do you enjoy reading?"

14. "Have you read any good books or written anything recently?"

15. "What kind of movies or TV shows do you like to watch?"

16. "Have you seen any good movies or series recently?"

17. "Do you enjoy traveling? What's a place you've enjoyed visiting?"

18. "Do you have any upcoming travel plans or dream destinations?"

19. "Do you enjoy cooking or trying out new recipes?"

20. "What's a type of cuisine or a dish you love to make?"

21. "Are you into video games or any type of gaming?"

22. "Do you follow any tech trends or enjoy working with new gadgets?"

23. "Do you like spending time outdoors? What are some outdoor activities you enjoy?"

24. "Have you been on any interesting hikes or nature trips recently?"

25. "Are you involved in any community activities or volunteering?"

26. "Is there a cause or organization you're particularly passionate about?"

27. "Do you enjoy learning new things? What subjects are you interested in?"

28. "Are you taking any courses or workshops right now?"

29. "What do you do to relax and take care of yourself?"

30. "Do you practice any mindfulness or wellness activities?"

31. "What are some personal goals or dreams you're working toward?"

32. "Is there a hobby or activity you've always wanted to try but haven't yet?"

33. "Would you be interested in trying out [specific activity] together sometime?"

34. "Is there a hobby or activity you've wanted to explore more?"

Understanding that shared interests do not equate to similarity helps in appreciating the diverse strengths and approaches individuals bring to the table. The 4Cross Love Framework highlights these differences, showing how each position's unique motivations shape their engagement with common interests, ultimately enriching collaborative efforts and interpersonal relationships.

In the next chapter, we will examine how, although they may appear the same, each position sees values differently and how you can navigate this reality.

Are you valuable?

CHAPTER 11

Checklist Point #4 Values

"Where there is love there is life." - Mahatma Gandhi

In the 4Cross Love Framework, each position views their values through the lens of their inherent characteristics and survival concerns. Understanding the values and characteristics of each position within the 4Cross Love Framework is crucial when navigating your relationships because it helps you better understand yourself and your potential partners.

Knowing these positions provides insight into each person's core motivations, strengths, and concerns, allowing for more effective communication, deeper connections, and better conflict resolution.

North individuals value wisdom, seeing it as a crucial element in their lives. They want to lead by instilling confidence and providing certainty to others. Driven by a need to be seen as certain and competent, they often feel that if others doubt their knowledge, it could jeopardize their identity.

East individuals value valor, embodying courage and enthusiasm. They thrive on freedom and the ability to inspire and motivate others. Their primary concern is maintaining their freedom, and they see their role as freeing others, often acting as negotiators and facilitators to gain buy-in for new ideas.

South individuals value justice, focusing on fairness, support, and emotional stability. They naturally gravitate toward roles that involve coordination and ensure harmonious relationships. Their survival concern centers around maintaining stability and avoiding conflict, making them reliable and supportive partners on any team.

West individuals value prudence, emphasizing careful planning, reflection, and thorough evaluation. They excel in creating order and structure. Their primary concern is thoroughness and ensuring that everything is well thought out before action is taken, making them methodical and organized.

Overall, this awareness allows individuals to tailor their approach to dating and relationships, ensuring they meet each other's emotional needs and create a balanced, fulfilling partnership. It fosters empathy and respect for each other's unique qualities, ultimately leading to stronger and more harmonious relationships.

Let's take a look at some common values and how each position might look at them.

Value: Leadership

Each position views leadership differently.

Norths see leadership as providing direction and certainty. They believe in taking charge, making decisive moves, leading by example, and seeing themselves as visionaries who guide others toward a clear goal. Leadership is central to a North's identity and their contribution to a team or organization.

Easts, on the other hand, see leadership as inspiring and energizing others. They lead with enthusiasm, innovation, and engagement, focusing on motivating the group and exploring new possibilities. For Easts, leadership is about creating an exciting and inclusive environment.

Souths perceive leadership as being supportive and ensuring everyone feels valued and included. They lead through empathy, reliability, and a focus on team harmony, viewing leadership as a way to ensure stability and support within the group.

Wests believe leadership is about meticulous planning and precision. They lead by organizing, evaluating, and methodically executing plans, valuing thoroughness and reliability in their leadership roles. Leadership for Wests is important for ensuring that everything is done correctly and efficiently.

Value: Religion

In the 4Cross Love Framework, each position has a distinct perspective on religion.

Norths view religion as providing a structured belief system that offers certainty and direction. They see it as a source of wisdom and guidelines for living, reinforcing their need for certainty and providing a framework for making decisions.

Easts, on the other hand, perceive religion as community, inspiration, and the freedom to explore spirituality. They value religion for its ability to forge connections and provide personal meaning, appreciating its community aspects and inspirational messages, provided it allows for personal freedom and expression.

Souths consider religion as a means to create a sense of belonging and emotional support. They view it as a source of comfort, stability, and moral guidance that is crucial for maintaining emotional security and fostering a supportive community.

Wests approach religion with a focus on tradition, order, and moral clarity. They see it as a systematic approach to ethics and life, valuing its detailed doctrines and practices. For Wests, religion is essential due to the structure and thorough, methodical approach it brings to understanding life and morality.

Value: Family

In the 4Cross Love Framework, each position has a unique perspective on family.

Norths consider family to be about leadership and ensuring the family unit is directed toward common goals. They see their role in the family as the provider of certainty and direction, making family a cornerstone of their identity where they can lead and impart wisdom.

Easts, on the other hand, view family as an environment of fun, freedom, and dynamic interaction. They see family as a source of energy and a platform for expressing creativity. They value the social and adventurous aspects it provides, as long as it does not restrict their freedom.

Souths perceive family as a source of support, emotional stability, and a nurturing environment. They consider family their core community, where loyalty and harmony are paramount, making family central to their sense of belonging and emotional well-being.

Wests view family as a unit that benefits from maintaining order, tradition, and a well-organized home. They see family as crucial for providing structure and ensuring that everything runs smoothly and according to plan. They also believe that a family benefits from detailed planning and systematic care.

Value: Cleanliness

In the 4Cross Love Framework, each position has a distinct perspective on cleanliness.

For Norths, cleanliness is about maintaining a controlled and efficient environment. They view it as essential for productivity and clarity, ensuring their environment is organized and free from distractions, enabling them to focus on their visionary tasks.

Easts, on the other hand, see cleanliness as a way to create an inviting and energetic space. They value cleanliness for maintaining a dynamic and pleasant atmosphere. To that end, they keep their environment lively and free from clutter that stifles creativity and freedom, though they may not be as meticulous as other positions.

Souths perceive cleanliness as providing a comfortable and welcoming space for themselves and others. They see it as a way to show care and respect for their environment and the people in it. To them, cleanliness is crucial for fostering a sense of stability and emotional well-being.

Wests view cleanliness as a reflection of their precision and order. For them, cleanliness is essential for maintaining order and efficiency. It aligns with their meticulous nature and is part of ensuring that everything is in its proper place.

Value: Fiscal Responsibility

In the 4Cross Love Framework, each position has a distinct perspective on fiscal responsibility.

Norths consider fiscal responsibility to be about ensuring certainty and enabling strategic investments. They view financial management as a way to secure the future and support their visionary goals, considering it critical for maintaining the resources they need to pursue their plans, vision, and projects.

Easts, on the other hand, sees fiscal responsibility as a means to explore opportunities freely. They view financial management as a way to ensure they can engage in new experiences and ventures without constraints, valuing it for sustaining their adventurous lifestyle, even if they might take more financial risks compared to other positions.

Souths perceive fiscal responsibility as a way to provide security and support for loved ones. They view financial management as essential for ensuring their family's well-being and stability, making it crucial for maintaining the emotional and physical security of their household.

Wests approach fiscal responsibility with precision and careful planning. They see financial management as a detailed process requiring meticulous tracking and prudent decision-making, considering it essential for maintaining order and avoiding unnecessary risks. This approach aligns with their methodical nature.

Value: Communication

In the 4Cross Love Framework, each position has a distinct perspective on communication.

Norths consider communication to be about conveying clear, decisive information. They view it as a tool for providing direction and certainty, believing that effective communication is vital for ensuring that their vision and plans are understood and followed.

Easts, on the other hand, sees communication as a way to engage and inspire others. They use it to connect, share ideas, and generate enthusiasm, considering it crucial for maintaining social bonds and motivating others.

Souths perceive communication as a means to foster understanding and emotional connection. They view it as a way to support and empathize with others, believing that effective communication is essential for maintaining harmony and ensuring everyone feels heard and valued.

Wests approach communication as a method for providing detailed and accurate information. They see it as critical for ensuring clarity and preventing misunderstandings, believing that precise communication is necessary for maintaining accuracy and ensuring all details are correctly understood and followed.

By understanding these nuanced perspectives, we can see how individuals from different positions might share the same values but interpret and prioritize them differently, enriching their interactions and relationships.

Shared values are critical for long-term compatibility. They influence decisions, behaviors, and how you navigate challenges as a couple. Aligning on core values ensures that your long-term goals and life philosophies are compatible, which is essential for a harmonious relationship.

Here are some great questions you can ask based on a common value.

Questions for the Value of Knowledge:

- What areas of knowledge are you most passionate about, and how do you pursue learning in those areas?

- What's the most exciting thing you've learned recently, and how did it inspire you?

- How do you use your knowledge to help and support the people around you?

- Can you share a detailed process you follow to deeply understand a new topic?

Questions for the Value of Courage:

- Can you describe a time when you had to take a significant risk to achieve a goal?

- What's the most adventurous thing you've ever done, and what did you learn from it?

- How do you support others when they need to find the courage to face difficult situations?

- Can you give an example of a situation where you had to stick to your principles despite pressure to do otherwise?

Questions for the Value of Fairness:

- How do you ensure that your decisions are fair and just, especially when leading others?

- How do you make sure that everyone feels included and treated fairly in social situations?

- What does fairness mean to you in terms of supporting family and friends?

- Can you describe a method you use to make fair decisions in complex situations?

Questions for the Value of Prudence:

- How do you balance long-term planning with taking action in the present?

- How do you decide when to be spontaneous and when to be cautious?

- How do you ensure that your actions today will positively affect the future for those you care about?

- What steps do you take to carefully plan and evaluate decisions before making them?

Questions for the Value of Leadership:

- What qualities do you think are essential for effective leadership, and how do you embody them?

- How do you inspire and energize people around you in leadership roles?

- How do you use your leadership to create a supportive and harmonious environment?

- How do you ensure that your leadership decisions are precise and well thought out?

Questions for the Value of Family:

- How do you balance your career goals with family responsibilities?

- What fun activities do you enjoy doing with your family to keep things lively?

- How do you ensure that your family feels supported and emotionally connected?

- What routines or traditions do you follow to maintain order and harmony in your family?

Questions for the Value of Cleanliness:

- How do you maintain an organized and efficient environment in your home and work?

- How do you incorporate cleanliness and order into your lifestyle?

- How important is a clean and tidy home for creating a comfortable and supportive environment?

- What detailed steps do you take to ensure cleanliness and order in your daily life?

Questions for the Value of Fiscal Responsibility:

- How do you manage your finances to achieve your long-term goals?

- How do you balance enjoying life with being financially responsible?

- How do you ensure that your financial decisions support your family's well-being?

- What detailed budgeting or financial planning methods do you use to stay organized?

Questions for the Value of Communication:

- How do you ensure that your communication is clear and effective?

- How do you keep communication lively and engaging in your relationships?

- How do you use communication to foster emotional connections with others?

- What techniques do you use to ensure that your communication is precise and thorough?

Speaking of communication…how do you think communicating effectively would help in all of your relationships?

Are you an effective communicator?

CHAPTER 12

Checklist Point #5
Effective Communication

"One word frees us of all the weight and pain in life: That word is love."—Sophocles

---

The number-one problem in all relationships is communication breakdown, which is why effective communication is the cornerstone of any successful relationship. Let's explore effective communication among the four positions as it relates to dating and romantic relationships.

Effective communication involves not just transmitting information but also receiving and understanding that information. It encompasses verbal and nonverbal cues, active listening, empathy, and clarity. In romantic relationships, effective communication is vital for several reasons: it builds trust and intimacy, resolves conflicts, fosters emotional connection, and prevents misunderstandings.

Clear and honest communication helps partners understand each other's needs, desires, and concerns, fostering trust and intimacy. Effective communication skills are essential for resolving conflicts amicably, ensuring that both parties feel heard and respected. Sharing thoughts and feelings openly strengthens the emotional bond between partners, and clear communication helps prevent misunderstandings that can lead to frustration and resentment.

Each position in the 4Cross Love Framework has a unique communication style that reflects their underlying values and motivations. Understanding these styles can enhance interactions and improve relationship dynamics.

Norths communicate with a focus on providing clear, decisive information. They view communication as a tool for providing direction and ensuring that their vision and plans are understood and followed. In a dating context, a North individual might prioritize discussions about goals, plans, and expectations. They appreciate partners who are straightforward and appreciate direct feedback. However, Norths may sometimes come across as overly blunt or dismissive of others' feelings, which can create tension if not balanced with empathy and patience. Effective communication with a North involves being clear and concise, showing appreciation for their strategic thinking and decisiveness, and balancing directness with empathy to ensure emotional connection.

Easts thrive on engaging and inspiring communication. They see it as a means to connect, share ideas, and generate enthusiasm. In dating, Easts are likely to enjoy lively conversations, spontaneous outings, and shared experiences that foster a sense of excitement and adventure. They value partners who are open to exploring new ideas and experiences. However, Easts may sometimes struggle with consistency and may be perceived as unfocused or scattered in their communication. Effective communication with an East involves engaging with enthusiasm, expressing interest in their ideas, embracing spontaneity, being open to new experiences, and providing gentle reminders to maintain consistency and follow through on commitments.

Souths prioritize supportive and empathetic communication. They see it as a way to foster understanding and emotional connection. In a dating relationship, Souths are likely to focus on creating a nurturing and harmonious environment. They value partners who are empathetic, attentive, and supportive. However, Souths may avoid confronting issues directly, leading to unresolved conflicts and built-up resentment. Effective communication with a South involves communicating with warmth and empathy, showing genuine care for their feelings, encouraging open discussions about any concerns or issues, and providing reassurance and support to build a stable and secure relationship.

Wests communicate with a focus on providing detailed and accurate information. They value precision and clarity and see communication as essential for maintaining order and preventing misunderstandings. In dating, Wests appreciate partners who are reliable and attentive to details, valuing structured plans and well-thought-out discussions. However, Wests may be perceived as overly critical or rigid, focusing too much on details and not enough on emotional aspects. Effective communication with a West involves being thorough and precise, acknowledging and appreciating their attention to detail, and balancing factual discussions with expressions of emotion to strengthen the emotional bond.

Effective communication in romantic relationships requires an understanding of both your own communication style and your partner's. Practicing active listening by giving your full attention to your partner, acknowledging their feelings, and responding thoughtfully fosters mutual respect and understanding. Cultivating empathy by trying to see things from your partner's perspective helps bridge gaps in communication styles and fosters a deeper emotional connection.

Being clear and honest in your communication prevents assumptions and misunderstandings, ensuring that your thoughts and feelings are expressed openly. It's crucial to be adaptable in your communication style and recognize that different situations may require different approaches. Providing constructive feedback to each other about what communication strategies work best and being open to adjusting also enhances communication.

Here are the key aspects of what effective communication in a relationship looks like:

1. Active Listening

- **What it looks like**: Active listening involves fully focusing on your partner when they speak, without interrupting, and showing that you value their perspective. This means giving your full attention, making eye contact, and offering verbal and non-verbal cues (such as nodding or saying "I see" or "I understand") to show you are engaged.

- **Why it matters**: It reassures your partner that their thoughts and feelings are important to you. It also helps prevent misunderstandings, as you're more likely to hear the full message rather than making assumptions.

2. Open and Honest Expression

- **What it looks like**: Effective communication requires expressing your thoughts, feelings, and needs honestly and clearly. This means being direct without being harsh, and stating your needs or concerns in a way that's easy for your partner to understand.

- **Why it matters**: When you communicate openly, you reduce the likelihood of bottling up emotions or creating confusion. Honest communication builds trust, showing that you are willing to be vulnerable and transparent with your partner.

3. Respectful Tone and Delivery

- **What it looks like**: The way you say something often matters more than what you're saying. Using a calm, respectful tone, even when discussing sensitive or difficult issues, helps prevent defensiveness and escalation. Avoid blaming, accusing, or using a condescending tone.

- **Why it matters**: A respectful approach ensures that your partner feels safe and understood, making them more open to resolving issues and engaging in meaningful dialogue. Disrespectful communication can lead to feelings of resentment or emotional withdrawal.

4. Non-Verbal Communication

- **What it looks like**: Effective communication is also conveyed through body language, facial expressions, and gestures. Being aware of your body language (like crossing arms, avoiding eye contact, or looking disinterested) can either reinforce or contradict what you're saying.

- **Why it matters**: Non-verbal cues can either strengthen the message you're communicating or create confusion. Positive non-verbal communication, such as leaning in, maintaining eye contact, and using gentle gestures, shows attentiveness and empathy.

5. Empathy and Understanding

- **What it looks like**: Empathy is the ability to understand and relate to your partner's feelings and experiences. In practice, it means validating their emotions by acknowledging what they're going through, even if you don't agree with their perspective. Phrases like "I understand why that upset you" or "That must have been difficult for you" show empathy.

- **Why it matters**: Empathy fosters emotional intimacy and helps your partner feel valued. It reduces defensiveness and opens the door for more constructive conversations, especially during conflicts.

6. Constructive Conflict Resolution

- **What it looks like**: In any relationship, disagreements will arise. Effectively communicating during conflict involves discussing the issue without resorting to blame, criticism, or anger. It's about focusing on the problem, not the person, and working together to find a solution. Using "I" statements, such as "I feel upset when..." instead of "You always...," helps keep the conversation constructive.

- **Why it matters**: Constructive conflict resolution prevents issues from escalating into bigger problems. It allows you to address concerns respectfully and productively, leading to a healthier, more resilient relationship.

7. Being Mindful of Timing

- **What it looks like**: Timing matters when it comes to discussing sensitive topics. Effective communication includes being mindful of when and where to bring up certain issues. For example, bringing up a serious issue in the middle of a stressful event or in public may not lead to the best conversation.

- **Why it matters**: Discussing important matters when both partners are in the right frame of mind creates an environment for thoughtful and productive dialogue. It reduces the chances of emotional overreactions and allows for a more focused and considerate discussion.

8. Checking for Understanding

- **What it looks like**: Communication doesn't end after you've said what's on your mind. It's essential to check that your partner has understood your message and vice versa. You can do this by asking, "Does that make sense to you?" or "How do you feel about what I just said?"

- **Why it matters**: This ensures that both of you are on the same page and prevents miscommunication or assumptions. It also provides an opportunity for clarification if something wasn't understood correctly.

9. Offering and Accepting Feedback

- **What it looks like**: Effective communication involves being able to give feedback gently and receive it with an open mind. When giving feedback, focus on the behavior, not the person, and offer it in a way that encourages improvement rather than making your partner feel attacked. When receiving feedback, try to stay open, even if it's difficult to hear.

- **Why it matters**: Feedback helps partners grow together. When given and received with respect, it strengthens the relationship by encouraging positive change and mutual understanding.

10. Balancing Speaking and Listening

- **What it looks like**: Effective communication is a two-way street. It's important to balance talking with listening, ensuring both partners have the space to express themselves. Avoid interrupting or monopolizing the conversation. Instead, create a rhythm where both people feel heard and valued.

- **Why it matters**: Equal participation in conversations leads to mutual respect and ensures that both partners feel their thoughts and feelings are important. It prevents one-sided communication, where one person dominates while the other feels ignored.

11. Sharing Vulnerabilities

- **What it looks like**: Sharing your vulnerabilities and fears is key to deep emotional connection. Effective communication means being willing to talk about what scares you, what you struggle with, and how you feel emotionally, without fear of judgment.

- **Why it matters**: Vulnerability fosters intimacy and trust. It lets your partner in, building a stronger emotional bond that allows for more open, honest conversations.

Summary:

Effectively communicating in a relationship is about fostering openness, trust, and understanding. It involves **active listening, honest expression, empathy**, and **constructive conflict resolution**, all while maintaining respect and mindfulness of timing. Communication that is **balanced, present, and vulnerable** strengthens the emotional connection, helping both partners feel valued and understood. By practicing these skills, partners can navigate challenges, enhance intimacy, and build a healthy, fulfilling relationship.

To thoroughly evaluate someone's communication effectiveness, consider incorporating multiple approaches to gain a comprehensive understanding. Here's how each method can help:

1. **Observation**: Observe the person in a variety of settings, such as meetings, casual conversations, and written communications (e.g., emails, texts). Pay attention to their body language, tone, clarity, and responsiveness. This gives you real-time insight into how they adapt their communication style depending on the context and audience.

2. **Feedback from Others**: Collect feedback from friends, family, peers, and coworkers. Getting diverse perspectives allows you to see how their communication style is perceived by different people. This feedback can highlight patterns, such as whether they tend to dominate conversations or listen attentively.

3. **Self-Assessment**: Encourage the individual to reflect on their own communication skills. Ask them to consider how they approach listening, clarity, and empathy in conversations. Self-assessment helps raise their awareness of personal strengths and areas where they may want to improve.

4. **Incorporating Communication in Feedback**: When providing feedback on performance, include specific insights on communication skills. For example, instead of just saying "be clearer," offer tangible examples like "During our last meeting, you tended to use jargon that confused me. Try explaining the concept in simpler terms."

By systematically evaluating these aspects, you'll gain a deeper understanding of how effectively someone communicates. This multi-faceted approach allows you to identify specific areas for improvement, helping to enhance both their communication skills and your own through mutual reflection and growth.

Understanding the unique communication styles of the four positions in the 4Cross Love Framework can greatly enhance romantic interactions. By appreciating each position's distinct perspectives and motivations, couples can tailor their communication to foster trust, intimacy, and emotional connection. Whether it's the directness of a North, the enthusiasm of an East, the empathy of a South, or the precision of a West, each style brings valuable strengths to a relationship.

We are going to get to the ultimate goal: choice.

Are you ready to choose?

CHAPTER 13

Checklist Point #6 Choice

"Every heart sings a song, incomplete, until another heart whispers back." – Plato

Let's talk about commitment and why it can be so difficult.

Making the choice to commit to somebody can be challenging due to several factors. Understanding the 4Cross Love Framework can provide valuable insights into these challenges and help you navigate your relationships more effectively so you can feel good about the process of making a commitment or recommitting wholeheartedly to the one you are with.

Here are some of the biggest challenges we all face when thinking about making a commitment to a relationship.

Self-Awareness and Understanding:

Without self-awareness, you may struggle with understanding your needs and motivations, as well as how you interact with others' needs and motivations. Understanding your own position within the 4Cross Love Framework is crucial.

Positional Awareness Opposites and Balance:

We are often attracted to people who balance our characteristics. For example, Norths and Souths, or Easts and Wests, complement each other well. However, this balance can also lead to conflicts, as each position has different needs and ways of interacting. If these differences are not understood and managed well, it can make commitment difficult.

Emotional Attraction:

Beyond physical attraction, emotional connections are crucial for a strong commitment. Making emotional connections can be challenging for various reasons. Here's a look at the difficulties involved in forming these connections.

Vulnerability: Forming a deep emotional connection requires vulnerability. Many individuals struggle with opening up and sharing their true feelings, often due to past experiences of rejection or hurt.

Emotional Intelligence Gaps: Differences in emotional intelligence can create barriers. If one partner is highly emotionally intelligent and the other is not, it can lead to misunderstandings and frustration.

Fear of Intimacy: Some individuals fear emotional closeness because it makes them feel exposed and dependent. This fear can lead them to avoid deep connections.

Communication Styles: Differences in how people express and handle emotions can lead to miscommunication. For example, Norths might be more reserved and logical, while Easts are expressive and spontaneous, leading to potential clashes.

Emotional Baggage: Past traumas and unresolved emotional issues can prevent individuals from forming new emotional bonds. These past experiences can create walls that are hard to break down.

Intellectual Connections:

Making intellectual connections can be challenging for various reasons. Here's an in-depth look at the difficulties involved in forming these connections.

Divergent Interests: Partners may have different intellectual interests, making it hard to find common ground for stimulating conversations.

Intellectual Compatibility: Differences in intellectual levels or cognitive styles can create a disconnect. One partner might find the other's ideas simplistic, while the other might feel overwhelmed by complex discussions.

Communication Barriers: Misunderstandings and communication issues can arise if partners have different ways of processing and articulating their thoughts.

Lifestyle Differences: Intellectual pursuits often reflect deeper lifestyle preferences. If one partner enjoys quiet, thoughtful activities while the other prefers more dynamic, hands-on experiences, it can be hard to connect intellectually.

Intellectual Insecurity: Some individuals may feel intellectually insecure and avoid deep conversations out of fear of being judged or not measuring up.

Knowing the 4Cross Love Framework helps you and your partner understand each other when emotional and intellectual connections are challenging. The framework gives you a structured understanding of your own and your partner's innate characteristics, strengths, and areas for improvement. This awareness fosters better communication, empathy, and conflict resolution strategies tailored to each position.

By recognizing and appreciating your unique needs and perspectives and your partner's, you both can find common ground, support each other's passions, and build a balanced, fulfilling relationship even when faced with differing interests or intellectual mismatches.

Common Interests:

Not having common interests makes the idea of commitment difficult because it reduces opportunities for shared experiences and quality time, which are essential for bonding and creating emotional connections. Without mutual activities, couples may struggle to find meaningful ways to engage with each other, leading to feelings of isolation or disconnection. Divergent interests can also reflect deeper lifestyle differences, causing tension in daily routines and long-term goals. Additionally, a lack of common ground can hinder intellectual compatibility, making conversations less engaging and preventing mutual growth. These challenges can create barriers to forming a deep, fulfilling relationship, making commitment seem less appealing and more challenging to maintain.

By understanding your own and your partner's position within the 4Cross Love Framework, you can both find ways to connect on deeper emotional and intellectual levels, build mutual respect, and identify new activities that honor your preferences and your partner's, ultimately strengthening your relationship.

Shared Values:

Not having shared values can be a deal breaker because values form the foundation of a person's beliefs, actions, and long-term goals. When partners do not align on core values, such as honesty, family, ambition, or financial priorities, it can lead to fundamental disagreements and conflicts that are difficult to resolve. These differences can create persistent tension and undermine trust and respect, making it challenging to build a cohesive and supportive relationship. Without a shared value system, partners may find it hard to navigate important life decisions together, ultimately making long-term commitment unsustainable. There is simply no way to get around it.

Knowing the 4Cross Love Framework can help you realize potential value misalignments before making a bad commitment decision. It does this by providing a clear understanding of your own and your partner's core characteristics and needs. By identifying each other's position within the framework, you can better recognize and articulate fundamental values and concerns. This awareness facilitates deeper conversations about essential life goals and beliefs, enabling you and your partner to address potential conflicts early on and reduce the risk of long-term commitment issues due to value differences.

Effective Communication:

Ineffective communication makes it difficult to commit because it leads to misunderstandings, unresolved conflicts, and emotional disconnection. When partners struggle to express their thoughts, feelings, and needs clearly, it can create frustration and resentment, eroding trust and intimacy. Poor communication hinders problem-solving and compromise, making it challenging to navigate differences and align on future goals. Without effective communication, partners may feel unheard or undervalued, causing doubts about the relationship's stability and long-term viability and ultimately making commitment seem risky and unwise.

Knowing the 4Cross Love Framework can help alleviate communication concerns by offering insights into each partner's natural communication style, strengths, and needs based on their position. This understanding fosters empathy and patience, enabling partners to adapt their communication methods to be more effective and considerate of each other's perspectives. By recognizing and addressing these differences, couples can improve their dialogue, resolve conflicts more efficiently, and build stronger emotional connections, thereby enhancing trust and making the idea of commitment more appealing and attainable.

Being intentional about the decision to commit to someone is crucial because it ensures that the relationship is built on a foundation of mutual understanding, compatibility, and shared goals. Thoughtful consideration helps you evaluate your own needs and values alongside your partner's, reducing the risk of future conflicts and misunderstandings. Intentional commitment fosters trust and a deeper emotional connection, as both partners enter the relationship with clarity and purpose.

Using the 4Cross Love Checklist enhances your likelihood of building a fulfilling, resilient partnership. It is the recipe for success in love, where both you and your partner are aligned in your expectations and dedication to each other's growth and happiness.

After going through the comprehensive process of the 4Cross Love Checklist, you will be ready to synthesize all this information to make an informed and confident choice about making a commitment to someone or reigniting the flame and recommitting to the one you are with.

Practical Steps and Considerations to Help You Make That Decision

Reflect on Your Awareness

Review Your Position: Revisit your own position within the 4Cross Love Framework. Reflect on your inherent traits, strengths, weaknesses, and what you need in a partner to complement and balance you.

Review Positional Compatibility: Evaluate how well your potential mate's or your mate's position aligns with yours. Consider how their characteristics, motivations, and ways of interacting with the world match your needs and complement your traits.

Reflect on Attraction

Physical Compatibility: Reflect on the level of physical attraction and chemistry you share. Physical attraction is important for intimacy and overall satisfaction in the relationship, but it should be balanced with other forms of attraction.

Emotional Connection: Consider the depth of your emotional connection. Ask yourself if you feel understood, valued, and emotionally supported by your potential mate. Think about how you handle emotional challenges together.

Intellectual Stimulation: Reflect on the intellectual connection. Assess whether your conversations are engaging and stimulating and whether you enjoy learning and exploring ideas together.

Positional Attraction: If they are not opposite of you positionally, are you able to identify, accept, and honor their position?

Review Shared Interests and Activities

Common Interests: Evaluate the activities and hobbies you both enjoy. Shared interests are important for building companionship and enjoying time together.

Potential for Growth: Consider whether you can introduce each other to new activities and interests and whether there is a willingness to grow and explore together.

Ensure Alignment of Core Values and Long-Term Goals

Core Values: Reflect on whether your core values align. Consider ethics, religion, politics, and personal beliefs. Values are the foundation of a strong and enduring relationship.

Long-Term Goals: Assess whether your long-term goals are compatible. Discuss and review plans for career, family, lifestyle, and other significant life choices. Ensure that your visions for the future are aligned.

Evaluate Communication Styles and Conflict Resolution

Effective Communication: Reflect on your communication styles. Consider whether you communicate effectively and whether your potential mate listens, understands, and responds in a way that makes you feel valued.

Conflict Resolution: Evaluate how you handle conflicts. Think about whether you can resolve disagreements constructively and whether you both approach conflicts in a way that promotes growth and understanding.

Identify Potential Problems and Deal Breakers

Potential Problems: Review any concerns that emerged during the dating process. Consider whether these issues can be addressed or if they represent significant incompatibilities.

Deal Breakers: Identify any deal breakers that are non-negotiable for you. Ensure that your potential mate aligns with these critical aspects to avoid future conflicts.

Consider Feedback from Trusted Friends and Family

External Perspectives: Seek feedback from trusted friends and family who know you well. They can provide valuable insights and perspectives that you may not have considered. But always keep in mind their positions in the game. It has a huge effect on their perspective.

Objective Assessment: Use their feedback to make a more objective assessment of your potential mate. Ensure that your loved ones see the same positive qualities and compatibility that you do.

Conduct a Trial Period

Test the Relationship: Consider a trial period where you and your potential mate commit to a more serious and exclusive relationship. Use this time to test the compatibility and see how you function as a couple in more every day, real-life situations.

Evaluate Daily Interactions: Pay attention to how you interact on a daily basis. Assess whether your relationship can handle the stress and routine of everyday life.

Trust Your Instincts and Intuition

Gut Feeling: Trust your instincts and intuition. Sometimes, your gut feeling can provide valuable insights that rational analysis might miss.

Emotional Resonance: Reflect on whether the relationship feels right on an emotional level. Consider whether you feel happy, secure, and fulfilled with your potential mate.

Create a Pros-and-Cons List

Objective Analysis: Write down the pros and cons of the relationship based on all the factors discussed. This can help you visualize and weigh the strengths and weaknesses.

Balanced View: Ensure that the list includes aspects of physical, emotional, intellectual, and positional attraction, as well as shared interests, values, and communication.

Have Deep, Honest Conversations

Open Dialogue: Sit down with your potential mate and have open, honest conversations about your future together. Discuss your findings from the checklist and ensure that you both are on the same page.

Mutual Agreement: Ensure that both of you agree on the key aspects of your relationship and are committed to working on any areas of improvement.

Deciding on a mate after using the 4Cross Love Checklist is a comprehensive and thoughtful process that integrates multiple dimensions of compatibility. You can make an informed and confident decision to commit or honestly reevaluate your relationship. This structured approach helps ensure that you build a strong, fulfilling, and lasting relationship with a partner who truly complements and aligns with you.

At 4Crosslove.com/resources you will find a free checkable PDF to check off each category.

CHAPTER 14

The Dynamics of Each Positional Pairing

"At the touch of love everyone becomes a poet." — Plato

So you've met someone. That's fantastic! Let's talk about what you may be experiencing and what you need to observe, realize, and understand with positional pairing.

In this chapter, we are going to explore all the positional pairings—North and South, East and West, and so on—to recognize and understand what happens when you find a match.

When you find a great match, there are still things to consider. If you are attracted to the opposite of you, how do you reconcile the other side? And if you have found yourself at ninety degrees, what do you need to consider in the positional pairings?

But first, let's start by understanding the magnetic attraction of opposites in the game of love.

Opposites Attract!

The allure of opposites enhances our experiences, providing a contrast that makes interactions more interesting and dynamic. This pull toward what we lack adds excitement and variety to our relationships, making our interactions richer and more flavorful.

Each person brings unique traits and qualities to a relationship. Alone, we may be delightful but one-dimensional. When paired with someone who complements us, we become part of a more complex and balanced partnership. This blend of differences creates harmony and satisfaction, enriching our lives.

Being with someone who's opposite to us can broaden our perspective. Initially, it may be disorienting, but over time, it helps us see the world in new ways. This expanded view fosters flexibility, empathy, and a more inclusive understanding of life.

Differences can lead to friction, which is a natural part of any relationship. However, these challenges also promote personal growth and deeper connections. Tensions and challenges are opportunities for self-reflection and evolution, leading to a richer, more nuanced relationship.

The attraction between opposites isn't just psychological—it creates a palpable chemistry. The excitement of being with someone different keeps the relationship dynamic and ensures ongoing curiosity and attraction.

Building a relationship with your opposite can be challenging. It requires open communication, respect, and a willingness to find common ground. These are essential tools for navigating the complexities of such a relationship.

The key to a successful relationship with your opposite lies in balancing contrast and complement. By embracing differences, we open ourselves to a fuller spectrum of experiences, celebrating the diversity that enriches our lives and the shared journey that unites us.

By appreciating and navigating the contrasts, we create unique and dynamic love stories, growing together and learning from each other.

Each position has a very different perspective on life. So, even if you are attracted to the opposite or perhaps a ninety-degree turn, these pairings face obvious challenges that can lead to misunderstandings and conflicts. We are going to discuss how these challenges appear and how to reconcile them.

Please remember these examples are described in general, for the most part, but not always. It would be impossible to describe every possible scenario. If you don't wholeheartedly agree with these examples, that's okay. Try to glean what you can from them rather than assuming you are exempt and throwing the whole thing out. You can learn something from all of them.

North - South

A North and South relationship often revolves around balancing action and stability. These two positions have very different approaches: Norths are driven by a need for certainty, control, and results, while Souths focus on creating a steady, supportive environment where everyone feels secure and cared for. If they learn to navigate their differences, they can create a relationship that combines leadership with emotional support.

Where They Complement Each Other:

- **North's Drive + South's Support:** The North brings direction, leadership, and the ability to push the relationship forward with clear goals and vision, while the South provides the emotional stability and support that helps the North feel grounded. The North can rely on the South's steady presence, while the South appreciates the North's ability to lead and make decisions.

- **Balancing Action and Stability:** The North's drive for action is balanced by the South's desire for steadiness. While the North ensures that progress is being made, the South makes sure that things don't move too fast and that the emotional needs of the relationship are cared for.

Areas to Watch:

- **Balancing Action with Stability:** Norths will need to slow down at times and recognize the South's need for consistency and emotional security. Souths, in turn, will need to understand that the North's drive for action is not a threat to stability but a way of ensuring progress. Finding a middle ground where both action and stability are respected is key.

- **Communication and Conflict Resolution:** Norths are direct and prefer to address issues head-on, while Souths may avoid conflict to keep the peace. Norths should practice patience and allow the South to express themselves without feeling rushed, while Souths should work on being more open about their concerns, even if it risks conflict.

- **Pace and Decision-Making:** Norths are quick decision-makers and like to see results fast, while Souths prefer to take their time and ensure that everything is done thoughtfully. Norths should be careful not to push the South too hard or make them feel overwhelmed, and Souths should try to be more open to change and progress.

In simple terms, a North-South relationship can be a strong partnership where leadership meets emotional support. The North brings clear direction and decisiveness, while the South provides a steady, nurturing foundation. Together, they can build a relationship that balances action and stability, as long as they respect each other's pace and communication styles.

East - West

When East and West are together, the relationship is often a balancing act between excitement and caution, spontaneity and structure. Both have very different ways of approaching life, which can lead to both complementing each other or clashing depending on how well they understand their differences.

Where They Complement Each Other:

- **East's Creativity + West's Structure:** The East brings fresh ideas and spontaneity, which can help pull the West out of their comfort zone, encouraging them to try new things. Meanwhile, the West offers structure and thoughtful planning, helping to ground the East's wild ideas and make them more practical.
- **Balancing Energy:** Easts' energetic and impulsive nature can complement the West's calm and measured approach. The West can bring a sense of peace and stability that helps the East find balance when things get too chaotic, while the East brings a sense of fun and unpredictability to the West's more routine life.

Areas to Watch:

- **Flexibility:** Easts need to learn to slow down sometimes and appreciate the West's need for careful planning, while Wests can benefit from embracing a bit of spontaneity and trusting that not everything has to be perfectly planned.
- **Communication:** Clear communication is key for this pair, as Easts tend to speak in broad strokes and big ideas, while Wests prefer detailed, well-thought-out plans. They will need to work on expressing their needs and listening to one another's concerns to avoid misunderstandings.

In simple terms, an East-West relationship can be a vibrant partnership full of exciting ideas and thoughtful decisions if both partners learn to appreciate the balance between spontaneity and structure. The East brings the spark, and the West keeps the fire under control, ensuring the relationship stays warm and stable without burning out.

North - East

A North and East relationship can be an exciting mix of leadership and creativity, action and adventure. However, these two positions have very different ways of navigating life, which can lead to both dynamic growth or occasional friction.

Where They Complement Each Other:

- **North's Direction + East's Creativity:** The North brings clear leadership and a sense of purpose, while the East adds creativity and enthusiasm. Norths help keep the East focused and on track, ensuring their ideas don't get lost in the excitement. On the flip side, Easts help Norths think outside the box, introducing fresh ideas and new ways of approaching problems.
- **Balancing Energy:** The North's decisive, action-oriented nature pairs well with the East's more spontaneous and flexible mindset. The North can guide the relationship forward, while the East brings a sense of fun and unpredictability, preventing things from becoming too rigid or dull.

Areas to Watch:

- **Compromise on Control:** Norths will need to learn to give the East some room to explore their creativity and freedom, without feeling the need to control every detail. Similarly, Easts will need to understand that too much chaos can make the North feel unsettled, and offering some level of structure will make the relationship smoother.
- **Balancing Planning with Flexibility:** While Norths are great at making and sticking to plans, Easts thrive on spontaneity. Both will need to find a middle ground where there's room for fun and flexibility without losing sight of the bigger picture.

- **Communication:** Norths prefer direct, straightforward communication, while Easts may speak more in creative or abstract terms. Clear, respectful communication will be key in avoiding misunderstandings or feelings of being dismissed.

In simple terms, a North-East relationship can be a vibrant partnership where leadership meets creativity. The North keeps the ship on course, while the East adds wind to the sails, making the journey both purposeful and exciting. However, both will need to respect each other's core needs—structure for the North and freedom for the East—for the relationship to truly thrive.

South - East

When a South is in a relationship with an East it can be a delightful mix of stability and spontaneity. These two positions have very different approaches to life, with the South seeking comfort and consistency while the East thrives on adventure and freedom. If they learn to balance their differences, they can create a relationship where both feel fulfilled.

Where They Complement Each Other:

- **South's Stability + East's Excitement:** The South provides a steady, supportive foundation that helps ground the East when their adventurous spirit takes them in all directions. Easts can help the South step out of their comfort zone, bringing fun and novelty into the relationship that the South might not seek out on their own.
- **Nurturing vs. Playful Energy:** Souths love taking care of others and making sure their loved ones feel secure and supported, which the East appreciates, especially when they feel overwhelmed or scattered. In turn, Easts bring an infectious enthusiasm that keeps things from becoming too

routine, adding a spark of excitement that helps the South experience more joy and adventure.

Areas to Watch:

- **Balancing Stability with Change:** Souths will need to learn to embrace change and spontaneity a bit more, while Easts can benefit from understanding the importance of routine and structure for their South partner. Both will need to respect each other's need for comfort and excitement.
- **Respecting Each Other's Pace:** Souths prefer a slower, more thoughtful pace, while Easts like to move quickly and dive into new things. Finding a middle ground where the South feels secure and the East doesn't feel held back is key to avoiding frustration.
- **Managing Communication Styles:** Souths tend to keep things inside to avoid conflict, while Easts are more likely to express their feelings openly. Souths need to feel safe enough to share their concerns, and Easts should practice patience, recognizing that the South may need more time to process their feelings.

In simple terms, a South-East Relationship can be a beautiful partnership where security meets excitement. The South provides a loving, grounded foundation, while the East keeps things fresh and lively. Together, they can create a balanced relationship that's both stable and adventurous, as long as they respect and appreciate each other's core needs.

South - West

When a South is in a relationship with West, the relationship is often built on shared values of stability, security, and dependability. Both positions are focused on creating a calm, predictable environment, but they express it in different ways. The South seeks emotional stability and support, while the West is more focused on creating structure and ensuring everything is carefully thought through.

Where They Complement Each Other:

- **South's Emotional Stability + West's Thoughtful Planning:** The South provides emotional warmth and a nurturing presence, helping to soften the West's more cautious and sometimes overly analytical nature. In turn, the West brings careful structure and planning to the relationship, which aligns well with the South's need for consistency and reliability. Together, they create a stable and secure environment that both partners value deeply.

- **Dependability and Thoughtfulness:** Both the South and the West are dependable in their own ways—Souths through their emotional support and caregiving, and Wests through their careful attention to detail and their ability to think ahead. This shared dependability creates a strong foundation for their relationship.

Areas to Watch:

- **Balancing Emotions with Logic:** Souths will need to recognize that the West's need for analysis and structure is not emotional neglect, while Wests should make an effort to express their feelings and show emotional support to the South. Both need to meet in the middle, with the South learning to appreciate the West's logical approach and the West understanding the importance of emotional connection.

- **Handling Conflict:** Souths tend to avoid conflict, while Wests may want to dive deep into problem-solving. Finding a way to discuss issues without overwhelming each other is key to avoiding frustration. The South needs to feel safe enough to express their concerns, and the West needs to ensure they don't overanalyze to the point of creating tension.

- **Pace and Decision-Making:** Souths and Wests can both be slow to embrace change, but for different reasons. Souths prefer to stick with what works, while Wests are cautious and deliberate. They need to be mindful of each other's decision-making process and find a way to keep things moving without making either partner feel rushed or too bogged down.

In simple terms, a South-West relationship can be a solid and dependable partnership where stability and security are at the forefront. The South brings emotional warmth and care, while the West provides thoughtful planning and order. Together, they create a safe and stable environment, as long as they balance emotional connection with logical decision-making.

West - North

When a West and North are in a relationship the dynamic is a mix of precision and action. Both partners are driven in their own ways—Norths by their desire for certainty and quick progress, and Wests by their need for careful analysis and structure. Together, they can create a powerful team if they learn to appreciate their differences.

Where They Complement Each Other:

- **North's Drive + West's Planning:** The North's decisiveness and desire to take action pairs well with the West's careful planning and attention to detail. The West can help the North slow down and consider all the possibilities before jumping into action, ensuring that decisions are well thought out. In turn, the North's decisiveness can help the West move forward when they are stuck in overthinking or analysis paralysis.
- **Balancing Risk and Security:** The North's willingness to take risks can push the relationship forward, while the West's focus on minimizing risk ensures that those decisions are made

with care. Together, they can strike a balance between taking bold actions and making sure they are well-planned and secure.

Areas to Watch.

- **Balancing Action with Thought:** Norths will need to learn to appreciate the value of the West's careful planning, even when it feels slow. Similarly, Wests will need to trust the North's instincts and be willing to move forward even when they don't have all the answers. Finding a balance between action and analysis will be key to avoiding frustration.

- **Respecting Each Other's Pace:** Norths want to act quickly, while Wests prefer to take their time. Both partners need to be aware of their differing approaches to decision-making and find ways to meet in the middle. Norths should try to slow down and allow the West time to process, while Wests should work on speeding up their decision-making when necessary.

- **Communication:** Norths are direct and often speak in terms of outcomes and goals, while Wests prefer to discuss the process and the details. Clear communication is key to avoiding misunderstandings. The North needs to be patient with the West's need for thoroughness, and the West needs to be concise and clear when sharing their concerns.

In simple terms, a North-West relationship can be a highly effective partnership where action meets thoughtful planning. The North's drive and decisiveness keep things moving, while the West's careful approach ensures that each step is well-considered. Together, they can create a balance between speed and security, as long as they respect each other's strengths and work together on timing and decision-making.

Relationships with the Same Position

While relationships between individuals of different positions can offer balance and mutual growth, relationships between individuals of the same position can be fraught with challenges. These challenges arise from the amplification of shared traits and the potential for conflict over similar needs and approaches. Here's an exploration of why it's not advisable and often impossible to sustain a romantic relationship with someone of the same position within the 4Cross Love Framework. This analysis will also shed light on the conflicts you may be having with family, friends, or coworkers in the same position as you.

When individuals of the same position enter into a relationship, their shared traits and characteristics can become amplified. While these traits may be strengths individually, they can create significant challenges when both partners exhibit them simultaneously.

Two Norths, who are logical, decisive, and strategic, may both strive to take control, leading to power struggles and conflicts over decision-making. Their combined assertiveness and need for certainty can result in rigidity, making it difficult for them to compromise or adapt to each other's plans.

Two Easts, who are adaptable, energetic, and social, may struggle with a lack of structure and stability. Their combined need for freedom and spontaneity can lead to chaos and inconsistency, making it difficult to establish long-term plans or commitments.

Two Souths, who are supportive, reliable, and emotionally intelligent, may focus excessively on maintaining harmony and avoiding conflict, potentially leading to unresolved issues and passive-aggressive behaviors. Their combined need for emotional security can result in stagnation, as neither partner may push for necessary changes or growth.

Two Wests, who are methodical and introspective may become overly focused on details, leading to analysis paralysis and an inability to make decisions. Their combined need for order and precision can create a rigid and inflexible environment, stifling spontaneity and creativity.

When both partners share the same position, their similar needs and survival concerns can become sources of conflict. Each partner's need for validation and fulfillment can clash with the other's, leading to competition rather than cooperation.

Two Norths may both seek to assert their authority and control over situations, leading to power struggles and conflicts over decision-making.

Two Easts may both seek constant novelty and excitement, making it difficult to establish stability and consistency in the relationship.

Two Souths may both seek reassurance and support, potentially leading to dependency and a lack of individual growth.

Two Wests may both seek to impose their own standards and methods, leading to conflicts over the "right" way to do things and an overly critical environment.

One of the strengths of relationships between individuals of different positions is the balance of complementary traits and perspectives. Each position brings unique strengths that can offset the challenges of the other, creating a harmonious and well-rounded partnership. In relationships between individuals of the same position, this balance is often lacking.

My hope in going through all the potential positional couplings is that you will see and start to become aware of how we communicate with others based on our positions and the crossing of all the positions. It's a dynamic, fluid, and interesting perspective once you recognize it, and it can obviously give incredible relief and help you understand how to maneuver and strategize each relationship. I hope it also allows you to reflect on how not knowing this has affected your ability to navigate, embrace, and enjoy all your relationships up to this point. And thus, how to move forward with grace.

Now let's get into watching Love Is Blind!

Part 3

CHAPTER 15

Introducing Love Is Blind

"Love is the greatest virtue of the heart." -Frank Lloyd Wright

---

Love Is Blind on Netflix is the perfect exhibition of the four positions in the game of love I have come across so far…but I just started watching 'Married At First Sight' and this may prove to be even more apparent in seeing the positions. We shall see. I have struggled to explain the four positions because it's so nuanced and personal, and if you are not in the same position as me—North— you see yourself and others from a different perspective. So, when I saw this show, I was thrilled because it allows us to observe the four positions in the game of love under stress, anxiety, fear, passion, jealousy, love, and potential loss. This brings out the best and worst in people. It's like *Wild Kingdom* for the four positions!

I watched every episode in every season two times because they were so fascinating. I was able to identify each person's position (for the most part), see how they chose their mate, spot the games they played, and recognize how they communicated with one another. Some people were much harder to identify than others because they were secure, determined, and committed or they were hiding their true feelings. With some people, I knew their position the moment they opened their mouths. It's priceless relationship-viewing gold! We can use this show as our backdrop by relating to and observing each position in this crazy game of love.

I'm going to give a case-by-case breakdown of each couple, gleaning insight from the examples in this show. You will see how the four positions play the game of love based on their concern and perspective. If I was able to get more information about how they went about choosing their mate, like more actual footage of their dates, I could have used the 4Cross Love Checklist for each one but I just couldn't get all the information I needed. But, this case-by-case analysis will be invaluable for seeing what position each person is and how to watch for clues in your position viewing investigation. Even if you watch only one season, you will be able to see and understand what I'm talking about because you now know the positions. You will learn from each person and circumstance.

The Concept of Love Is Blind

The core concept of the show revolves around the intriguing premise that emotional connections can be formed and even lead to engagement without the need for physical presence or visual assessment, challenging the conventional norms of physical attraction in relationships. This innovative approach unfolds in three distinct phases over a span of thirty-eight days.

The first phase consists of over twenty participants of the opposite sex wanting to get married. On one side of the labyrinth are all the women, and on the other are all the men. On the first day, they date every participant of the opposite sex via pods, where they cannot see one another. After the first day, they have to start ranking their potential mates. Each date in the secluded pods allows for deep, meaningful conversations without visual distractions, emphasizing the "blind" aspect of love. At the end of this dating carousel, participants are encouraged to get engaged if they feel like they have a connection. Then they meet in person as doors open, allowing them to see each other for the first time. The man asks the woman for her hand in marriage, getting on bended knee and offering a ring. This phase is about ten days.

Enter the second phase. As the journey progresses, engaged couples transition from the abstract world of the pods to an in-person group vacation with the other engaged pairs. This means everyone is on vacation with their engaged mate and other people they may have dated in the pods. This phase serves to encourage all players to explore and solidify their physical and emotional bonds outside the isolated environment of the pods.

The third and final phase of the experience grounds the couples. They cohabit in a specially arranged apartment, facing the day-to-day challenges and distractions of real life. This ultimate test is designed to evaluate the durability and depth of the connections formed under unique circumstances.

Initially, participants' conversations tend to revolve around surface-level commonalities and life aspirations, facilitating a rapid assessment of compatibility on fundamental issues, such as lifestyle preferences, family planning, and personal values.

However, as the process accelerates, participants are encouraged to delve deeper, sharing personal vulnerabilities and past experiences, thereby fostering a profound level of trust and emotional intimacy. These heartfelt disclosures forge the genuine human connection needed in lasting relationships.

The idea and creation of the show itself embodies the cycle of human coordination and action, starting with the North position, where the innovative concept of *Love Is Blind* is conceived, challenging traditional paradigms of love and attraction, and then moves East in a clockwise direction.

The East position encapsulates the brainstorming phase, addressing logistical and ethical considerations to bring the concept to fruition.

Then it moves to the South, where executing the show involves practical arrangements, from selecting contestants to setting up the infrastructure the show's unique format requires.

The West position entails a reflective evaluation of the outcomes, successes, and potential improvements, ensuring the concept's evolution and refinement. Then it goes back to North with all this gathering of information to start the sequence over on the second season.

Ok, let's break down each couple and really talk about what happens in *Love Is Blind*. We'll observe the players in the game so you can watch it with your eyes wide open.

The key to observing and identifying positions is paying attention when people lose control of their biology in a stressful situation and show their insecure side. They are trying to get their survival concern vs. giving it. The positions are also apparent when the other person involved speaks about their mate's annoying or troubling traits that are concerning to them.

Getting vs. Giving Concern

In stressful relationship situations, individuals often shift from a state of balance (where they can give their concern) to a state of insecurity (where they try to get their concern). This means they are more focused on fulfilling their own unmet needs rather than contributing positively to the relationship. For example:

North: Instead of providing direction, they might demand control.

East: Instead of inspiring creativity, they might seek constant stimulation and validation.

South: Instead of offering emotional support, they might seek reassurance and comfort.

West: Instead of ensuring accuracy, they might seek validation for their meticulousness.

Practical Relationship Example

Imagine a stressful situation in a relationship, such as planning a big move or dealing with a financial setback:

North: Normally provides clear plans for the future but now becomes overly directive, insisting on her way without considering her partner's input.

East: Usually brings fun and spontaneity to the relationship but now becomes erratic, suggesting impulsive solutions to escape the stress.

South: Typically offers emotional support but now seeks constant reassurance, agreeing with everything to avoid conflict and maintain harmony.

West: Generally, ensures that all details are covered but now obsessively focuses on minor details, seeking validation for every decision and delaying necessary actions.

Observing partners in stressful situations can reveal their true 4Cross Love position because they show their insecurities and primary concerns more clearly. Understanding this behavior helps us accurately identify their position and better manage interactions and expectations within the relationship. This awareness can lead to more effective support and communication, fostering a stronger, more resilient partnership.

Identifying someone's position (North, East, South, or West) can be challenging during normal, controlled interactions because people often manage their behavior to present their best selves. However, in stressful relationship situations, individuals are more likely to lose control of their usual composure and reveal their innate, biological tendencies. This is when true positions become more apparent.

All right, Cupid's warriors, get ready to dive into the game of love with the ultimate reality TV guide: *Love Is Blind*. Whether you want to watch one season or all of them, you'll find your cheat sheet, with all the seasons and the positions of each player on my website 4Crosslove.com/resources .

Let's explore the clues and insights each couple on the show reveals. You will see that, in truth, love is not blind. Instead, it's an enlightening journey that calls for vision, understanding, and the courage to see beyond the surface.

The secret to finding true love isn't about seeing the person but seeing the world through their eyes.

I want to express my gratitude to the participants who bravely put themselves out there, taking a leap into this vulnerable situation. Their experiences provide us with valuable insights and lessons. I understand that there were moments, and perhaps entire journeys, that some participants may wish they could take back. However, the key takeaway here is how unaware of ourselves we often are. Understanding your position and the position of others will illuminate why you may be in the dark about your approach to the game of love. Thank you to all the participants for helping us see what's really going on.

Here are all the seasons, the players, and their positions if you can't make a copy of the cheat sheet.

Season 1: Atlanta, Georgia

Damian Powers (West) and Giannina Gibelli (East)

Mark Cuevas (South) and Jessica Batten (North)

Matt Barnett (West) and Amber Pike (East)

Kenny Barnes (West) and Kelly Chase (North?)

Cameron Hamilton (West) and Lauren Speed (East)

Season 2: Chicago, Illinois

Jarrette Jones (South) and Iyanna McNeely (North)

Nick Thompson (West) and Danielle Ruhl (East)

Shayne Jansen (East) and Natalie Lee (North)

Shake Chatterjee (North) and Deepti Vempati (South)

Salvador Perez (West) and Mallory Zapata (North)

Kyle Abrams (South) and Shaina Hurley (North)

Season 3: Dallas, Texas

Cole Barnett (East) and Zanab Jaffrey (North)

SK Alagbada (West) and Raven Ross (North)

Bartise Bowden (North) and Nancy Rodriguez (South)

Matt Bolton (North) and Colleen Reed (South)

Brennon Lemieux (South) and Alexa Alfia (North)

Season 4: Seattle, Washington

Brett Brown (North) and Tiffany Pennywell (South)

Kwame Appiah (South) and Chelsea Griffin (North)

Paul Peden (West) and Micah Lussier (North)

Zack Goytowski (West) and Bliss Poureetezadi (East?)

Marshall Glaze (West), Jackie Bonds (East), and Josh Demas (North)

Season 5: Houston, Texas

James Milton Johnson (West) and Lydia Gonzalez (East)

Izzy Zapata (South) and Stacy Snyder (North)

Jared "JP" Pierce (South) and Taylor Rue (South)

Uche Okoroha (North) and Aaliyah Cosby (South)

Christopher Fox (South) and Johnie Maraist (West)

Season 6: Charlotte, North Carolina

Johnny McIntyre (South) and Amy Cortes (North)

Clay Gravesande (North) and Amber "AD" Desiree (South)

Jimmy Presnell (West) and Chelsea Blackwell (East)

Kenneth Gorham (South) and Brittany Mills (South)

Jeramey Lutinski (West), Laura Dadisman (North), and Sarah Ann Bick (North)

The Brazilian Season 1-

Hudson Mendes (South) & Carol Novaes (North)

Lissio Fiod (North) & Luana Braga (South)

Thiago Rocha (East) & Nanda Terra (West)

Shayan Haghbin (North) & Ana Prado (East)

Rodrigo Vaisemberg (West) & Dayanne Feitoza (East)

The Brazilian Season 2-

Alisson Hentges (East) & Thamara Terez (West)-

Robert Richard (North) & Flavia Queiroz (South)-

Tiago Chapola (East?) & Vanessa Carvalho (West)

William Domiencio (South) & Veronica Brito (North)

Guilherme Martins (West) & Maira Bullos (East)

The Brazilian Season 3-

Renan Justino (South) & Agata Moura (North)

Menandro Rosa (South) & Maria Carolina Caporusso (North)

Jarbas Andrade (West) & Bianca Sessa (North)

Daniel Manzoni (West) & Daniela Silva (North)

Valmir Reis (East) & Karen Bacic (West)

The Swedish Season-

Rasmus Hedenstedt (South) & Krisse-Ly Kuldkepp (North)

Sergio Rincon (North) & Amanda Jonegard (South)

Oskar Nordstrand (East) & Meira Omar (West)

Lucas Gustavsson (North) & Emilia Holmqvist (East)

Christopher Pocock (East) & Catja Lovstrand (North)

Season 1- Atlanta, GA

Damien Powers (West) & Giannina Gibelli (East)

Mark Cuevas (South) & Jessica Batten (North)

Matt Barnett (West) & Amber Pike (East)

Kenny Barnes (West) & Kelly Chase (South)

Cameron Hamilton (West) & Lauren Speed (East)

Giannina (East) and Damien (West)-

Giannina is an East that at least recognizes she is a lot to handle but doesn't know how to navigate herself effectively or understand why she does what she does. She doesn't know how to act any other way. So far it has been enough to get her where she is in life.

She tells herself and Damien that she self-sabotages which is a preempt to a way out if she needs it. As an East she is setting up an exit just in case she needs one. Easts have a tendency to be anxious and become more so if they feel trapped. Easts also have a tendency toward being contrary, untraditional. They like to do things on their terms which is why she decides that she is going to propose to Damien after he did. It certainly made him squirm, putting him at the ready, just like she likes. She's on edge and this is comfortable for her. She creates it. She fuels the flame of challenge constantly.

As they continue on through the season it's clear she needs more energy from Damien so she continues to provoke, tease, and cajole him into emotional drama. She has certain expectations about what she wants in life and she realizes that Damien needs to be tested to see if he is going to live up to her expectations.

Giannina has been taught by her East mother that the Latina woman is a crazy, expressive, hot mess and isn't afraid to show it. This is simply not always true and is a damaging narrative. When we buy into and make excuses for ourselves based on cultural stereotypes, we rob ourselves of acting the way we want to. Giannina is a nice person; I don't think she necessarily meant to hurt Damien, but she didn't give him the respect that he gave to her, and in the end, that was not going to work for either of them.

Damian is a thoughtful, calculated, and pensive West who can have fun, but he doesn't realize that his persistent, measured, and dull approach can be perturbing, especially to an East. Several times, he suggests that he listened and listened to her, but he didn't feel listened to. I could see that, but also maybe he didn't express enough that he needed her to listen, but honestly good luck with a contrary East. He needs order, discipline, and adoration for his strength. She didn't give it to him nearly as much as he needed, while he told her how beautiful she was constantly, and she knew it. She played all the games knowing he would endure it but she pushed him too far and he does have standards and intuition.

In the end, Damien made the right choice by saying no to Giannina. Even though position wise they were a good fit, they were not a good fit any other way. Giannina wasn't mature enough to realize how she created drama and thrived in the theatrics of it all.

Damien knew that it wasn't right, it wasn't correct, something was off, and things were out of order. He had to decide. I think it was one of the hardest decisions he has made, and, in the end, he will be happy he did because she wasn't as physically attracted to him as he was to her, and her way of showing it was by tormenting him. She wouldn't do that as much if she really wanted him. I think it was a wise decision for both of them.

I would say that Giannina was aware of how anxious, dramatic, and insecure she was but had no idea why or how to deal with herself. She surely didn't understand her strengths as she mostly saw her beauty as a strength. She was almost proud of her weaknesses, using them as an excuse to 'be her.' This is often what we do with our inability to see and handle our challenges. We use them as an excuse. I'm not saying there is fault, merely blindness.

Damien has no idea why he does what he does and he's insecure. He does stand up for himself but you can see it's an attempt, albeit valiant but not effective, to get a grip on a volatile situation. He is trying to create order and peace but Giannina lives for the drama. This is an impossible situation to be in. And instead of walking away and holding his ground throughout the season, Damien is back and forth, undecided, which only fuels more drama because Giannina is clever and recognizes she can get away with being a pill because of her beauty. Neither is self- aware enough to ground this relationship.

Jessica (North) and Mark (South)-

Jessica is an opinionated North that is, for the most part, used to getting her way. She states from the beginning that she is picky. She has standards. What she doesn't realize is she is rude, outwardly snide and judgmental.

She and Mark connected in the pods based on him being able to listen to her and appease her. She wasn't into Mark from the moment she saw him. He wasn't going to measure up, literally. They both wanted to play the game and be on the show, so I think they both tried. Well, Mark tried. Jessica played the role as if she was on a soap opera. Jessica showed us almost every unhealthy North attribute that she could have possibly demonstrated. It was an embarrassment from beginning to end.

From the moment she attacked Barnett in the Pods for 'f**king with her' because he was having trouble deciding, to the very end when she tries to give a gift to Amber and Barnett. She was a conniving, manipulative train wreck.

It was hard to watch her say one thing and then lie to try and hide her obvious games. Norths can, especially when under the influence, say what they believe are obvious truths in a very hurtful way under the guise of speaking hard truths that nobody else will say. Then, the next day, or within hours, act like nothing happened. It's their way of getting what they are feeling out because they aren't the best at expressing feelings.

Mark tries so hard to work through it. He's on defense as a South. He says he wants to go back and build a foundation of trust. That could not be a more South statement. He thinks they can work through it and bust through the wall to get to love. He tolerates so much from her, and she knows he will. She says one thing one day and something totally different the next. She is trying to find every excuse in the book to get out of it but somehow stay on the show. Somehow, a 10-year difference is a huge deal with her and Mark, but an 8-year difference with Barnett wouldn't be. She is a mess of contradictions and justifications for trying to make herself right and get what she wants.

I was honestly hoping Mark would have a chance to say no, but he didn't. I wonder what he would have said. Note that at the wedding, after she said no, she had nobody there for her. And then, she said rather sternly, that she wouldn't apologize because she had nothing to apologize for. That was the epitome of a spiteful North. She dragged Mark through that and couldn't even say she was sorry.

This was an obvious choice. Jessica continues even after the wedding to mess with Barnett and Amber, but fortunately, Barnett has enough gumption to stand up for his wife and see what a mistake he would have made choosing Jessica. They would not have been a good fit. She is a demanding North, obviously, and he is a rather sheepish West. Not a good fit.

I do think when Jessica saw herself on the show she was mortified. She clearly recognizes what an ass she made of herself. She can grow and probably has grown a lot from it. If she studied the 4Cross Love Framework, she could be a mature and responsible North that could have healthy relationships. And Mark, of course, could learn a great deal about himself and how to choose wisely in the future.

Amber (East) & Barnett (West)-

Amber is a beautiful, fun, and extreme East on the show. Easts have a tendency to 'put on a show' when in the spotlight and Amber does not disappoint. She is extremely competitive and constantly trying to convince Barnett, and everyone else, that she is good enough, hot enough and bad ass. She is demonstrating so many East tendencies it's impossible to miss her position in the game of love. She's so extreme it's hard to watch at times but after she got to the end and Barnett said yes, she simmered a bit.

Barnett is a likable, handsome West. His sensitivity and somewhat charming demeanor are clearly the reason he was getting some attention. But as you can see his inability to make a clear choice got him in trouble. He was declared a 'player' by Jessica, but I promise you, Barnett is no player. He wants to believe he is in some way, but it's just in jest.

Amber says several times that he is analytical and hard to read because he doesn't talk about his feelings. That is not going to change, but if he learns to be more expressive and less guarded for fear of feeling exposed or embarrassed, this will help their relationship a lot. He has to learn to trust her, but she is so spontaneous in her actions I can see why he might be guarded.

It would help them both immensely to learn their positions and each other's.

They could see into each other's concerns and be able to alleviate so much anxiety within themselves and between each other. They could make huge leaps forward in discovering their strengths and playing the game of love more effectively.

I'm glad they both said yes. They are a great fit. She is a high-strung, dynamic and lovable East, and he is a kind, calm, clever West.

Kenny (West) and Kelly (North?)-

Kelly is a pretty calm North but also has a certain drive and tenacity about her. She's got a sense of determination. I thought for some time she was South and I could be wrong by identifying her as North. She is one of the only ones throughout the seasons that I struggled to be certain about her position. If she is a North, she needs the supportive yet strong energy of a South partner. And when she meets the right South, a mature and self-aware South that knows 4Cross, they could move mountains.

Kenny is so calm, sincere and concerned about doing things the right way. His maturity and ability to be patient in the situation was remarkable. I'm sure he will find a vivacious and mature East that will be able to embark on a great adventure together. He might also do well with a mature North.

I think they both handled the situation the best they could while playing the game of "Love is Blind," maintaining their dignity and respect for one another.

Kelly made the right choice. As much as I loved Kenny and how mature and adorable they were, it wasn't going to work.

This had to be an extremely hard decision for Kelly to make. And I guarantee you that looking back on its Kenny would agree with her choice. I'm sure it hurt in the moment, but Kenny, being the analyzing West that he is, had to have known that something was off. What a genuine and mature person he was to address the wedding party with such grace and composure at the end.

Sure, the dramatics help make the show exciting, but the composure and grace of these two give us hope in reality TV that it's not all about the car crash scenes.

Cameron (West!) and Lauren (East)-

They are the quintessential sweet and adoring couple that we were all rooting for to be married and live happily ever after. Lauren is a gorgeous, mature, and fun East who continually had to calm her desire to run, and Cameron had to keep himself from overanalyzing her moods. He could have easily sent her running by being too demanding of her to make a choice. He needed to step back and give her some space as it was. Had Lauren's dad not been a part of her life and willing to let things unfold it may have been a different story altogether. But in the end, their love did persevere.

We all admired Cameron for his calm demeanor and steadfast support and love for Lauren. He was unflappable. But I did want to slap him and wake him up a couple of times. This is who he is. He proved it. He never overheated. He is measured in every way.

It will be hard for Cameron to keep up with Lauren's Eastness. She's an exciting, charming, and loveable person. I can tell from the 'after the altar' episodes that she is trying too dapper him up. She seems to respect his Westness and, at the same time, pushes him to be more adventurous. They made a great choice, and knowing their positions in the game of love will only make their marriage more engaging, solid, and fun.

Season 2- Chicago, IL

Jarrette Jones (South) & Iyanna McNeely (North)

Nick Thompson (West) & Danielle Ruhl (East)

Shayne Jansen (East!) & Natalie Lee (North)

Shake Chatterjee (North) & Deepti Vempati (South)

Salvador Perez (West) & Mallory Zapata (North)

Kyle Abrams (South) & Shayna Hurley (North)

Jarrette (South) & Iyanna (North)-

I think everyone wanted these two to get married, but we all kind of knew that it was going to be a tough road. Jarrette was not mature enough and or ready to make the kind of commitment that Iyanna needed. He said and did some things at the resort that made us all cringe. It must be so hard to look back and watch after the fact.

They have divorced. Jarrette being a South is very committed to his friends and to his lifestyle. He thinks the party will not go on without him and he's likely right. He used it as an excuse. Had it been a small part of his life that he had to reel back, it might have worked, but it was clearly a need that marriage to Iyanna was not going to fill, at least not at this time.

Iyanna, although being a fun and caring North, had her role in the demise as well. She had her way of doing things and was not going to compromise too much. She is stern in her approach not realizing that her curt tone can come off as uncaring. She loves Jarrett but as her mom says at the dinner table, 'there are two sides to the story.' Had Iyanna been more accepting of Jarrett perhaps he would have made more compromises for her. I think they both tried. Had they both been more self-aware and aware of the other person's position in the game of love, it might have turned out differently.

Nick (West) & Danielle (East)-

These two are pretty extreme versions of East and West. Danielle is so quick to react and make the situation bigger than it is, and on top of that, she's self-conscious. She is a sweet person, but on the other side of that, when she loses control of her biology, it gets ugly quickly. Her inability to see herself in the moment, which is where she lives and how she plays the game of love, torments her. You can tell after she has spiraled out of control that she almost can't believe what she's done. Obviously, she keeps it in check enough to keep Nick curious and interested because she is so completely opposite of him.

Nick is a measured and super considerate West who wants order and a way to look at things rationally. His mom mentioned his OCD-type behavior when he was little. Danielle is engaging, fun and beautiful, so Nick very much wants to stay with her, but she is a lot. His compassion and love for her are noble and prudent. He really wants to do the right thing.

I have read that they are divorced but perhaps getting back together. It would be super helpful for them to see and understand their positions in the game of love. I think their appreciation and love for one another could grow to the point of realizing how truly wonderful their relationship has been, how incredible it is that they have come this far considering their challenges.

Shayne (East) & Natalie (North)-

Shayne was one of the most East people I have seen on the show. He tops Amber from the first season. His high energy came out in so many ways. He is very likable in that his energy is attractive, and at the same time, he's too much. Natalie is such an interesting choice for him. I'm guessing he has tried to date Wests who end up being too calculating and critical and or Easts who seem like a good idea at first but get way too competitive and out of control.

Natalie is a controlling North that has a hard time expressing herself. For an East like Shayne, who needs a lot of atta boys, he could not have chosen a more incapable person to give him the loving, kind, and constant reassurance that he craves. For him, as an East, it's like he is trying to give himself a challenge. He also thinks in some way that he can save her or, in a sense, challenge her to be more adventurous and loving. But he quickly finds out that this is not a challenge he can win.

He is so willing to put himself out there and love her for who she is, and she is so scared to let any of her guard down and give him what he needs. I find it interesting as well that the other person whom he was considering was Shayna, who is obviously a pretty extreme North as well. In the pods, at one point, he was gone; he was just going to leave because it was too much for him, migrate, classic East. This is the East so concerned about relationships that he couldn't take the idea of hurting anyone… and it created drama; there's always room for drama.

For both North and East, there is something intriguing about not being status quo, seeking the opposite for the sake of being contrary to what you're supposed to do.

At the end of all the episodes, he and Shayna decide to create more drama by taking a picture of themselves together at her fiancé's (South) restaurant to create more drama, and then he's dramatically going to run off to Panama! Ha! Ok, Shayne, we see you, Easty. Clearly, Shayna has also realized that Shayne wasn't going to be enough for her, and she marries the workaholic, Christos. Clearly, these two could benefit significantly from studying the 4Cross Framework and knowing their positions in the game of love.

Shake (North) & Deepti (South)-

Deepti was nothing but sweet and considerate the entire time, as far as I could tell. I never saw a moment on the show that she was hurtful or inconsiderate to Shake or anyone, for that matter. And you only see that continue afterward. I really enjoy watching the reunions and the other get-togethers after the wedding episode. It's interesting to watch. It would have never worked with her and Kyle; they are both Souths, which is why they had so much fun together, but if you had a suspicion that they were better off as friends, you were right. Deepti would benefit from knowing her position in the game of love so she can understand what it is she needs and is unknowingly looking for. She felt the North energy that Shake was putting off, which is attractive for a South. He's just was clearly the wrong North for her.

Shake is a North that comes off as super confident but so superficial. He was cringy. When we see him open up to Deepti in the pods, I think we all had some hope that Shake would realize that his tactics are off-putting, to say the least. But as the show continues, his need to speak the 'hard truth' continues not only into the day of the wedding but afterward into the reunion. He is not liked because he thinks he's right and he would rather be right than have it work. He's rude, blunt, and inappropriate. Now, are some of the things he said true, yes, but that doesn't mean he needed to say it the way he did. He is not self-aware, and Deepti makes a wise decision not to marry him. He needs to grow up and, of course, learn his position in the game of love so he has a chance of being a good person and being kind and considerate to others.

Salvador (West) & and Mallory (North)-

I was surprised that Mallory chose Salvador in the pods. I could see why Salvador picked Mallory because her North energy was reassuring and gave him a sense of direction. It was obviously close between Salvador and Jarrett, but I think Mallory realized that although Jarrette was fun and charming, she had been there and done that with his type. She was looking for something different; that's what Norths do.

Salvador is so calm, kind, considerate, and clever enough that I think he fits the bill because Mallory was searching for something new. I'm guessing she has gone through some dull and unimaginative South boyfriends, so the idea that Salvador was sophisticated, smart, and different was intriguing to her, especially after the Ukulele serenade, which was the deal cincher.

It was clear from the moment they met that Mallory was not happy with her choice. Although Salvador is handsome and smart, something about him is off to her, and it's because he's West. She thought that she could keep trying and see if it worked out, but it was hard for her to pretend. Norths are truthful, and they have a hard time hiding what they think.

Obviously, Salvador felt this but proceeded to try and work it out with her throughout the show, but I'm guessing behind the scenes Mallory was a lot more cold and abrupt than she let on. There was a hint of something happening where Mallory stood Sal up and was running around with friends. Also, the scene at the bar with Jarrett was not good.

Salvador made the right choice; he knew something wasn't right, and he wasn't going to be made a fool of by saying yes. Later in an episode, he brings a very East girlfriend to the birthday party. She is clearly so smitten and competitive and loud. She is everything that Salvador needs, but he isn't quite sure why. I love this for him. He deserves to be happy. If he understood his West position in the game of love, he could see what happened between him and Mallory. He was not being a victim. He was being vulnerable.

Mallory is a nice person; she just doesn't understand what happened and how to deal with her natural instincts. She deserves to be happy, and the best way to do that is to learn her North position in the game of love and learn the other 3 positions so she can relate, learn, and grow.

Kyle (South) & Shayna (North)-

I can't be the only one who thought Kyle and Shayna were Mark and Jessica from the first season all over again. And for all intents and purposes, it was, except Shayna thought she really wanted Shayne the East instead of a West like Barnett, which ironically wouldn't have worked either. It will take a very strong, handsome, and solid South man to appease Shayna and Jessica's assessing eyes. And from what I can tell, that's what they both went and got. Good for them. It's just too bad they had to go about it the way they did. Although for all of us, they were a great/tragic demonstration of what not to do as a North.

Ok, so back to Kyle and Shayna. We knew the moment Shayna saw Kyle that he wasn't going to be good enough for her, but she tried, sort of. She should have never said yes to him knowing that her faith was such a hurdle for him, but hey, it made for good drama. And even though I was not a fan of Shake, he was right. She wanted to be on the show.

Kyle wanted to try, and I think her looks certainly affected his desire. It wouldn't have worked, even if he was Christian. She wasn't into him, and that's okay, but where she really made a mistake was getting her big nose in Natalie and Shayne's business. That was not cool.

I wasn't surprised that Kyle and Deepti ended up as friends and considered being together, but the reason they got along was because they are both Souths and, in a sense, were commiserating with one another over their two unfortunate North choices. I wanted to tell them not to be more than friends, it would not work and from what I can tell it didn't. I wish them all well. And, of course, if they knew their positions in the game of love, they could all make sense of what happened and could have prevented a lot of heartache and anxiety.

Season 3 Dallas TX-

Cole Barnett (East) & Zanab Jaffrey (North)

SK Alagbada (West) & Raven Ross (North)

Bartise Bowden (North) & Nancy Rodriguez (South)

Matt Bolton (North) & Colleen Reed (South)

Brennan Lemieux (South) & Alexa Alfia (North)

Zanab (West) & Cole (East)-

These two attracted because Zanab heard the fun and engaging Cole as a chance for her to be around someone that she wasn't and vice versa. Because Cole is an outgoing and fun East, he senses the strength and determination of a North might be a great choice for him, at least in the pods.

They are both very attractive, but it's clear from the moment they are on vacation that Zanab is very particular, and Cole is open about his 'type.' She is not fun at all in person. She's so concerned about her hair and makeup getting messed up that she won't go in the water. I knew it was doomed from the start. She is so uptight that it starts creating a contrary and outspoken Cole to start second guessing and looking for an exit even though he said he wanted to stay. He tries hard to keep it light, but clearly, he starts picking up on her critical and condescending nature. I think Zanab tried hard to lighten up, and she did recognize that she was being demeaning, but by that point, Cole was gone, and his immaturity came out in his need to criticize her without overtly putting her down, so he thought. The pool comment to Colleen and the comment to Zanab that evening was his way of being contrary to her.

This dynamic played out until the very end. She was clueless about how her need to make sure things were done her way. She went back and forth about being incredibly critical but also being in love with him. He was clueless and bewildered about how his lack of maturity and cleanliness perturbed her. The dinner scene was about as perfect of an example as you could get to demonstrate their misunderstandings. He wants to have fun; she wants it done her way. It was not going to work. But they can learn their positions in the game of love so they can both see that neither of them was necessarily wrong. They were just blind to the game of love.

Bartise (North) & Nancy (South)-

These two had such a fun and engaging emotional connection in the pods. Bartise is an outgoing and confident North who is not afraid to tell the honest (brutal) truth. Nancy is a bubbly, solid, adorable South who is looking for that North energy but with a side of fun, unlike Andrew, who is North but too rigid for Nancy.

The moment Bartise meets Nancy, he tells her you better run over to me. He is a commanding and arrogant man who needs to find some grace. But hey, that's what Nancy wanted. She was smitten with his looks and his energy. He was reluctant but willing to give it a go. As soon as Bartise sees Raven, he regrets his choice, but he realizes quickly that Raven (North) is not even remotely interested in him, and it would not have worked. But Bartise had to tell Nancy the honest brutal truth because he was already looking for a way out. Who knows what he would have done had Raven given him even a glimmer of interest? We may have had Jessica and Shayna in male form all over again.

Nancy, even after Bartise humiliates her, is willing to tolerate his truth and is unwavering in her loyalty and commitment to Bartise. At some point, it's hard to watch. I thought for sure when they moved into their apartment and he started distancing himself from her, that she would have pulled the plug, but it speaks to South's incredible ability to try to maintain stability and push through.

Even at the end, when she is talking to her North mother and North brother, she still wants to try and remain friends while they are warning her to stay away from him. Her mom says she is too nice. Nancy keeps telling her she does not like to cut ties like her mom does. She doesn't want to be excluded. She wants to be in the Bartise club. By the end, she finally decides, after he suggests that they can still be friends, that she has had enough. That took a lot for her to do that, but good for her, there was nothing good to come of that relationship going forward. Her North mom and North brother were right. And if they could learn to see their positions in the game of love by studying the 4Cross Love Framework they could help themselves immensely going forward.

Sk (West) & Raven (North)-

These two bonded on their maturity and knowing better than those other silly couples. Sk is an analytical, traditional, and serious West that doesn't have a huge sense of humor. He is calculating and considerate. You won't see him out wrestling steers. He's too mature for that nonsense. He was sincere and different. That is exactly what Raven thought she was looking for. She has had enough of choosing men for their muscles, she wanted to get as far away from someone like Bartise as she could, and that she did.

They were awkward on vacation because he was so reserved, and she wasn't going to let her guard down and be lovey-dovey, either. At one point, she suggested he needs to bring the energy and some direction, but what she doesn't understand is that she exudes and commands the lead, so for a West in this situation with such a dominant, beautiful North, he was constantly second guessing what to do. He has a hard time deciding, so he's stuck in a rock and a hard place.

You can see how their need to govern themselves plays out in their relationships with others. They are both guarded; this is what they think bonds them, but SK's indecisiveness and standards around how things are supposed to be throw him for a loop, which is why, in the end, he just can't figure out what is really going on and decides to not go through with it. He knows something is out of order but just can't put his finger on it. He says downstairs that he wishes there was a textbook to tell him how to do this.

I was really surprised at the reunion that they were still dating. It took a lot for Raven to consider that. She must have really loved him. Then, when they were engaged again, I can't imagine what it took for her to say yes to him again. Wow! She really put herself out there for a North in that situation, good for her. And then he betrayed her again. I was shocked. The West and North dynamic would be hard to maintain. In the end, even though I feel that it was probably the best for Raven, I just wish it didn't have to go down like that. But don't worry, Raven, you will find a solid, mature, outgoing, and honest South man, I'm sure of it. If they both could dive into the 4Cross Love Framework and learn their positions in the game of love, they could decipher what happened and move on with eyes wide open.

Matt (North) & Colleen (South)-

Matt is a troubled soul because of what happened to him in his previous marriage. Being cheated on and then knowing that his wife is pregnant with another man's child must be devastating. Plus, for him as a driven North, that sense of losing control is bewildering. It threw him for a loop, but he did sign up for this experiment to get married again. Colleen is a sweet, hardworking, and bubbly South who wants a strong, commanding, and stable husband.

She loves him. I think she struggles a little bit with wanting more man, but Matt certainly brings the North energy, maybe a bit too much sometimes. His insecurity comes out in his controlling nature. He has realized that when he starts feeling out of control, he better leave because he will start yelling, and I'm sure that was part of the issue in the past. He knows it. His fear of being played messes with his ability to be rational and patient. Part of the issue is that Colleen's need for stability has put her in a situation of compromise in a way, she is settling to settle, and hence why they bicker a bit, as was said at the last party. They are not the star couple like Brennon and Alexa because everyone can sense some angst. Matt's angst and insecurity is coming out by antagonizing Colleen and she hates it. She is tolerating to her highest ability; you can see it when they are on the couch. She's not moving in with him for a reason. We'll see how this one goes.

Matt needs to relax and quit antagonizing her. Colleen needs to decide that this is what she really wants and stop the back-and-forth energy that makes Matt nervous.

Obviously if they knew their positions in the game of love, they could have a far better understanding and appreciation for one another.

Brennan (South) & Alexa (North)-

These two are a perfect match. He's a South that was committed to the process and to her from the beginning, and he has been a solidly stable man with an unwavering connection to her since.

She is as North as they come. She is harsh and straightforward in her criticism of others. She seems to be exceedingly in love with Brennon, and as best as she can, she compliments and adores him. She seeks the confirmation of his love to get the certainty she needs from him throughout the process.

He's so solid in his foundation that he barely wavers when push comes to demand. She may get bored of him, but he needs to learn, as she said, to throw her around and put her in her place while surfing the line of not going too far. Ha! Good luck with that Brennon. But he is as loyal and supportive as they come. He backs her up with the whole Cole situation. He backs her up in front of the family, to the point where even her dad tells him he might be a little too appeasing of her demands.

One of the hardest positions for a man is to be married to a strong, demanding, extravagant, bull-headed, righteous North woman. He may get tired of her need to be extravagant and always right. I wish them the best.

The best thing they could do is learn their positions in the game of love so they could grow their already strong bond, creating greater connection, understanding, and love.

Season 4 Seattle WA-

Brett Brown (North) & Tiffany Pennywell (South)

Kwame Appiah (South) & Chelsea Griffin (North)

Paul Peden (West) & Micah Lussier (North)

Zack Goytowski (West) & Bliss Poureetezadi (North?)

Marshall Glaze (West) & Jackie Bonds (East) & Josh Demas

Brett (North) & Tiffany (South)-

What an adorable couple. I was having a hard time deciding if Brett was West or North until I saw his place, his boujeeness, and then of course the wedding pant issue. There is no way a West would spend that much on luggage. His entire concern around his look speaks volumes about how he wants the world to see him. He is a very mature North with a conviction for truth and adherence to his values and the process.

I can't imagine how he was not married or had a serious girlfriend already, but my guess is his criteria was high. Also, for a driven North like him, it can be difficult to find a South that is individualistic, entrepreneurial, and energetic. Souths are hardworking and driven in different ways, more of a nose-to-the-grindstone kind of drive. He says several times in the show that he is attracted to Tiffany because she is driven and enthusiastic even though her voice and mannerisms are South.

Tiffany is a mature South who is not interested in the drama created in the Pods. She was trying to make sure people were getting along, except for Micah and Irina, who she soon realized were toxic to the group as a whole. What's not to like about Tiffany? She is loyal, supportive, honest, and truly beautiful on the inside and out. When she and Brett meet up with Tiffany's friends, you hear how loyal she is and, hence, how loyal and protective they are of her. She is likely friends with several other Souths who are looking out for her.

Brett is unwavering. He is liked immediately and given blessing by Tiffany's Dad and Tiffany is welcomed into Brett's family with open arms. I thought it was funny that Brett's brother asked her if his hairdo was ok. Ha, the South wants acceptance from the other South. What a fun couple.

As with most couples, their challenge will be keeping it interesting. Tiffany seems motivated and willing to try new things. Brett will need to check himself in his innate need to be right and potentially righteous approach.

It would be extremely helpful for them to know the 4 positions in the game of love so they could learn how to play better.

Kwame (South) & Chelsea (North)-

These two are adorable and a great match. She is a loud and critical North but not so much so that she's off putting in the show. She has a commanding presence but because of her pink outfits and her fun approach to life she attracts people rather than pushing them away with her abrupt nature. She's mature enough in the pods to get what she wants and doesn't get caught up in the drama too much. A very mature, manipulative, and North orchestration.

Kwame's lack of maturity showed up in the pool scene with Micah and it was not cool. I thought Chelsea handled this very well and was a big part of the reason that they ended up together by the end. If Chelsea hadn't commanded the respect she deserved with such grace, it could have been ugly. It was cringy to watch Kwame and Micah, but it did make for juicy, awkward reality television.

Kwame is so adorable, kind, and supportive. He is very likable to all the guys in the pods and to everyone throughout the season. He is a mostly mature South who is strongly connected to what I'm guessing is a commanding North mother, which is why it was so hard for him to commit to going through with the marriage. Which I don't understand, because he signed up for it knowing his mother was likely not going to be supportive no matter what. He obviously didn't think this all the way through. Kwame not having the blessing of his mom was tough. Having his sister and brother there was the deciding factor in Kwame saying yes. And what a ray of light his sister Barbara was and a stabilizing and confident show of support from his brother Jerry. Jerry also said that Kwame's Dad was excited for him.

In the show following the weddings, it seems like the bond between them is only getting stronger, and Kwame owns up to his immature display around the Micah issue. He has grown up. Micah was not a good match for him even though she is North. I'll leave it at that.

Paul (West) & Micah (North)-

This is not a good match, and not just because they are not opposites. Micah is immature and her friends are even more so. The suggestion that somehow Micah deserves a great love/mate because she's so beautiful goes against what the show is all about and is honestly a display of exactly why the dating world is so superficial. Micah proves her immaturity and devious behavior in the Pod lounge with Irina (South). By the end of the series Micah has realized her behavior was inappropriate and does apologize to Chelsea. I think it was interesting that at the flag football gathering Chelsea basically told Micah to leave Seattle because her match was not in Seattle. This is North (Chelsea) being brutally honest in a manipulative way, joking but not joking.

Paul is so West. He is indecisive and laborious in every decision. For me, as a North, it was hard to believe that Micah not only chose him but also kept on talking to him after the wedding. Maybe she wanted to be more like Paul and not the superficial crowd she hung around. I don't know. But I did have a feeling, as was suggested later in the series, that she wasn't as into him as she was professing. Hence why she asked him to answer first because she didn't want to look stupid if she did say yes. She knew something was off and wasn't totally sure herself.

He speaks several times about being in his head and not being able to decide because he's so analytical. His friends suggest the same. He knows that something is not right/correct. Wests are very introspective and able to sense when things are off but he just can't put his finger on it. He is right in that he doesn't get or sense the loving, compassionate, nurturing energy from Micah that he is looking for. His mom is an East and even though she and Micah look alike they are not at all alike in how they express themselves. It's not that Micah is incapable of being nurturing, expressive, and compassionate, it shows up in different ways than what Paul is used to or looking for.

I think more than anything, Micah is playing the victim when she knows deep down, she was manipulating and hiding her true feelings. That was a hard decision for Paul to make, but it was the right one. By the end of the series, you can tell he knows it; he just isn't clear on why.

If they knew how to see themselves through the lens of 4Cross Love, they could open their eyes to the game of love and learn to play a whole lot better!

Zack (West) & Bliss (South?)-

Zack was trying to be clever and hide his true self from the beginning, which was quite the turn-off for a lot of the girls, but he soon realized in order to win at this game, he was going to have to be vulnerable and tell the truth, which took a lot of courage because it sounds like he has been judged for not being 'good enough' quite a lot in his life. Which for West is very difficult. They thrive on being 'better' in some way than others at something. It's what drives them. They don't rely on boldness like a North or charisma like an East or being part of a group like a South. They have to find a way to claim their domain of some expertise or knowledge. For Zack, being a lawyer gives him identity and a sense of confidence in something he can have 'over' others. I don't mean this in an arrogant way but in a purpose-driven way. It was hard for all of us to watch him choose Irina over Bliss, but there was a sense that Irina was going to be his rock, someone who was going to fight for him. He needs someone to back him up because he can't always do it for himself. He can't decide. Which is why Bliss will be great for him.

Bliss is strong, she has conviction and she's honest. She was forthcoming about what was happening in the women's Pod lounge with Irina without being conniving and gossipy. It had to have hurt to not be chosen over Irina after all that. And then to go back to Zack after the obvious disaster of Zack and Irina took a lot of tolerance, compassion, and trust. And then to keep going to the altar with Zack even after her North dad basically told her she was crazy. She is resilient. I have her at South but I'm not 100 on her. Because Irina was a big part of the story, I wasn't able to fully get where Bliss was coming from.

The potential issues they might have been Zack not being secure in his skin and his decisions. He is kind of an odd duck, but in a good way. I felt bad for him even though there were some things about him that were kind of awkward. But let's face it: we're all weird in our own quirky way, and if this couple can learn how to see their positions in the game of love, they can play better and live happily ever after.

Marshall (West) & Jackie (East)-

Jackie knows she needs the calming, nurturing, and patient West in her life, which is why she chose Marshall. She is trying to, in a sense, to force herself toward a partner that has the potential to bring out the part of her she doesn't have. She's fun, loud, spontaneous, and full of energy, but on the flip side of that, when she's worn herself out with drama, she is done, tired, and fed up. She yo-yos from being crazy and fun to spiraling into a victim of her own doing. She sees it, she kind of knows it, and confesses as much to Marshall, but she can't help herself. She needs, craves, and is most comfortable in drama… until she's not.

Marshall is so patient, compassionate, and loyal. He wants this to work and he's willing to put in the time and outlast her episodes. But it quickly becomes apparent that it's not just her need for drama and her family's potential disapproval that is making her annoyed, it's that she needs more excitement. She is used to more drama and excitement, and Marshall's grounded and calm nature is just not going to create it; in fact, he is the antithesis.

We all see it coming. I would say she gave it a great effort. So, although they were opposites in position and seemingly a great match, they are not compatible in maturity, hence why Jackie is attracted to Josh (North). Not only will he give her the 'manly' energy that she craves, but he will also create the drama through his immaturity that she needs. By the time she says she doesn't want drama at the end of the show with Josh's first fiancé Monica (North), she's already been in the thick of her drama enough to be tired of the drama she creates and hence creates more victim-driven drama. And the cycle goes around and around and around. I'm not surprised Jackie and Josh are not still together.

They all could learn a great deal about themselves and the game of love by investigating and learning the 4 positions so they can play much better.

Season 5 Houston TX-

James Milton Johnson (West) & Lydia Gonzalez (East)

Izzy Zapata (South) & Stacy Snyder (North)

Jared Pierce JP (South) & Taylor Rue (South)

Uche Okoroha (North) & Aaliyah Cosby (South)

Christopher Fox (South) & Johnie Maraist (West)

Milton (West) & Lydia (East)

Milton is so West it's hilarious. I thought it was funny when he said that he's a risk-taker because, from his parallel of perspective, he is. He says he has his standards about how things should or shouldn't be handled, as he mentions several times, but what he doesn't understand is that is how he sees it. What's ironic is that he loves Lydia for her passion, charm, and outgoing nature as well as her family but at the same time he struggles to embrace it and accept the parts that he doesn't agree with.

He is mature and wise, but he is also condescending and forthcoming about the way he thinks things should be done. There is a right way to do things and a wrong way, and he thinks he knows the proper way. He is traditional. He wants Lydia to take his last name, and that is that. He is very much like his mom, who is also West. I could also tell that his dad was used to giving up on the conversation, knowing that he was not going to be listened to. I imagine he and his wife have had some very heated and stubborn discussions. Milton is patient, calculated and kind while at the same time having that very clever West sense of humor.

Lydia is very East. She, as Alyiaah said, can be so much that she smothered her a bit in the pods, and she also couldn't shut her mouth when Alyiaah was clearly asking her to. In stressful situations Lydia overreacts and can't help herself from talking too much and creating drama. It's what she does. She had matured by the end of the show and at the reunion. I think she realized, and I'm sure Milton has pointed it out that she needs to learn how to manage her emotions, but that's also what makes her so engaging and fun to be around.

These two really love one another and I hope they build a happy and satisfying life together. It would help them immensely to understand their positions in the game of love so they could see what is really happening underneath their concerns, comments, and misinterpretations.

Izzy (South) & Stacy (North)

Izzy is a caring, calm, and enduring South. He falls for the directness, boldness, and loudness of Stacy. He struggled to decide if he wanted to go for someone softer and more soothing like Johnie (West), or what felt more stable and certain in Stacy. But once he decided he was loyal, hardworking, and consistent. Notice how he tries to stand up for his friend Chris (South). He is concerned about his loyalty and having his buddies back. And he does the same for Stacy. He is a loyal, supportive South.

Stacy is a hard person to satisfy, she has very high standards of what she does and doesn't want and will not tolerate otherwise. She isn't afraid to tell Izzy or anyone else for that matter what she needs. She says she wants a man to take the lead, but it's always on her terms, so it's hard for a South man to do that when, in a sense, they want to be told what to do. Which, in her defense, she does. She tells him exactly what to do; he just doesn't do it exactly how she wants, and that is the conundrum of being a South husband to a very strong-willed North woman.

I thought it was interesting how her family was suggesting as much. They were basically saying how she needed her 'personality' tempered by someone like Izzy. And did you notice how quickly Izzy moved his way into her family? He was trying to gain loyalty with them, and they genuinely liked him. He was dying for that family connection. She has a tough shell to crack, but as Izzy said, she is also kind, warm, and loving underneath all her toughness. I think they both gave the idea a sound effort.

Had Izzy told her from the beginning about his mistake regarding his credit score that he was correcting, he would have given her the certainty she needed at the altar. But once she had any doubt, as she said, she needed 100% certainty; she used that as an excuse to be done. And this North was done. Stacy really opened up and did her best to be vulnerable. Given her intense nature and her need to be right, she was mature and honest. It was so funny when she said she's always right on her wedding day when she was sitting in the chair getting her makeup done. It's so funny when people know their position without knowing it and have the self-awareness to be honest about it.

Learning the 4Cross Love Framework would clearly help these two gain a lot of self-awareness. They could play the game like champions.

JP (South) & Taylor (South)-

I'm not 100 about the positions for these two but because it was so obvious from the beginning that this wasn't going to work, I have a feeling they are both Souths connecting on the notion of friendship and not loveship. Perhaps JP was a West, but his attire and need to identify with the USA flag as his ode to a group was interesting.

The tension may have been partly by JP being turned off by Taylor's 'gaudy' eyelashes and what he perceived as 'fakeness,' as he puts it, but it was more about neither of them taking the lead. It's a weird energy not to know who to look for in guiding the energy.

It was glaringly obvious that JP was uncomfortable and awkward, but it was made even more apparent by his unwillingness to relax and at least try to play along. That was a tough position to be in. Taylor is adorable and she tried hard to push through the awkwardness and get him to feel comfortable but as he said it was a bit badgering rather than supportive. But honestly, I don't think there was anything she could have done. They bonded in the pods on the sameness not realizing how awkward that would be in real life.

Uche (North) & Aaliyah (South)-

Uche is very straightforward about what he believes is the truth. He wants honesty but was unwilling to also admit that he may have had some shortcomings. I'm not sure what the truth is behind how he and Lydia somehow managed to be on the same show, but as Milton says, 'everyone is on their own parallel of perception about the truth.' I would suggest that Lydia probably did act a little odd and perhaps erratic in the past with their relationship. Uche was so concerned about his identity and what he saw as the truth that he lost the reason behind the experiment. This can be a hard thing for North. They are more concerned about being right than having it work. He let his concern for people thinking that he was right ruin the experiment for Aaliyah and potentially Lydia and Milton.

Fortunately, Milton was mature enough to realize something was off, not correct, and outlasted the silliness. I did feel badly for Aaliyah because Lydia, in all her need for a relationship, wanting to show her sincerity and being a true friend, also couldn't shut her mouth. Had

Lydia not told Aaliyah more than she should have, it may have worked out with her and Uche. I don't know, but it was an unfortunate situation for all of them. I don't think Uche is a bad guy. He just needs to be more self-aware.

Had they known their positions in the game of love, they could have gone about the experiment with more awareness, kindness, and compassion.

Johnie (West) & Chris (South)-

Johnie had a calming energy, but she was also a bit of a smooth talker. She talked on both sides of her mouth because she couldn't decide what she wanted. And there was a good reason for this. Her true love, who was likely an East, died of an overdose. It was such a scare for her that she was looking for something not like him but at the same time knew that the safe choice, as she called Chris, wouldn't be exciting enough for her. She was looking for excitement, not realizing, of course, that Izzy wasn't going to be exciting enough for her either. Which she found out later. It's similar to Milton and Lydia in that Wests love the high energy of East because it's something they don't have but it also scares the heck out of them. It's a conundrum.

Chris was a calm, slow, and nice South guy. As Johnie said, he's' one of the kindest souls she has ever met. He was loyal to her even after the craziness in the pods. He defended her when he knew that maybe she wasn't totally honest or straightforward. I imagine he knew not too long afterward that it wasn't going to work, which is why he found someone else, probably a North. He didn't want to confront the situation and tell her, but I imagine part of that was subliminal payback. Johnie also knew it wasn't right; you could tell at the reunion she wasn't too upset by it; in fact, she called him her bud.

They could save themselves a lot of anguish and hurt feelings by knowing their position in the game of love by studying the 4Cross Love Framework.

Season 6 Charlotte NC-

Johnny McIntyre (South) & Amy Cortes (North?)

Clay Gravesande (North) & Amber Desiree AD (South)

Jimmy Presnell (West) & Chelsea Blackwell (East)

Kenneth Gorham (South) & Brittany Mills (South)

Jeramey (West) & Laura (North) & Sarah Ann (North)

Johnny McIntyre (South) & Amy Cortes (North)-

Johnny is a supportive, caring, and loyal man who got lucky in love with a caring, independent, and charming North woman in Amy. I was thinking for a bit that maybe they were both Souths connecting on friendship and not on love, which you can have in a friendship, but it's not the same as romantic love. There is a lack of zing when it's friendship love.

Johnny is head over heels for Amy. He feels like he has hit the jackpot because not only is he in love with her emotionally, but he couldn't be happier with her physically AND they are opposites. They are an adorable couple.

Amy is a very steady North. She exudes wisdom and certainty while also having some vulnerability. She is able to express herself to Johnny because he is so open and honest. They make a great couple.

Her North father was more than willing to hold court and represent his family. I found him to be endearing and was glad that he gave them the North certainty that Amy and Johnny needed. I don't know what else to say about such a solid couple.

Of course, if they knew the 4Cross Framework, navigating their marriage going forward they could gain a whole new level of peace and understanding now and in the next phase of their life, having a family. If they ever figure out the whole birth control thing.

Clay Gravesande (North) & Amber Desiree AD (South)-

I think we all wanted to like Clay. He tried hard to break out of his North shell and be honest and vulnerable, but his smooth talking, as emulated by his father, is buried deep in his identity. He struggled from the beginning to make any commitment, which I find interesting, being that is the whole premise of the show… marriage, kind of a big commitment. He fell for the supportive nature of AD recognizing he needed someone completely different than him. Someone who could tell the truth and hold strong in challenging times.

Clay's mom was a shining example of a South wife who put up with a lot from her former husband, who blatantly tried to interject his achievements from years ago on camera on his son's wedding day! I wonder where Clay got it!?

I think we all saw this one coming to a degree. Clay was not as attracted physically to AD as she was to him.

AD tolerated so much through that season: all the ups and downs of Clay trying to figure out what to do while using her kind heart to play with her emotions.

Do you see where Clay was giving AD the certainty she needed up until the very end? Up until he said no. This, to me, was cruel punishment to a woman of such grace, beauty, and loyalty.

When Clay's parents are talking after the, 'I don't' from Clay, was one of the most profound moments of all. His dad, even after it was abundantly clear that his wrongdoing and mistreatment of Clay's mother had a huge impact on Clay's outlook on marriage, still could not apologize! He still is trying to blame it on his upbringing. Wrong is wrong, and we all know it. So, I have to say I do feel for Clay, but the truth is he knows, just like his dad, what is right and wrong no matter who raises you.

Jimmy Presnell (West) & Chelsea Blackwell (East)-

Here we go with the indecisive West and the crazy emotional East that can't see her own need for drama and neediness driving away love.

It starts in the Pods with Jimmy not being able to decide between Jessica (North) and Chelsea. It's very similar to Barnett (West), Jessica (North), and Amber (East) from the first season. In the end, Jimmy realizes he must decide and plays it as long as he can to try and get as much information as he can to be forced into a decision. I find it fascinating that so many West men come on this show to force themselves to decide because they have such a hard time doing it in life.

Jessica, being the strong and forceful North, realizes this and lashes out, just like Jessica did to Barnett. If you can't decide, you're (Jimmy) an idiot. She's a catch, and he's an idiot.

Well, of course, this forces Jimmy to ask Chelsea, who is having a hard time deciding between him and Trevor. For East indecision is based on possibility, too many choices. For West it's about wanting to get more information for security.

The insecurity and neediness demonstrated by Chelsea from the pods to the outside world is very evident and heartbreaking. I won't go into that further as it is so profoundly obvious that her desire to feel wanted outweighed Jimmy's capacity to outlast her insecurities.

I think it was interesting that he thought there was any doubt that we all knew he had slept with one of his 'friends' the minute he introduced Chelsea to them. I was just wondering which one or if it was both. I thought that the second they saddled up. And I know I'm not the only one. That's kind of a West thing. They think they can hide things. They think they are clever in some way and funny but can be cheesy and deceitful.

I think we all saw this breakup coming and I thought it was at least graceful and honorable that Jimmy did it before they went to the altar knowing he just couldn't take it anymore. And he and Jessica would have never made it. As he said, he was rightfully scared of her.

Kenneth Gorham (South) & Brittany Mills (South)-

This relationship was hard to figure out. I think I finally realized by the reunion that they were both South bonding on friendship and Southness. They never really had any pizazz, zing, or zip. There was nothing.

For a while, I thought Brittany was a nice North but then realized, as she said to Ken, that she was lacking the very zing that we all knew wasn't there. If she was a North, she would have been trying to whip him into shape, but instead, she was tolerating. And then he seemed not to be fazed by it after momentarily looking up from his phone while connecting and touching base with all his 'people', as he put it.

I found it interesting that it was up to her to prove that she was capable of being with a black man. She had to prove to his people that she could handle it. And yet it wasn't mentioned, on camera anyway, that she was marrying a black man and to prove anything to anyone. He even said that his best female friend would be questioning his sanity. I believe it was part of his hesitancy.

Kenny was sweet, loving, and fair. He was going along to get along. I think they were more like brother and sister than husband and wife, and of course, as two Souths, that's exactly how it would be. Kind of like Deepti and Kyle end up thinking that maybe there was a romantic connection.

Of all the positions, the South is likely the only one that could be together, confusing love with friendship. The other positions, especially the two on offense, North and East, would be a tornado of domination or massive dramatic energy.

Jeramey (West) & Laura (North) & Sarah Ann (North)-

Well Jeramey had his work cut out for him with either Laura or Sarah Ann because they are both very domineering Norths. Again, we have a West that can't decide, which gives off being a 'player,' which Jeramey is not…he's a West that can't decide, even though he put himself on a show knowing he had to decide.

Jeramey is a fun and outgoing West. His sense of style is to have no real style at all, and that is why Laura was so perturbed. He thinks he's charming, clever, and fun, which he is for the right person, but not for Laura. She's annoyed by him from the moment they meet, and it doesn't get any better. She has the right way to do things, and he has his way of doing things. Both stubborn and self abosored. Not going to work. I think seeing his house was quite the eye opener in her realizing she was dealing with an entirely different level of clean, order, and specificity than even herself.

So, he's feeling torn, indecisive, and hurt. And instead of being upfront about it, he sneaks behind her back and betrays Laura with Sarah Ann. Not cool. Sneaky.

She has no problem calling him out bluntly on his indiscretion, and rightfully so.

Sarah Ann decides she is going to get what she wants. She could have waited, been patient but it's clearly all about her, she doesn't care, as she says. So off they go on the jet skis to create the waves of drama. That is not going to end well.

Laura is a strong beautiful woman. She will find what she's looking for but it would behoove her to learn her position so she can see how her forceful and sometimes rude energy can be off-putting. She could learn to use it and navigate it to get the love she wants.

Jeramey could learn a lot about why and how he operates in the game of love and recognize how he can become a more self-aware person who can play the game of love like a champion.

The Brazilian Season 1-

Hudson Mendes (South) & Carol Novaes (North)

Lissio Fiod (North) & Luana Braga (South)

Thiago Rocha (East) & Nanda Terra (West)

Shayan Haghbin (North) & Ana Prado (East)

Rodrigo Vaisemberg (West) & Dayanne Feitoza (East)

Hudson Mendes (South) & Carol Novaes (North)-

Although Hudson is his own man, he is willing to get along with Carol to appease her. He's supportive, sweet, funny, and works hard to figure it out. He's full of energy and enthusiasm. What a sport. He loves Carol, but I think he is overwhelmed by her at the beginning.

Carol is a demanding and outspoken woman who has no problem declaring her thoughts. I'm sure she has a sensitive side, but it's not apparent until we see her start to unwind and really buy into this experiment. She falls for Hudson. I think it's real, and she is having a hard time reconciling her need for control and her desire to have a man in her life.

By the wedding, you could tell that she really fell for him, and he started to feel like maybe he was enough for her. They are adorable, but…He said several times that he was embarrassed by her need to be right, especially about the wine tasting at dinner on their honeymoon. The thing is, he likes that she takes control and leads the way; for the most part, he just doesn't understand why. It's confusing and unstable, a very uncomfortable place for a South.

It's going to be really hard for Hudson in this relationship. He has married a strong, outspoken, feminist North who wants him to be a man but wants to run the show. She will definitely test him to his wits' end, and at some point, he will break, and she's not going to like it.

What gets me about this is that Hudson is expected to be a traditional gentleman, open doors, pull out her chair, and dote on her, but she doesn't want to follow traditional roles when she thinks they are stupid. This generation seems to be in a conundrum. It's contradictory and confusing. This dilemma can be really hard for North, they want to change the rules as they see fit, because they're stupid, but also wants the rules to remain when it suits them. North is all about if it suits them, it's good for them, at any given time.

Lissio Fiod (North) & Luana Braga (South)-

Lissio is an ant agonizer, and for the most part, Luana likes his charm and sense of humor, but he pushes it too far too often. He needs to realize that part of his antagonizing is his way of controlling the power struggle and the insecurity he feels around being analyzed by her because she's a therapist. He's sweet and seems to come from a caring and sweet family. He struggles with his desire to want to be right and control things and his desire to be a good person and a family man.

Luana is supportive, kind, and has a big heart, as Lissio says. She is a feisty, smart South that has learned to take care of herself, so she is not going to be a pushover by any means, and as with most relationships, the struggle to keep the upper hand in some way is always there, especially in a new relationship like theirs.

I read that they have split up. I'm guessing it was a power struggle and Lissio felt threatened by her. Not sure. I could be wrong, but I doubt it.

Thiago Rocha (East) & Nanda Terra (West)-

When Nanda couldn't decide on the two Easts that she was dating, Mack and Thiago, it was apparent that Nanda was West. It has been an issue for almost all the Wests in these shows because they have a hard time deciding and want more time and information. It's either this way, or they jump in and decide because they know they must so they can stay on the show and not get left behind. It has turned into the West being perceived as a 'player,' but that couldn't be further from the truth; they just can't decide, so they drag it out. Nanda is coy and believes she is clever, but Thiago is swoony, and I think she realizes she has a challenge on her hands.

Thiago is a pretty calm, cool, and mature East. He doesn't fly off the handle or create a lot of drama, at least not that I saw on the show. But you can see how sensitive he is, and of course, his lifestyle is very

East. He's a risk taker and a thrill seeker who does not have a lot of responsibility in his life because he runs from it. Which is why I find it interesting he's on the show. He is obviously handsome and he clearly has no problem finding people to date.

They definitely have a power struggle, and it is likely what broke them up. He had a strong sense of what he wanted and I'm not sure she met those challenges. I read that they have split, and she is now with Mack, and they have a baby.

Shayan Haghbin (North) & Ana Prado (East)-

Shayan is a pretty extreme antagonist who likes to stir the pot in sometimes overtly awkward ways to prove in some way that he is in control. He has a domineering air about him, and he's tall and handsome. From what I can gather he was even more so off camera. He seems like a genuine guy who doesn't understand how he 'comes off.' You can tell this when Ana is telling him basically how condescending he is, and he reacts as if he has no idea what she's talking about. I think underneath it all, he probably has an idea, but he doesn't understand how much it affects others. Which is likely why he struggles in relationships. And, of course, he comes from a different culture; he makes that very clear.

Ana was attracted to the feeling of certainty and leadership that he brought, but for an East like her, it can be too much. Both North and East are on offense and don't like to be told what to do or how to do it, so this was going to be a tumultuous relationship from the start.

Ana is obviously concerned about her relationship with her daughter, which is her number one priority. The time that Shayan didn't spend with her daughter is blown out of proportion and made it to be something that it wasn't, like an East would in a stressful situation. She wanted him to be all in and he is a pretty aloof, avoidant North. It would be hard for this relationship to work with just Ana and Shyan, but when you bring a child into the picture, and the mom is an East, the relationship aspect is huge. Shayan not trying hard enough, just added to an already rocky relationship. Of course, if they knew 4Cross, they could have recognized this from the beginning and perhaps been able to work things out if they really connected as they did in the pods.

Rodrigo Vaisemberg (West) & Dayanne Feitoza (East)-

I don't know if Rodrigo feels like he made a mistake by not saying yes to Dayanne. He was caught in a situation where he felt like something was out of order and wrong, but he couldn't quite figure it out, so when push came to shove, he fell back to needing more time and information to decide. They seemed to be perfect for each other but Rodrigo's need for Dayanne to live up to his standards of what seemed to make perfect sense to him was the barrier to them getting a chance to figure it out. And as Dayanne said, it wasn't just that he wanted her to be different, more like him; he said it in a judgmental, condescending West way. They don't see themselves doing it, but also know they are doing it, because they don't have a problem pointing things out. It's important to note that he doesn't really understand how he comes off.

Dayanna is so East. She's fun, crazy, and loud and does things her way in whatever outfit she decides works in the moment. She did have a disaster for organization, but she was willing to work on it. She needs touch, love, kisses, and kindness, and because Rodgrigo's natural reaction to his concern not being met is to avoid, hibernate, and clam up, you could slowly see this relationship unraveling.

He said she was too much, needed too much, wanted too much. Dayanne tried hard to satisfy Rodrigo's need for order, but by the end, she was ready to migrate because nobody was going to tell her how to do things, and not give her what she needed. They were a really cute couple, and had they known 4Cross Love, they could have laughed at all their differences and realized what each of them needed to feel safe. I think they could have worked it out and had a great life together.

The Brazilian Season 2-

Alisson Hentges (East) & Thamara Terez (West)-

Robert Richard (North) & Flavia Queiroz (South)-

Tiago Chapola (East) & Vanessa Carvalho (West)

William Domiencio (South) & Veronica Brito (North)

Guilherme Martins (West) & Maira Bullos (East)

Alisson Hentges (East) & Thamara Terez (West)-

Thamara is yet another example of a West that is being labeled as a player because she has a hard time deciding and she wants to make sure she is not left behind. It's her way of being in control by choosing several men and suggesting she has chosen all of them as her number one. This gives her the illusion of control of choice. She thinks she is clever like nobody is privy to her game. But in an environment like this, it becomes clear that she is caught. West likes to play behind the scenes in a sense, they are covert, hiders, thinkers thinking that nobody can see their hand, but not so much in 'Love is Blind.' Everybody talks, the stakes are high, and the game is fast.

Thamara is sweet, fun, interesting, and smart. She is always thinking about how to make her next move. And she has no problem pointing out when she doesn't like something about how Allison is behaving.

I thought it was interesting how she challenged Allison with her ex when they got back. Had the shoe been on the other foot, I'm pretty sure she would not have handled it the way he did. That was a very mature approach by Allison, but I'm sure with his competitive East side, he was likely freaking out inside.

Allison grew up a lot in 38 days. I think he came into the experiment with a cavalier approach that kept him from opening up, likely because he learned very early on in life to keep things to himself. He started off as a non-typical East with the guys and grew to really enjoy and embrace the whole experience. When East don't feel like they can really be themselves they will go inward and be more introverted. But if you listen closely, and then, of course, by the end, you can see how open, fun, and silly he is.

He and Thamara are a great fit, and if they knew 4Cross Love, they could really learn to appreciate their differences and enjoy their adventure together on so many more levels.

Robert Richard (North) & Flavia Queiroz (South)-

Flavia is an outgoing, fun, and adventurous South that you can't help but love. She has no problem standing up for herself throughout the show. You see her kindness towards Robert. She supports him in opening up and being there for him. He feels her commitment to their relationship. Her mom is supportive, just like her, wanting the best for everyone involved.

Robert says that he didn't know if he could open up and get past his cold nature several times. He tries really hard to let go of his controlling nature and fully buy into the experiment with Flavia. I think it's because of his willingness to be vulnerable and his intention to be a strong man for Flavia that it is easy to root for them. He never suggested or said anything negative about her. He was certain.

I really thought they were going to make it but evidently, he couldn't quite keep to his commitment after they were married. Although it didn't sound like he physically cheated on her, he admitted he had made a mistake and had insinuated to someone else that he was interested in them through some sort of dating app. He was very apologetic and sincere, but I believe it's too late. It's hard for a South to trust again if you break trust.

Of course, if they had known 4Cross Love, they could have been so much further in their understanding of one another; perhaps this could have been avoided.

Tiago Chapola (East) & Vanessa Carvalho (West)

This was one of the hardest couples for me to figure out. I'm quite sure Vanessa is a somewhat extroverted West, and Tiago played an introverted East. All the stories of his history led me to believe he is East, but his actions on the show were kind of contrary to that, which is what East can and will do if they are running inside.

I feel like he started running while still playing the game from the moment he met her. I don't think he was physically attracted to her, so he played along as best he could. I don't know. This one is a conundrum for me. I would love to interview both of them to get some clues as to what was going on for both of them, but in particular, Tiago.

Vanessa is a fun and confident West who clearly has her standards as to how to approach a relationship. Tiago, although handsome and, I'm sure, sometimes engaging, was not enough to give her the confidence to decide to marry him. I understand her concern. He was hiding something, not honest about what was going on for him, and she knew it.

Tiago was hard to like because of this. You can tell that he is struggling to be authentic, and I'm not sure where this comes from. We don't get much insight from his family or his life after they get back from the honeymoon. Only that he is unemployed and a 'sales' guy but that could be a circumstance for a lot of people.

I wasn't surprised that they both said no by the end. They could certainly help themselves going forward by studying 4Cross Love so that when they find the 'right' person, they understand how to relate at a much higher level and get past the blindness.

William Domiencio (South) & Veronica Brito (North)

Veronica is such a mature, lovely, majestic, and honest North. The way she handled herself throughout the entire season was a lesson in grace. Looking back, I imagine it was overwhelming for William. I'm sure a part of him felt her graceful dominance as destabilizing and flared his insecurity that he couldn't live up to her needs. He was certainly going to marry up. And this was profoundly evident when William's mother came into the picture.

William's mom is true North. She had no problem speaking her truth and letting everyone know how she felt. Had she been supportive in any way, William may have had the fortitude to say yes. In hindsight,

William's mom may have been right, as I'm not sure William could live up to Veronica's needs at this time in his life. He is young. He still lives with his controlling mother, and Veronica doesn't need a son; she deserves a man.

I have nothing against William. He is a sweet, smart South who had a hard choice to make, but in the end, I think he knew what was fair for Veronica was actually to say no. By the end, he didn't feel like he could be the stabilizing contribution to the relationship that he was expecting himself to be or that his mother basically said he was incapable of.

The fact that William's mom couldn't even suggest that perhaps she was wrong by being so controlling and mean by apologizing was a glaring demonstration of a brute force North versus a graceful one like Veronica.

Going forward, they would hugely benefit from knowing 4Cross love so they can see how positionally they were matched, but maturely, not so much. It's okay. They are both good people and if William can see how much his North mom is manipulating him, he will be more apt to stand on his own. Veronica will be able to see what really happened, not that she doesn't, and find someone who is worthy of her grace and strength.

Guilherme Martins (West) & Maira Bullos (East)

This was a hard one to watch because Guilherme gave us every reason to believe that he was into it, but as with many Wests, it seems, behind the scenes, when nobody was watching, he was not as on board as he was playing it out to be. I'm not even sure if more time and information would have led him to be a great companion for Maira. It's so hard for a West to make the choice and fully commit when there might be other options. And it sounds like, at the reunion, he had already started talking to somebody else. Which he adamantly wanted Maira not to reveal.

Wests do not like their 'stuff' out in the open; they are covert and reserved, thinking that somehow, they won't be exposed if they can keep it under the radar. They don't give up personal information unless pushed, and even then, they will keep some things to themselves. They are the mysterious ones, at least in their mind's eye.

Maira is a dramatic East that craves action. She can exaggerate and create a scene with the best of them. She is fun, charming, and beautiful. Her need to feel needed can be a bit of a burden for her partner no matter if it's Guilherme or anyone else. She really loved him and was rightfully confused by his back-and-forth indecisive commitment to the experiment. It was confusing to the end when he acted like he wanted to keep trying but was clearly not into it.

I gather that her son was a huge factor for him. I don't blame him. That was a huge commitment without even being introduced to him. I can see why he needed more information. I don't think it was fair not to introduce the two of them. I wonder if Maira already knew that Guilerme was not committed at that point and didn't want to involve her son in something she had a sense wasn't going to work out.

It was interesting meeting Maira's West Dad. He had no problem confronting the situation that he believed was not up to his high standards. That was certainly an interesting dynamic. We'll leave it at that.

Knowing 4Cross love will help them see what happened so they don't feel bad about how it played out in the end. Self-awareness in love is the key to getting what you need and recognizing what others need so you can create a relationship of understanding, thoughtfulness, and truth.

The Brazilian Season 3-

Renan Justino (South) & Agata Moura (North)

Menandro Rosa (West) & Maria Carolina Caporusso (North)

Jarbas Andrade (West) & Bianca Sessa (North)

Daniel Manzoni (West) & Daniela Silva (North)

Valmir Reis (East) & Karen Bacic (West)

Renan Justino (South) & Agata Moura (North)

I thought at first that Renan was North, but the more we got into the show, the more I realized he is South. He is very concerned about his friends, in particular his group of girlfriends, and making sure they like and accept Agata. He also wanted to be sure that he included all the guys in the group and had trouble considering leaving Valmir out even if Agata didn't care for him. And then the real clincher was how his exes treated him. He said that he has rolled over in his past relationships and was threatened by several of them. A North would never allow that. He was also concerned that Agata was aware that he was involved in his 'causes' (groups), and he was not going to give up on those things for anyone. He is a solid, grounded, stable man who needs to be appreciated for who he is and his contribution to his people/friends/causes rather than his looks, which is why he signed up for this experiment. If he gets that, he will grow up and be the solid man that Agata needs him to be.

Agata has a magnetizing beauty. She is elegant. She is constantly assessing the situation and is concerned about not looking stupid. She needs to be different, and she will not be one more floozy in the line of Renan's admirers, she is not having it. I don't blame her. Nobody wants to be the last stop on the train of many non-endearing romances. Now, this is not necessarily Renan's fault; he simply keeps falling for out-of-control Norths who want to dominate his life and tell him what to do and where to go. Which is why he is so lost. Agata has her own desire to control him and will be another mark on his long list of loves if she doesn't learn to control herself. If Agata is a caring, supportive, and not too controlling North, this couple can certainly make it. Not only make it but reach the obvious potential that is so clearly available.

Menandro Rosa (West) & Maria Carolina Caporusso (North)

Ah, Menandro, the sweet, sensitive, and patient West that is craving some direction and security for his life and his daughter. This is why he chose Maria, the very opinionated, dominant, and assuring North. He oozes compassion, empathy, and sincerity, which is why it hurt so bad when he was accused of being secretive. The thing about West is that they are calculating their moves. They are not necessarily trying to be covert, sly, or distant; they are simply weighing out all the logical possibilities. He is scrutinizing, analyzing, and thinking while leaving the game open for potential new information to come to light. This is why it is so hard to decide. They wait. They outlast.

They hide (hibernate). He is lost. You can see it in his mannerisms, but she is his guiding light. He is who he is. It will be hard for him to man up the way she needs him to. He is adorable, but they will end up feeling more like siblings than lovers.

Maria is outspoken, truthful, dominant, and not going to take any nonsense. She makes this abundantly clear to Valmir who would not have been a good choice. She does not put up with nonsense, which Valmir was full of. The issue with her mother, Maria (North), is they are constantly having right fights, and neither is willing to back down. They would rather be right than have it work. This will also be an issue for Maria with Menandr, just in a different way, because she will continually override him with her concern for being right. She needs an upstanding man who can tell her when she is wrong and stand up for themselves. I can't see Menandro doing this consistently enough to alleviate the craving she has to be dominated. A dominant person needs the opposite and equal primal feeling of dominance. It's human nature. This is why, especially in the new culture of women's power, the North women might find themselves frustrated and alone.

Maria chooses and marries Menandro because, in some ways, he is the opposite of her: soft, caring, and sweet. However, this will fade quickly, and he will start to hibernate and perhaps betray in other ways.

Of course, if they knew their positions in the game of love, they could learn to navigate their 90-degree positions in a way that could benefit them for the rest of their lives.

Jarbas Andrade (West) & Bianca Sessa (North)

I feel like I never really get anything from Jarbas, and that is a sign you are dealing with a West. He's sweet, kind, and seems to be glowingly in love with Bianca. I have a hard time with him. I don't know what to think. You can tell he doesn't want to get the door tattoo and then he says that he was joking later, like he joked at the altar. Is it a joke? I don't think it is. I could be wrong, he might be a sincere and straightforward person, I just sense something. He's charming, caring, and adorable. But the day he was drunk after the dress fitting was a sign and Bianca knew it. She's a wise North but also in love. She sensed something.

Bianca. She is strong. She is adorable. I could sense that she was assessing and, in a way, watching from above most of the time. She was trying to figure out the truth. Was there anything glaring, missing, underneath it all? She will not be duped but love is a duper. I like Bianca. I think we all like Bianca. She is a fighter and a winner, and she will find someone to love if she learns to recognize how she plays from her position in the game of love. It was telling that her brother said in one of the scenes that Bianca is always right. That's what I mean by listening for clues. Very often, you will hear from the closest people to the person you are trying to figure out the clues to their position.

I wasn't surprised when they separated.

Daniel Manzoni (West) & Daniela Silva (North)

These two are adorable. Daniel is a fun and charismatic West who clearly loves chocolate! He doesn't get too up or too down on the entire show. That would not be the correct way to do things. Which is what will come up often for him. It was clear that Daniela walking around naked in her house with neighbors watching was inappropriate and not respectful in his mind. This was one of the times Daniela's

Northness was clear. She doesn't care what others think; they can deal with it.

I thought it was interesting how Daniel used his standards of not talking about sex to dismiss one of the contestants but continued to talk about it most of the season. This can be a West thing to do, suggesting others should live by their standards but not uphold them themselves. It's that 'do as I say but not as I do' approach, and it's not attractive. When we meet Daniel's mom (East) and his East brother, it's apparent why they have such a strong bond. Daniel's mom is his energy source, his funny and interesting side. How good of her to recognize the security that Daniel counted on in his mother and suggest that he now needs to look to his wife for that. What a smart woman.

Daniela is a wise and mature North, but several times during the show, you can see how controlling she wants to be, starting with the chocolate and the diet. She has had a very specific set of do's and don'ts up to this point, and nobody has lived up to them. Hence why her family was chanting… finally! Ha! Daniela is going to struggle because although Daniel has an outgoing and fun side to him, his analytical and preservation approach to life is going to perturb her need to try new things and do it her way.

Obviously, the best thing they can do is learn the 4Cross Love Framework so they can work together in the long run.

Valmir Reis (East) & Karen Bacic (West)

Valmir is very East. He is fun, competitive, outgoing, outspoken, A LOT! The problem is he's immature and clueless. He also has a devious side to him, like the whole game of life is a competition for attention, and he does not disappoint in showing his true colors on this show. He thinks he's clever, but he doesn't have any idea what he's up against, especially with a straightforward, no-nonsense woman like Karen. Well, first Maria, a North with no time for his nonsense. Which is why he gets the rap that he deserves with the women. He's obnoxious. The guys mostly like him because he's a guy's guy. Of course, his best buddy is Daniel, the West. Daniel sees the fun and intense side of Valmire, just like his mom, but in best buddy form. Valmir goes along to go through with it and plays the role in the movie. That's what East will do. It's dramatic and fun. It's a great story to him. I was surprised he said yes. I was more surprised Karen said yes! But we all knew that wasn't going to last.

Karen was kind of a pain in the ass but look what she was up against. She knew in the pods; she knew on the honeymoon, and she knew at the altar. I thought for sure she was going to say no. During most of their time together, she was calling him out on his crap and pretending it was in some way a joke, but we all knew it was a sideways way of pestering him. Karen is too abrupt. She has her way of doing things correctly and in the order, she expects, but she needs to be more self-aware; she is extremely judgmental and hurtful. The way she kept calling Menandro short was demeaning and rude. You can just see her looking down her nose at others, and although she is likable, her air is not always. At the reunion, she and Italo got engaged, but evidently, that didn't last long either (two days!)

And of course, if they knew 4Cross, all three of them, they could get a grasp on the games they are playing and grow up.

This was the only season that everyone said yes and got married. Obviously, Valmire and Karen didn't last that long, but that was interesting.

The Swedish Season-

Rasmus Hedenstedt (South) & Krisse-ly Kuldkepp (North)

Sergio Rincon (North) & Amanda Jonegard (South)

Oskar Nordstrand (East) & Meira Omar (West)

Lucas Gustavsson (North) & Emilia Holmqvist (East)

Christopher Pocock (East) & Catja Lovstrand (North)

Rasmus Hedenstedt (South) & Krisse-Ly Kuldkepp (North)

Rasmus is a sweet guy. He's kind of a teddy bear, but he does stand up for himself, which is why this couple is such a great match. He is supportive, patient, and a little smooth. He tries to play the game of being suave, but I think we all see through that, as he isn't the most svelte specimen. But who cares. He is going to be a great husband and a wonderful father if Krisse-Ly doesn't push him too much.

It seems like she was humbled by a pretty tumultuous upbringing. This has kept her from blossoming into the woman she knows is inside. This show and Rasmus's support and love are just what she needed to leap to the next chapter in her life—and leap she will, I'm sure.

But the more 'famous' and confident Krisse-Ly gets, the bolder she will become. If kept humble, which seems likely, and Rasmus holds his ground when he needs to, they will make it. They seem to be genuinely smitten with one another. The physical and emotional connection is there, there seems to be mutual respect and admiration. It will be fun to watch how it all goes with them. They are a very likable, mature, and honest couple. Of course, knowing their positions in the 4Cross Love Framework could take their relationship to an entirely different level and perhaps epic proportions of success.

Sergio Rincon (North) & Amanda Jonegard (South)

Sergio rubs people the wrong way because he's trying to be somebody he's not. He tries to be bold, debonaire, and funny, but his jokes are cheesy and his bravado is transparent. He makes you feel like he is hiding something, holding back, or trying to make an excuse to get out, and I have no idea why.

I'm not sure if he's really hurt by Amanda not giving him a ring or wearing his bracelet or if it's just a ploy to run. This is a strange circumstance. Maybe the translation to English threw me, but it was awkward. He was awkward. He seemed never to really go all in but somehow made it to the altar and said yes. I was kind of shocked. I'm not sure we ever got an answer to the rumor about him having a child with a woman in Spain.

Amanda was about as South as South could be, always trying to smooth things out, calm things down, and keep going. She tolerated so much postering, and indecision, especially after Kriss-ley brought up that perhaps he was going to be the father of a child in Spain, where he was from! I was flabbergasted that Amanda almost didn't flinch while Kriss-ley was about to lop his head off.

There were several times I thought Amands was going to throw in the towel, and the next day, they were still together. That's the North saying something one day and turning it around as if nothing happened the next and the South almost pretending like it didn't happen. Tolerating. I don't know how many times I was thinking to myself, Amanda, you can find someone that truly loves you, but I think I am wrong with this one, at least that's how it appears as I see they are having a baby! Well, of course, if they knew the 4Cross Love Framework, this duo could rocket into the next hemisphere of love.

Oskar Nordstrand (East) & Meira Omar (West)

Oskar, don't you just want to hug this sweet man? He is so jovial and fun and wants to please Meira. His almost desperate need for her was a little cringy, and his willingness to go above and beyond when she was questioning his every move, chino, and food choice was hard to bear. His family was so happy to see him getting married that they were practically pushing him along rather than questioning him.

Meira is a caring and beautiful woman, but her continual questioning and indecision were enough to make me want to slap her. She was, in some ways, trying to get out of it, making every excuse in the book, especially the one about their cultural difference. But like a Labrador retriever, Oskar kept coming up for more pets.

This couple seems more like great friends than a married couple. There seems to be a lack of admiration and respect. Meira takes advantage of Oskar's willingness to please. It could work if they both knew how to navigate their love playing from their position in the game, but honestly, it seems like a struggle already. I could be wrong. I think they are still together.

Lucas Gustavsson (North) & Emilia Holmqvist (East)

I think we all saw this one coming. It was hard for Lucas to hide, and he said it several times. He was just not attracted to her. There is no shame in that. I believe he gave it every effort. He was mature and upfront, for the most part. It had to be a tough situation to be in because I think he really liked her; he just didn't love her. It was apparent at the wedding how bad he felt, and I'm sure in hindsight he would probably not have taken it that far, but there is also pressure to try and take the experiment all the way to the end. That is part of 'doing it right,' and it's important for a North to do it right. To prove a point, to be right.

Emilia is a beautiful, fun, outgoing, and charming East. She is a lot. And for a pretty uptight and rigid North like Lucas, it was going to be tough anyway, even without the mismatch in physical attraction. She kept coming back to giving her all and going all in, but the feedback was there, and she knew it.

There is no fault in this relationship. They were both super likable and will find love if they knew their position in the game.

Christopher Pocock (East) & Catja Lovstrand (North)

Who wanted to tell Christopher to stop with the purple hair, weird scarves, and awkward necklaces if he wanted any chance with Catja? But let's face it, even then, he was not going to win her over. He is a sincere, fun, and charming East, but he's no match for Catja, and he knows it. She knew it. Everyone knew it. He is so willing to please, compliment, and love Catja. And nothing. He got nothing but a 'you're stupid' look. She loathed his quirky ways and mocked him ruthlessly. I don't think that was fair of her, but in her way, she tried the best she could. Ok, she didn't really, but for her, she did.

He's adorable and should be allowed to be himself and be loved for it, just like in the pods, but a North with her looks and confidence is not going to relent.

This was another one of those Easts that is hard to watch them give and give and give and get not much in return but grief. This can be why Easts turn to addiction because they desperately want to be loved for their quirkiness and the energy they bring, yet they can't see when they need to hit the brakes on their effort and need for drama and excitement, so they find it in something else.

Catja is bold, confident, and needs an upstanding South who can be strong on his own and build all the things she wants, including a grand lifestyle. It's the only way she will be satisfied. With her vision and a strong partner, she could be a driving force no matter what she chooses, especially if she learns her position in the game of love by studying the 4Cross Love Framework.

The Glaring 'Stars'-

Having this show to help us see the positions is priceless. I know it's a reality show, and some of it seems dramatic and perhaps fake because I'm sure many of the contestants 'played' to the camera, but even with that, it was very revealing and apparent position-wise.

Here are some of the clearest people of each position per Season:

North: Jessica Season 1, Shake Season 2, Iyanna Season 2, Shayna Season 2, Raven Season 3, Bartise Season 3, Alexa Season 3, Chelsea Season 4, Micah Season 4, Brett Season 4, Stacy Season 5, Uche Season 5, Clay Season 6, Sergio Swedish, Catja Swedish, Carol Brazil 1, Veronica Brazil 2, Maria Brazil 3

East: Giannina Season 1, Amber Season 1, Danielle Season 2, Shayne Season 2, Cole Season 3, Jackie Season 3, Lydia Season 5, Chelsea Season 6, Oskar Swedish, Dayanns Brazil 1, Ana Brazil 1, Thiago Brazil 1, Maira Brazil 2, Valmir Brazil 3

South: Mark Season 1, Jarrette Season 2, Deepti Season 2, Kyle Season 2, Nancy Season 3, Brennan Season 3, Kwame Season 4, Tiffany Season 4, Izzy Season 5, Johnny Season 6, AD Season 6, Amanda Swedish, Hudson Brazil 1, William Brazil 2

West: Damien Season 1, Barnett Season 1, Kenny Season 1, Nick Season 2, Salvador Season 2, SK Season 3, Paul Season 4, Zack Season 4, Marshall Season 4, Milton Season 5, Jimmy Season 6, Meira Swedish, Rodrigo Brazil 1, Nanda Brazil 1, Guilherme Brazil 2, Menandro Brazil 3

Now that you have started to get a feel for each position, I hope you will find a sense of grace, calm, empathy, sympathy, and understanding that you have never had before, not only for others and how they are coping with life based on their need to relieve their concern but also for how you relate to yourself and with others.

It is such a breath of fresh air and sigh of relief. 4Cross Love brings such light to the dynamic of all relationships. The key is to take responsibility for your position and not use it as an excuse. The more you do this the better you will play the game of love.

Let's get to who is red flagging!

Potential Red Flags by Position

CHAPTER 16

"At the heart of all things is love." -Sadaharu Oh

In the intricate dance of relationships, understanding the forces that drive our behaviors and interactions is key to fostering meaningful and lasting connections. The 4Cross Love Framework offers a revolutionary perspective on the game of love, revealing that our actions in relationships are not random but deeply rooted in our biological positions. These positions—North, East, South, and West—each come with distinct strengths and challenges that shape how we relate to others and navigate the complexities of love.

This exploration delves into the potential perception of red flags that each position may exhibit in relationships, shedding light on how these behaviors can impact both partners and the relationship as a whole. By understanding the perception of red flags, we gain insight into the underlying concerns and motivations that drive our actions, allowing us to approach love with greater self-awareness and empathy. In this journey, we will see that recognizing and addressing these red flags is not about placing blame, but about embracing our inherent tendencies and learning to balance them in ways that strengthen our connections with others.

The following examples provide a look at how each position in the 4Cross Love Framework may express their concerns in ways that could potentially hinder a relationship. By bringing these behaviors to light, I aim to empower you with the knowledge to not only identify these patterns in yourself and others but also to transform them into opportunities for growth and deeper understanding. In the game of love, awareness is your greatest ally, and the 4Cross Love Framework is your guide to playing the game more skillfully, with compassion and wisdom.

Here are 20 potential ways you are red flagging in the North position in the game of love:

1. Dictating Orders: Tendency to give commands with certainty, even when unsure themselves.

2. Need for Control: Using yelling, berating, or forceful methods to maintain control over situations and people.

3. Manipulation: Strategizing and manipulating to achieve desired outcomes without regard for others' feelings.

4. Always Needing to Be Right: Willingness to go forward with bad ideas rather than admit they are wrong.

5. Judgmental Attitude: Disdain for perceived stupidity, often calling people or situations "stupid."

6. Confusing Ideas with Accomplishment: Belief that having an idea is as valuable as executing it successfully.

7. Impatience and Intolerance: Quickly becoming perturbed or impatient if others don't understand their ideas.

8. Micromanagement: Tendency to micromanage and insist on doing things themselves to ensure they are done right.

9. Difficulty Apologizing: Reticence to apologize genuinely, often using non-apology apologies like "I'm sorry you're offended."

10. Imposing Ideas: Insisting on their ideas even when modifications or different approaches would be better.

11. Lack of Sensitivity: Often seen as insensitive or uncaring when communicating bluntly or dismissively.

12. Procrastination on Implementation: Struggling to finish projects due to constantly shifting to new ideas.

13. Overlooking Others' Efforts: Invalidating the contributions of others, focusing on their ideas as the primary driver of success.

14. Coldness: Can be perceived as condescending and cold, particularly when feeling threatened or challenged.

15. Failure to Communicate Clearly: Often failing to convey their ideas clearly, leading to misunderstandings.

16. Ego and Arrogance: An air of arrogance, assessing others for their competence and judging them harshly.

17. Impatience with Small Talk: Preferring to skip idle chitchat, which can make social interactions seem brusque and uninviting.

18. Resistance to Being Told What to Do: Difficulty accepting instructions or advice, preferring to do things their own way.

19. Antagonistic Behavior: Engaging in antagonistic actions, like getting in the last word, jab, or splash, to feel in control.

20. Overriding Others' Opinions: Expecting others to adopt their ideas without question, often dismissing alternative perspectives.

Here are 20 potential ways you are red flagging in the East position in the game of love:

1. Impatience: Easts can come off as impatient, making others feel rushed and undervalued.

2. Lack of Focus: They often struggle with consistency and may be perceived as scattered in their communication and actions.

3. Attention-Seeking: Easts have a competitive side and often need or want to be the center of attention, which can create tension in relationships.

4. Impulsivity: Easts may act impulsively, making decisions without fully considering the consequences, leading to instability.

5. Easily Distracted: They tend to be distracted, often thinking about other things while in conversation, which can make partners feel neglected.

6. Inconsistency: Struggling to maintain consistency in their actions and commitments, which can create trust issues.

7. Overbearing Nature: Can become overbearing and intense, especially when their competitive nature is triggered.

8. Drama-Prone: Easts may create or thrive on drama, making relationships tumultuous and emotionally draining.

9. Difficulty with Routine: They often resist routines and structured plans, preferring spontaneity, which can be challenging for partners who need stability.

10. Hyperactivity: Displaying hyperactive behavior, such as fidgeting or constantly needing to move, which can be distracting and unsettling.

11. Superficial Engagement: Engaging with enthusiasm but lacking depth in emotional connections, which can lead to superficial relationships.

12. Lack of Emotional Regulation: Difficulty in regulating emotions, leading to outbursts or intense emotional reactions that can strain the relationship.

13. Need for Novelty: A constant need for new experiences and excitement, which can make it hard to settle into long-term commitments.

14. Inconsistent Communication: They may communicate in an enthusiastic and engaging manner but struggle with follow-through, leading to misunderstandings.

15. Neglect of Partner's Needs: Focusing on their own desires for fun and adventure, potentially neglecting the more practical or emotional needs of their partner.

16. Avoidance of Deep Conversations: Preferring light-hearted or exciting conversations over deeper, more meaningful discussions about the relationship.

17. Competitive Nature: Their competitive drive can lead to conflicts, especially if they feel their position or status is being challenged.

18. Spontaneity Over Stability: Preferring spontaneous activities, which can be unsettling for partners who value planning and stability.

19. Intolerance of Boredom: Easily bored and needing constant stimulation, which can lead to dissatisfaction with routine aspects of a relationship.

20. Self-Centered Behavior: At times, their enthusiasm and need for excitement can make them seem self-centered, prioritizing their own enjoyment over their partner's needs.

Here are 20 potential ways you are red flagging in the South position in the game of love:

1. Avoidance of Conflict: Tendency to avoid addressing issues directly, leading to unresolved conflicts and built-up resentment.

2. Over-Reliance on Group Approval: Excessive need for validation and acceptance from their group, which can lead to neglecting the relationship.

3. Gossiping: Inclination to gossip and talk about others to feel included or to deal with conflicts indirectly.

4. Struggling with Boundaries: Difficulty in setting and maintaining boundaries, often saying yes to everything and everyone.

5. Fear of Being Alone: Deep fear of isolation, which can lead to unhealthy attachments or staying in toxic relationships for fear of loneliness.

6. Impatience with Change: Resistance to change and preference for routine, which can make adapting to new situations challenging.

7. Over-Tolerance: Tendency to tolerate too much, leading to burnout and frustration when their efforts are not reciprocated or appreciated.

8. Passive-Aggressiveness: Indirectly expressing dissatisfaction through subtle jabs or sarcasm instead of addressing issues head-on.

9. Difficulty Prioritizing Tasks: Struggling with prioritizing tasks, which can lead to inefficiency and stress.

10. Overworking: Tendency to overwork and take on too many responsibilities, leading to physical and emotional exhaustion.

11. Dependency on Routine: High dependence on routine and predictability, making it hard to cope with spontaneous changes.

12. Undermining Behavior: Potential to undermine others through rumors or passive actions if feeling undervalued or threatened.

13. Neglecting Self-Care: Often putting others' needs before their own to the detriment of their own well-being.

14. Insecurity about Competence: Feeling insecure about their contributions and needing constant reassurance from their partner.

15. Resistance to Delegation: Difficulty in delegating tasks because they believe they should do it themselves, leading to further stress.

16. Sensitivity to Criticism: High sensitivity to criticism, which can lead to defensive or hurt reactions in the relationship.

17. Overdependence on Partner's Emotional State: Their mood and well-being can be heavily dependent on their partner's emotional state.

18. Tendency to Exclude: If upset, they might exclude others or withdraw emotionally, creating distance in the relationship.

19. Overemphasis on Fairness: Extreme focus on fairness and equality, sometimes to the point of nitpicking or creating unnecessary conflict over perceived injustices.

20. Involvement in Drama: Inclination towards drama and gossip, especially within their social group, which can spill over into their romantic relationship.

Here are 20 potential ways you are red flagging in the West position in the game of love:

1. Over-Critical Nature: Wests can be overly critical, focusing too much on details and often pointing out what's wrong, which can make partners feel judged and inadequate.

2. Analysis Paralysis: They may become paralyzed by over-analyzing situations, leading to an inability to make decisions.

3. Inflexibility: Wests often struggle with being rigid and inflexible, making it difficult to adapt to new situations or compromise with their partners.

4. Detail Obsession: Their obsession with precision and order can overshadow the emotional aspects of a relationship, leading to a lack of spontaneity and warmth.

5. Avoidance of Responsibility: They might hide behind rules and regulations to avoid taking personal responsibility for actions.

6. Difficulty with Spontaneity: Struggling to embrace spontaneity, they can stifle the natural flow of the relationship.

7. Communication Overload: Tendency to provide excessive detail in communication, which can overwhelm or bore their partner.

8. Scarcity Thinking: Wests often operate from a scarcity mindset, finding it hard to envision new possibilities and focusing on conserving what they have.

9. Procrastination: Under stress, they may procrastinate by over-studying or over-analyzing instead of taking action.

10. Imposing Standards: They might impose their high standards and meticulous nature on their partner, leading to conflicts over the "right" way to do things.

11. Concealed Emotions: Often concealing their emotions with a poker face, which can make it hard for their partner to connect with them emotionally.

12. Competence Projection: Projecting an air of competence (know it all), sometimes trying too hard to impress others with how much they know.

13. Fear of Mistakes: Fear of making mistakes in front of others, leading to a lack of vulnerability and openness.

14. Impedance to Progress: Often impeding progress by focusing on potential risks and consequences rather than moving forward.

15. Authority Dependency: Relying heavily on established systems and authority to effect change, which can stifle innovation and personal growth.

16. Perfectionism: Allowing their need for perfection to get in the way of higher progress, missing the bigger picture by focusing too much on details.

17. Historical Focus: Preferring to look to the past for evidence and decision-making, which can hinder forward movement and growth.

18. Betrayal Risk: Under stress, their indecision can lead to feelings of betrayal in others, as they may support different sides until the last moment.

19. Rigid Conflict Resolution: Preferring detailed and methodical approaches to conflict resolution, which can feel overly analytical and dismissive of emotional concerns.

20. Emotional Detachment: Focusing on facts and logic can lead to emotional detachment, making their partner feel unheard and unsupported emotionally.

These behaviors can create challenges in relationships if not balanced with empathy, flexibility, and effective communication.

In concluding the exploration of how each position in the 4Cross Love Framework may exhibit red flags in the game of love, it's crucial to recognize that these are not merely isolated behaviors but reflections of deeper, underlying concerns intrinsic to each position. The 4Cross Love Framework illuminates how these biological positions drive our interactions, decisions, and ultimately, the dynamics of our relationships. Each position—North, East, South, and West—carries its unique strengths, but when these strengths are misaligned or left unchecked, they can manifest as behaviors that strain relationships.

For those in the North position, the drive for control and certainty can lead to rigid, domineering behaviors that may alienate partners. Their strategic mindset, when not balanced with empathy and flexibility, can become a source of conflict, as they may impose their ideas and judgments without considering the emotional impacts on others.

Easts, with their love for freedom and spontaneity, may struggle with consistency and depth in relationships. Their need for constant stimulation and attention can lead to impulsive decisions and emotional volatility, creating a sense of instability for their partners. This unpredictability, while exciting, can also be a source of stress in a long-term commitment.

Souths, who are naturally nurturing and supportive, may exhibit red flags related to their deep need for harmony and fear of conflict. Their tendency to avoid direct confrontation and over-rely on group approval can lead to passive-aggressive behaviors or a lack of assertiveness, which can create unresolved tensions in relationships.

Wests, with their meticulous and analytical nature, may become overly critical or detached in their relationships. Their focus on precision and order can overshadow emotional needs, leading to a sense of coldness or rigidity that can stifle the natural flow of the relationship.

Understanding these red flags through the lens of the 4Cross framework not only highlights potential pitfalls in relationships but also provides a pathway for growth. By recognizing these tendencies, individuals can work towards balancing their inherent strengths with the needs of their partners, fostering healthier, more harmonious relationships. This awareness is the key to navigating the complexities of love and human interaction, allowing each position to contribute positively to the game of love. The ultimate goal, as emphasized in the 4Cross framework, is to know thyself and others, creating a more empathetic and coordinated approach to love and life.

CHAPTER 17

Sexual Relationships by Position

<hr>

"Love is the cause of unity in all things." -Aristotle

<hr>

Sexual relationships are deeply influenced by the 4Cross positions because each position brings different needs, desires, and approaches to intimacy. Here's how sexual relationships might be affected by each position:

Let's break down and elaborate on the North's approach to intimacy and how it relates to their broader characteristics:

Approach:

Norths are naturally strategic, decisive, and driven, and this goal-oriented mindset often extends into their intimate relationships. For Norths, sex can be approached with the same focus and efficiency they apply to other areas of life. They like to be in control and may approach intimacy with a sense of structure, often with a focus on "getting things right." This can mean they are very clear about what they want and how they want things to go. Norths are likely to prefer direct communication about their needs.

- Goal-Oriented in Intimacy: Norths often see sex as something that needs to be successful or have a specific outcome, such as mutual satisfaction or achieving a desired level of connection. They may focus on performance, seeing it as another area in life where they want to excel.

- Decisive and in Control: Norths often like to take the lead in the bedroom, setting the pace and direction of the encounter. They may be less comfortable with spontaneity or giving up control, as they prefer to know what's going to happen next and feel in charge of the situation.

Effect:

While Norths bring a lot of energy and decisiveness into their sexual relationships, this can sometimes lead to a few challenges:

- Lack of Spontaneity: Because Norths like structure and control, they may struggle with being spontaneous or flexible during intimacy. This can create tension if their partner values more free-flowing, emotionally connected, or playful sexual experiences.

- Focus on Physicality: Norths can become overly focused on the physical aspects of sex, such as technique or achieving a particular outcome, and may unintentionally neglect the emotional connection that their partner might be craving. This goal-driven focus can sometimes make sex feel more like a task to accomplish rather than an experience to share.

- Difficulty with Emotional Vulnerability: Norths can find it difficult to open up emotionally during intimate moments. Their natural inclination to stay in control can prevent them from fully relaxing and being vulnerable, which can limit emotional intimacy with their partner. A North woman may say they want to be dominated or taken but they don't leave the space for their partner to do it. And if their partner does take the lead, or try to, it's very rarely the 'right' way as determined by the North.

To Improve:

For Norths, the key to enhancing their sexual relationships lies in balancing their need for control and precision with a greater focus on emotional connection and flexibility. Here are some ways they can improve:

- Learning to Relax and Let Go: Norths can benefit from slowing down and allowing themselves to be more present in the moment, rather than focusing on their specific outcome. This could mean letting go of the need for everything to go according to plan and embracing the natural flow of intimacy.

- Focusing on Emotional Connection: By tuning in to their partner's emotional needs, Norths can deepen the connection during intimate moments. This might mean asking open-ended questions about what their partner enjoys emotionally, not just physically, and allowing themselves to be more vulnerable.

- Practicing Spontaneity: Norths can work on being more spontaneous by letting go of control and allowing their partner to take the lead sometimes. This helps them move away from a rigid approach and fosters a more balanced, reciprocal connection.

- Clear Communication with Emotional Sensitivity: While Norths are great at direct communication, they can work on incorporating more emotional sensitivity into their conversations about intimacy. Instead of focusing purely on logistical preferences, they could explore how their partner feels during these moments and express their own emotions as well.

In summary, while Norths bring a lot of drive, clarity, and decisiveness to their intimate relationships, they can improve by softening their approach, allowing more emotional connection, and embracing spontaneity. By shifting some focus from physical goals to emotional experiences, they can create a more balanced and fulfilling sexual relationship.

Let's dive deeper into how the East's traits influence their approach to intimacy and what they can do to enhance their relationships:

Approach:

Easts are known for being energetic, spontaneous, and free-spirited. These traits strongly influence how they approach their sexual relationships. For Easts, intimacy is an adventure—an opportunity to explore, play, and try new things. They are naturally curious and drawn to variety, which can make them exciting and engaging lovers who enjoy experimenting and keeping things fresh.

- Spontaneity and Playfulness: Easts thrive on keeping things fun and lighthearted in the bedroom. They love surprises, exploring fantasies, and are often the ones to suggest something new or unexpected. This can make sex with an East feel exciting and full of possibilities, as they are always looking for ways to make the experience more dynamic.

- Adventure and Exploration: For Easts, intimacy is often about the thrill of trying new things. They aren't afraid to push boundaries or suggest ideas that others might shy away from. This adventurous spirit can lead to a wide range of experiences and a sense of playfulness in their relationships.

Effect:

While Easts' spontaneous and adventurous nature brings a lot of excitement to their sexual relationships, it can also create challenges, particularly when it comes to maintaining consistency and emotional depth.

- Engaging but Sometimes Inconsistent: Easts are fantastic at keeping things exciting, but their love for novelty can sometimes make it difficult for them to maintain consistency in their relationships. If things start to feel too routine or predictable, they may become restless or lose interest, which can leave their partner feeling disconnected or uncertain.

- Emotional Depth vs. Variety: Easts can sometimes focus so much on the fun, exploratory side of intimacy that they may unintentionally neglect the emotional connection that their partner craves. While Easts love keeping things fresh and adventurous, they might struggle to dive deeper into emotional intimacy, especially if they feel that this limits their freedom or makes things too "serious."

- Dislike of Feeling Trapped or Restricted: If Easts feel that their sexual relationship is becoming too predictable, restrictive, or emotionally demanding, they might start to feel trapped. This sense of restriction can dampen their enthusiasm and cause them to pull away, as they thrive on the feeling of freedom and spontaneity.

To Improve:

For Easts, the key to enhancing their intimate relationships lies in finding a balance between their need for novelty and their partner's need for emotional connection and stability. Here are some ways they can improve:

- Balancing Novelty with Emotional Intimacy: Easts should work on blending their love of adventure with deeper emotional intimacy. This doesn't mean giving up their spontaneity, but rather taking time to connect emotionally with their partner, ensuring that their relationship isn't just based on excitement but also on trust, vulnerability, and genuine emotional connection.

- Creating Emotional Stability Amidst Change: While Easts may love variety, they should also recognize the importance of consistency in a relationship. It's possible to have both—Easts can work on creating emotional stability within the context of their adventurous spirit. This might mean being emotionally available even during the most spontaneous moments, showing their partner that they are reliable despite their love of change.

- Focusing on Emotional Communication: Easts are great communicators when it comes to expressing excitement and sharing ideas, but they can benefit from working on emotional communication as well. This means taking time to discuss feelings, not just activities, and asking their partner how they're feeling emotionally about their intimate connection.

- Finding Joy in Routine Moments: Easts might struggle with routine, but they can find ways to infuse even the predictable moments with joy and creativity. This might mean finding small ways to make routine encounters feel special or approaching them with the same sense of curiosity and playfulness that they bring to more adventurous experiences.

In summary, while Easts bring a lot of spontaneity, fun, and creativity to their sexual relationships, they can improve by working on building emotional depth and consistency. By blending their adventurous spirit with emotional vulnerability, they can create a relationship that is both exciting and deeply connected, ensuring that both partners feel satisfied on a physical and emotional level.

Let's expand on how the South's supportive, loyal, and nurturing nature shapes their approach to intimacy, and how they can enhance their relationships by addressing some of their tendencies.

Approach:

Souths are supportive, loyal, and nurturing in all areas of their relationships, including intimacy. They see sex as an opportunity to deepen their emotional bond, offer comfort, and express their love and care for their partner. For Souths, the emotional connection is often more important than the physical aspects of intimacy, and they approach sex as a way to reinforce that closeness.

- Emotional Closeness and Bonding: Souths prioritize emotional intimacy in their sexual relationships. They often see sex as a way to emotionally connect with their partner, providing them with love, security, and a sense of belonging. For them, intimacy is less about excitement or novelty and more about reinforcing the stability and emotional bond in the relationship.

- Nurturing and Care: Souths tend to be very giving lovers, focusing on their partner's needs and making sure they feel comfortable and cared for. They may go out of their way to create a safe, comforting atmosphere for intimacy, often placing their partner's desires and happiness above their own.

Effect:

While Souths' nurturing and supportive approach makes them attentive and loving partners, this focus on their partner's needs can sometimes lead to imbalances in the relationship, especially if they neglect their own desires.

- Prioritizing Partner's Needs Over Their Own: Souths are naturally inclined to put their partner first, which can mean they often prioritize their partner's sexual satisfaction and emotional comfort above their own. While this makes them extremely caring lovers, it can also lead to them suppressing their own desires or avoiding discussing what they truly want. Over time, this can cause them to feel unfulfilled, even if they are meeting their partner's needs.

- Avoiding Conflict or Disruption: Souths tend to avoid conflict and prioritize harmony in the relationship, which can make it difficult for them to openly communicate about their own needs or boundaries. They may fear that asking for something different or discussing what they want could upset their partner or disrupt the emotional closeness they value so much. As a result, they may remain silent about what's important to them in order to maintain peace.

To Improve:

For Souths, the key to enhancing their intimate relationships lies in learning to balance their natural desire to care for and nurture their partner with an openness about their own desires and boundaries. Here are ways they can improve:

- Focusing on Open Communication: Souths should practice being more open and honest about what they need and desire in their intimate relationships. While they are great at taking care of their partner, they also need to ensure that their own needs are being met. This can start with small conversations about what feels good for them, what they would like to try, or even what boundaries they need to set.

- Being Assertive: Souths can practice being more assertive in the bedroom. This doesn't mean being aggressive or demanding, but rather being open to the opposite of what makes them always feel safe. It could be as simple as trying something new, or giving a different approach to affection. Not doing the same thing over and over.

In summary, while Souths bring a lot of care, loyalty, and nurturing energy to their sexual relationships, they can improve by focusing on open communication and ensuring that their own needs are met. By balancing their natural desire to please with the courage to express their own desires and boundaries, Souths can create a more fulfilling, mutually satisfying intimate relationship that thrives on both emotional and physical connection.

Let's break down how the West's methodical, thoughtful, and precise nature shapes their approach to intimacy, and explore ways they can enhance their sexual relationships.

Approach:

Wests are known for being methodical, thoughtful, and precise, and these traits extend into their sexual relationships. They often approach intimacy with the same care and attention to detail that they bring to other aspects of their lives. For Wests, sex is something that should be carefully considered, structured, and approached with thoughtfulness and precision.

- Focus on Details and Technique: Wests tend to focus on the mechanics of intimacy, ensuring that everything is just right. They may pay close attention to technique, timing, and creating the perfect environment for their partner. They want the experience to be smooth, controlled, and efficient, which can make them very attentive lovers.

- Preference for Predictability and Structure: Wests are not usually comfortable with surprises or spontaneous moments. They prefer predictability and a structured environment for intimacy, where they feel they know what's going to happen. They may enjoy planning out how things will unfold and feel more comfortable with a routine that allows them to stay in control.

Effect:

While Wests' thoughtfulness and attention to detail can make them very attentive and precise lovers, this approach can also create challenges, especially when it comes to spontaneity and letting go.

- Overthinking and Analyzing: Wests may find themselves overthinking or overanalyzing sexual experiences, focusing on whether everything is going as planned. They might worry about whether they are doing things "right," whether their partner is enjoying the experience as much as they should, or whether the environment is perfect. This tendency to overanalyze can create tension and make it difficult for them to fully relax and enjoy the moment.

- Struggles with Spontaneity: Because Wests prefer predictability, they may struggle with being spontaneous in their intimate relationships. They might resist going with the flow or trying new things on the spur of the moment, as they prefer to know what to expect and plan accordingly. This can sometimes make their partner feel that the experience lacks excitement or playfulness.

- Perfectionism in Intimacy: Wests often seek to create a perfect experience, which can lead to stress if things don't go exactly as planned. They may place too much emphasis on making sure everything is just right, which can prevent them from fully enjoying the experience or cause them to feel frustrated if their partner doesn't respond as expected.

To Improve:

For Wests, the key to enhancing their intimate relationships lies in learning to balance their attention to detail with a greater willingness to let go, embrace spontaneity, and be present in the moment. Here are ways they can improve:

- Letting Go of Perfectionism: Wests should work on letting go of the idea that everything in the bedroom needs to be perfect. Intimacy is about connection, not performance. By relaxing their need for control and accepting that things may not always go as planned, they can create a more enjoyable and less stressful experience for both themselves and their partner.

- Embracing Spontaneity: Wests can benefit from loosening up and allowing for more spontaneity in their intimate relationships. This might mean being open to trying new things without planning them in advance or allowing their partner to take the lead sometimes. By embracing spontaneity, they can bring more playfulness and excitement into their relationships.

- Being Present in the Moment: Wests should focus on being more present during intimate moments, rather than thinking ahead or worrying about details. This can mean tuning into their partner's emotional and physical cues and letting the experience unfold naturally. Being present allows for a deeper connection and prevents the stress that comes from trying to control or analyze every aspect of the encounter.

In summary, while Wests bring a lot of thoughtfulness, precision, and care to their sexual relationships, they can improve by letting go of perfectionism and embracing spontaneity. By focusing on the emotional and experiential side of intimacy, they can create a more relaxed, playful, and deeply connected relationship with their partner. Allowing themselves to enjoy the moment, rather than worrying about every detail, will ultimately lead to a more fulfilling and less stressful intimate experience.

Craving who we are:

The very thing we give is the thing we crave from our mate sometimes.

North

For a North, intimacy is about balancing control with moments of surrender. They have a natural drive to lead and structure things, yet they also long to experience being led in a way that doesn't compromise their need for confidence and decisiveness. Here's how that dynamic might unfold:

Ironically, Norths thrive on control and decisiveness in intimacy, but they also secretly crave moments where they can let go and trust their partner to take the lead. The challenge is that this "letting go" needs to happen in a way that feels confident and seamless. It's a delicate balance for a North: they desire control, but also want the thrill of being guided by a partner who knows how to take charge without missing a beat.

Complaint: "I'm always the one steering the direction, and sometimes I want you to take the lead. But when you do, I need to feel like you're just as sure and intentional as I would be. I want to be able to let go and still feel that sense of direction."

East

For an East, the dynamic is about balancing freedom and connection in intimacy. They crave spontaneity and novelty, but they also want their partner to bring in that same spirit of adventure. Here's how that might play out:

Ironically, Easts crave freedom and excitement in intimacy but also desire their partner to introduce the spark of something new. While they want the space to be expressive and spontaneous, they also want their partner to surprise them—just enough to keep things fresh without feeling too predictable. It's a fine line for an East: they need freedom but also long for their partner to bring a sense of spontaneity into the relationship, ideally without planning or overthinking it.

Complaint: "I love that I bring the fun and excitement, but sometimes I wish you'd surprise me, too. I want to feel like we're both exploring together."

South

For a South, intimacy is about creating emotional closeness and a sense of security. They naturally focus on nurturing their partner's needs, but they also long for their partner to reciprocate with the same care and attentiveness. Souths want to feel supported and cherished, yet they often struggle to voice this desire openly, as they fear it could disrupt harmony. Here's how that dynamic might play out:

Ironically, Souths are deeply attuned to meeting their partner's needs, but they also long for their partner to prioritize their emotional and physical needs in the same way. While they often create a comforting, stable environment in intimacy, they secretly yearn for moments where their partner takes the initiative to nurture and support them. It's a fine line for a South: they want to feel cared for and safe without having to ask, yet they hesitate to make their needs known.

Complaint: "I love being there for you, but sometimes I wish you'd take the lead in showing care for me. I want to feel like my needs matter too, without feeling like I'm asking for too much. It'd be nice to feel as cherished as I try to make you feel."

West

For a West, intimacy is about feeling genuinely considered and thoughtfully appreciated, much like the careful attention they give to their partner. They are meticulous in their approach to intimacy, taking time to ensure their partner feels valued and understood. Wests want to feel that same level of thoughtful consideration in return, yet they may struggle to voice this desire openly. They long for moments when their partner shows that they truly understand and appreciate the details that matter to them.

Ironically, Wests are highly attentive and precise in how they show love, but they also long to feel that same careful consideration from their partner. They want to be thoughtfully appreciated and understood, with their partner noticing and valuing the small details that make them feel seen. It's a subtle balance for a West: they crave connection that feels intentional and carefully crafted, without having to ask for it directly.

Complaint: "I put so much thought into making you feel valued, but sometimes I wish you'd take the time to consider me in the same way. I want to feel like you're noticing the little things that matter to me, that you're as thoughtful about our connection as I am."

By understanding these tendencies, partners can develop better communication strategies and navigate their differences in the bedroom more effectively:

- Open communication is key: Each partner should feel comfortable expressing their needs, desires, and boundaries.

- Respect for each other's approach: Recognizing and respecting the differences between each position will allow both partners to find a balance that works for them.

- Finding common ground: Each partner can learn to adapt to the other's style by incorporating their strengths into the relationship—whether that's embracing spontaneity, deepening emotional connections, or finding ways to bring excitement and predictability together.

Tailoring the Relationship:

When partners use this understanding to communicate and adapt, they create a more tailored, fulfilling sexual relationship that respects both emotional and physical needs. By addressing the unique challenges and strengths of each position, they can foster a dynamic that combines connection, excitement, stability, and playfulness in a way that works for both of them.

CHAPTER 18

Positional Projecting and Procrastination

"It is love alone that gives worth to all things." -Teresa of Avila

How Each 4Cross Position Might Project Their Survival Concerns onto Others

In the 4Cross Love Framework, each position—North, East, South, and West—comes with a core survival concern that shapes how individuals perceive and respond to the world. These concerns are deeply rooted and drive the behaviors, decisions, and emotional needs of each position. What's fascinating is how these survival concerns, often unconsciously, get projected onto others, influencing how people expect others to think, act, and respond.

Projection occurs when we take our own internal needs or concerns and assume that others share them. In relationships, work, and social settings, this can lead to misunderstandings or frustrations, as each position expects others to prioritize the same things they do. By understanding how each position projects their survival concerns, we can gain insight into the unique ways people relate to one another, fostering better communication and empathy.

This guide will explore how each position—North with their need for certainty, East with their need for freedom, South with their desire for stability, and West with their need for security—projects their survival concerns onto others, and how these dynamics play out in everyday interactions. Recognizing these tendencies is key to improving relationships and creating a deeper understanding of the core motivations behind each position's actions.

The North position projects their survival concern of certainty onto others by trying to take control of situations and expecting those around them to align with their plans, strategies, and decisions. They naturally assume leadership roles and may impose their need for clarity, structure, and decisive action onto others.

In relationships or teamwork, this projection can show up as:

- Micromanaging: Norths may insist on handling everything themselves because they believe no one else can do it the way it should be done or fast enough.

- Impatience with indecision: They struggle with others who hesitate or take too long to make choices, often pushing for quicker, more direct action.

- High expectations: They may hold others to the same standards they set for themselves, expecting everyone to operate with the same level of certainty, logic, and determination.

- Dismissing emotional complexity: Because they focus so much on logical outcomes and certainty, they might unintentionally disregard or downplay others' emotional needs, seeing them as distractions from getting things done.

Ultimately, the North's drive for certainty can lead them to push others into clear-cut, decisive paths, sometimes overlooking the nuances of different perspectives or the emotional aspects of situations. They project their need for stability and control, expecting others to match their pace and decisiveness.

An East projects their concern for freedom onto others by encouraging spontaneity, flexibility, and open-ended possibilities in their interactions. They value creativity and exploration, and they project this onto others by resisting limitations, avoiding routine, and expecting others to go with the flow.

In relationships or group dynamics, this projection can manifest as:

- Pushing for flexibility: Easts may struggle with rigid plans or commitments and expect others to be as adaptable as they are. They might suggest spontaneous changes or last-minute shifts, assuming everyone is comfortable with constant fluidity.

- Encouraging experimentation: They often push others to try new things, embrace the unknown, and leave comfort zones behind, projecting their love for adventure onto those around them.

- Avoiding commitment: In projecting their need for freedom, Easts might resist long-term plans or commitments, expecting others to be comfortable with a more casual or open-ended approach to relationships or projects.

- Frustration with routine: Easts may become easily frustrated with others who prefer structure or predictability, viewing such preferences as confining or dull.

Ultimately, an East projects their concern for freedom by expecting others to embrace flexibility, spontaneity, and creativity. They may struggle to understand why others want stability or structure and instead push for more open, unrestricted experiences, assuming everyone shares their desire to avoid confinement. Their tendency toward being contrary is a reflection of not wanting to be told what to do, it's a reaction to feeling confined, even to others viewpoints.

A South projects their need for stability onto others by emphasizing emotional security, harmony, and consistency in relationships and interactions. They seek to avoid conflict and keep the peace, and they expect others to value and prioritize the same emotional balance.

In relationships or group dynamics, this projection can show up as:

- Avoiding conflict: Souths may encourage others to avoid difficult conversations or disagreements in order to maintain harmony. They may downplay or dismiss issues, assuming that everyone prefers to keep things calm and stable rather than confront challenges.

- Over-nurturing: They may project their nurturing tendencies by trying to take care of everyone's emotional needs, assuming others want the same level of support and reassurance they seek. This can sometimes come across as overbearing or smothering.

- Expecting loyalty: Souths often expect unwavering loyalty and reliability from others, projecting their own sense of commitment and dependability. When others are unpredictable or unreliable, it can deeply unsettle them.

- Resisting change: Because Souths value emotional stability, they may resist changes that could disrupt the status quo, expecting others to share their desire for consistency. They might project their fears of instability onto others by discouraging risks or new directions.

Ultimately, a South projects their need for stability by encouraging others to avoid conflict, maintain loyalty, and prioritize emotional harmony. They often assume that others are just as invested in keeping relationships peaceful and secure, sometimes overlooking the need for confrontation or change when it's necessary for growth.

A West projects their need for security onto others by emphasizing precision, thoroughness, and careful planning in all aspects of life. They seek order and predictability, and they expect others to share their focus on careful analysis and structured decision-making to avoid risk and ensure stability.

In relationships or group dynamics, this projection can manifest as:

- Overloading with details: Wests may provide extensive information, expecting others to value the same level of precision and analysis. They might overwhelm others by insisting on covering every detail to ensure nothing is missed.

- Pushing for preparation: They often expect others to plan and prepare as meticulously as they do. Wests may become frustrated when others make decisions or take action without carefully weighing all options or gathering enough information.

- Reluctance to embrace spontaneity: Wests may resist spontaneous or unplanned actions, expecting others to stick to a set plan or follow a structured approach. They can project their discomfort with unpredictability by discouraging risks or impulsive behavior. They want others to follow the rules like they do. It makes them feel safe.

- Demanding reliability: Because Wests value predictability, they project an expectation of reliability onto others. They may become unsettled if others are inconsistent, expecting the same level of discipline and thoroughness they bring to the table.

Ultimately, a West projects their need for security by expecting others to prioritize planning, order, and careful analysis. They assume that everyone shares their desire for predictability and minimizing risk, which can lead them to push for precision and preparation in ways that may feel rigid or limiting to others.

By exploring how each 4Cross position—North, East, South, and West—projects their survival concerns onto others, we begin to uncover the deeper motivations driving human interaction. Whether it's the North's need for certainty, the East's desire for freedom, the South's pursuit of stability, or the West's focus on security, these concerns shape how we view the world and expect others to respond.

Understanding these projections allows us to step outside of our own perspectives and recognize that others may not share the same priorities or approach to life. It encourages empathy and helps us avoid frustration or misunderstanding when others act in ways that conflict with our own survival concerns.

By acknowledging and respecting these different needs, we can improve our relationships, communicate more effectively, and create a more harmonious environment—whether in love, work, or family dynamics. Ultimately, knowing how each position projects their survival concerns is a powerful tool for deepening our connections with others and fostering greater understanding in every interaction.

Procrastination By Position

Procrastination manifests differently for each 4Cross position based on their core concerns and approaches to tasks and responsibilities. Here's how it plays out:

Let's break down and elaborate on how procrastination manifests for Norths and their relationship with tasks, responsibilities, and decision-making.

How Procrastination Plays Out for North:

Norths are naturally strategic, decisive, and goal-oriented, and they typically thrive on taking control and getting things done. However, procrastination for a North tends to occur when they feel unsure about the best course of action or when they lack control over a situation. Unlike Easts, who may procrastinate due to distraction, Norths delay tasks when they are uncertain or don't feel confident that the task can be executed perfectly or with the desired outcome.

- Delaying Until There's a Clear Plan: Norths often procrastinate when they feel they don't have a clear plan or strategy in place. They prefer to act when they feel prepared and have all the steps mapped out, which means they can delay tasks until they are sure they have the right approach. They seek certainty and can get stuck if they don't feel they are making the "right" decision.

- Seeking Control: Norths tend to delay action when they feel they don't have control over the situation. They are reluctant to move forward unless they know they can steer the task or project in the direction they want. This need for control can result in procrastination when they feel things are too chaotic or unclear.

Reason for Procrastination:

Norths procrastinate due to a fear of making the wrong decision or appearing incompetent. They are driven by the need to achieve success and be seen as capable and confident. If they don't feel like they can deliver excellence or if the path forward is murky, they will hold back until they can get more clarity or gain control over the situation.

- Fear of Failure: Norths have a strong desire to avoid failure, especially in front of others. They procrastinate when they feel unsure about the best course of action because they don't want to risk looking like they made a mistake. This fear of failure is often tied to their identity as leaders and achievers, and they may hold off on tasks to avoid the possibility of falling short.

- Perfectionism and Over-Control: Norths also tend to procrastinate because they want things to be done right and may struggle to move forward until they feel everything is lined up perfectly. This need for perfection can slow them down, as they hold off on tasks until they have absolute certainty that things will go smoothly.

How They Handle It:

Despite their procrastination, Norths are decisive and results-driven once they commit to action. If they realize that waiting for the perfect moment is impractical, they will make calculated compromises to push the task forward, prioritizing results over perfection when necessary.

- Taking Control and Moving Forward: Norths may procrastinate initially, but once they decide it's time to act, they take charge of the situation. They excel at driving tasks to completion, especially when they feel like they have regained control and can direct the outcome.

- Strategic Compromise: When Norths recognize that perfection is unattainable, they will often make strategic compromises to keep things moving. Their desire for success outweighs their need for everything to be flawless, and they will find ways to work around obstacles to ensure they reach their goals.

To Overcome Procrastination:

Norths can overcome procrastination by recognizing that waiting for perfect certainty can sometimes hinder progress. They can benefit from learning to move forward even when conditions aren't ideal, trusting their strategic skills to make adjustments along the way.

- Accepting Imperfection: Norths need to work on accepting that not everything will go according to plan. They can improve by recognizing that some action is better than no action, and that adjustments can be made along the way. By embracing this mindset, they can avoid getting stuck in the paralysis of indecision.

- Prioritizing Action Over Perfection: Norths can benefit from focusing on progress rather than perfection. While they are naturally driven to achieve excellence, they should learn that perfectionism can lead to stagnation. By prioritizing action, they can break through the initial hesitation and get things done without needing to control every detail.

- Delegating to Regain Control: Norths often struggle with delegation because they feel no one else can do the task as well as they can. However, learning to delegate tasks when they feel overwhelmed or uncertain can help them regain control and reduce the pressure to do everything themselves. This will allow them to focus on what they do best—strategic planning and leading.

Overall Pattern:

For Norths, procrastination is driven by their desire for control and their fear of making the wrong decision. They tend to delay tasks when they feel uncertain or lack a clear plan, waiting for the perfect moment when they can confidently move forward. To overcome procrastination, Norths need to focus on taking action, even when the path isn't perfectly clear. By trusting in their ability to adjust and lead as they go, they can break through their hesitation and achieve results without getting stuck in analysis paralysis.

How Procrastination Plays Out for East:

Easts are energetic, spontaneous, and free-spirited, preferring to live in the moment and follow their curiosity rather than sticking to rigid plans or routines. For them, procrastination often manifests in the form of distraction and seeking novelty. They are easily drawn to exciting new ideas, projects, or activities, which can lead to them putting off more mundane or routine tasks.

- Chasing Excitement Over Routine: Easts are naturally drawn to activities that spark their interest and bring them joy. When faced with tasks that are repetitive, boring, or don't offer immediate excitement, they tend to put them off in favor of more stimulating or adventurous pursuits.

- Difficulty with Focus and Commitment: Easts may start multiple projects or explore several ideas at once, but they often struggle to stick with them through to completion. Their need for constant stimulation means they may abandon tasks midway if something more interesting comes along.

Reason for Procrastination:

Easts procrastinate largely because of their desire for freedom and their discomfort with tasks that feel restrictive or monotonous. They thrive on variety and often resist activities that require a lot of structure or planning, as this can feel confining to their free-spirited nature.

- Fear of Boredom: Easts avoid tasks that feel tedious or unexciting. If a task doesn't offer immediate gratification or doesn't align with their sense of adventure, they'll likely procrastinate, waiting for the motivation to strike or for something more exciting to distract them.

- Aversion to Routine: Easts dislike being boxed into routines or repetitive tasks. The idea of having to follow a step-by-step plan can make them feel stifled, and they'll often procrastinate on these kinds of tasks because they crave flexibility and spontaneity.

How They Handle It:

Despite their tendency to procrastinate when it comes to routine or mundane tasks, Easts excel at improvisation and can often catch up quickly once they find something engaging or when deadlines loom. When Easts feel pressure or excitement, they can dive into a task with renewed energy and creativity, quickly making up for lost time.

- Working Under Pressure: Easts tend to thrive when there's a sense of urgency. They might put things off until the last minute, but they can often pull things together in a burst of energy, relying on their creativity and adaptability to get things done.

- Switching Gears Quickly: Easts are highly adaptable and can switch focus rapidly when something piques their interest. While they may procrastinate on tasks, they don't find appealing, they can also surprise others by jumping into action when their curiosity or excitement is sparked.

To Overcome Procrastination:

Easts can improve their productivity and overcome procrastination by finding ways to make mundane tasks more engaging or aligned with their sense of freedom and creativity. By integrating fun, variety, or novelty into their routine, they can motivate themselves to stay on track.

- Adding Novelty to Routine: Easts can make routine tasks more enjoyable by finding ways to introduce variety or excitement into the process. This could mean breaking tasks into smaller chunks, rewarding themselves after completing tasks, or finding a new way to approach an old problem.

- Setting Creative Challenges: Easts thrive on creativity, so they can turn even mundane tasks into a challenge by finding new, innovative ways to approach them. For example, they might set time limits, use creative tools, or try unconventional methods to keep things fresh and engaging.

- Using Spontaneity to Their Advantage: Instead of fighting their spontaneous nature, Easts can embrace it by allowing themselves to jump from one task to another when they feel the motivation. As long as they come back to the important tasks, this flexibility can help them maintain their energy and avoid feeling stifled by a rigid schedule.

Overall Pattern:

For Easts, procrastination is often driven by a need to avoid boredom, routine, or anything that feels too restrictive. They may delay tasks that don't excite them, but when they find something that captures their interest, they can act quickly and with enthusiasm. The key for Easts to overcome procrastination is to infuse creativity and spontaneity into their tasks and to embrace their natural energy while staying mindful of deadlines and goals. By blending novelty with responsibility, Easts can harness their strengths without losing focus.

How Procrastination Plays Out for South:

Souths are naturally supportive, loyal, and nurturing, and their procrastination tends to stem from their desire to maintain harmony and avoid conflict. For them, putting off tasks often relates to a fear of upsetting others or disrupting the balance of their relationships and environment. They may procrastinate on tasks that involve confrontation or situations where they have to put their own needs above others.

- Avoiding Conflict: Souths tend to avoid anything that might create tension or conflict, which means they may delay tasks that require tough conversations or decisions. For example, they might put off discussing issues with a partner, addressing problems at work, or dealing with uncomfortable situations, preferring to keep the peace rather than face the discomfort head-on.

- Overcommitting to Others: Souths often prioritize other people's needs above their own, which can lead to overcommitting and taking on too many responsibilities. As a result, they may put off tasks that are important to them because they're too busy fulfilling the needs of others. They tend to put their own desires and responsibilities on the back burner, leading to procrastination on personal goals.

Reason for Procrastination:

Souths procrastinate because of their strong need for stability and their aversion to disrupting harmony. They fear making decisions that could upset others or cause emotional upheaval, which leads them to delay difficult or emotionally charged tasks. Additionally, they often struggle to say "no" to requests from others, which leaves them overwhelmed and stretched too thin, causing further delays in handling their own priorities.

- Fear of Causing Disruption: Souths' primary concern is maintaining stability in their relationships and environment. They may procrastinate on tasks that could disrupt this balance, especially if they involve confrontation or emotional vulnerability. Souths often feel guilty about putting their own needs first, which can make it hard for them to prioritize personal responsibilities.

- Neglecting Self-Care and Boundaries: Because Souths are so focused on taking care of others, they often neglect their own self-care and boundaries. This leads to procrastination when it comes to their personal needs or tasks, as they constantly prioritize others' well-being over their own.

How They Handle It:

Despite their tendency to procrastinate when it comes to confrontation or personal tasks, Souths are very dependable and focused when it comes to supporting others. They thrive in structured environments where they can nurture and maintain stability, so once they commit to a task, especially one involving other, they will see it through. However, they may continue to delay tasks that don't directly impact the emotional well-being of those around them.

- Following Through on Commitments to Others: Souths rarely procrastinate when it comes to helping or supporting others. Their sense of responsibility to their family, friends, or community drives them to complete tasks related to caregiving or providing emotional support, even if it means sacrificing their own time and energy.

- Avoiding Personal Priorities: When it comes to their own needs or tasks, Souths may struggle to take action. Their nurturing nature leads them to believe that their needs are secondary to others', and this can result in them putting off personal goals or self-care indefinitely.

To Overcome Procrastination:

For Souths, overcoming procrastination involves learning to prioritize their own needs and set boundaries without feeling guilty. They must work on recognizing that taking care of themselves and addressing difficult tasks doesn't mean neglecting others—it actually strengthens their ability to support those around them.

- Setting Boundaries and Saying "No": Souths can improve by learning to set boundaries and say "no" when they're overextended. This will free up time and energy for their own priorities and help them avoid procrastinating on personal tasks. Setting small, manageable goals for themselves can help them focus on their own needs without feeling overwhelmed.

- Addressing Conflict with Care: Souths should work on becoming more comfortable with addressing difficult situations or conflict. By reframing confrontation as a way to maintain stability in the long run, they can approach tough conversations with the same care they apply to other nurturing roles. This will help them avoid procrastinating on emotionally charged tasks.

- Balancing Care for Others with Self-Care: Souths can create a more balanced approach to life by focusing on self-care and making time for tasks that are important to them. This means acknowledging that their needs are just as important as the needs of those they care for and that taking care of themselves ultimately helps them support others more effectively.

Overall Pattern:

For Souths, procrastination is often driven by their desire to avoid conflict, maintain emotional harmony, and prioritize others' needs over their own. They may delay tasks that require them to assert themselves, address uncomfortable issues, or focus on personal goals. To overcome this, Souths need to work on balancing their nurturing nature with self-care, boundary-setting, and recognizing that sometimes putting themselves first is the best way to maintain long-term harmony. By addressing procrastination in a thoughtful and structured way, Souths can create a more balanced life that honors both their needs and those of the people they care for.

How Procrastination Plays Out for West:

Wests are methodical, thoughtful, and precise, and their procrastination is usually rooted in their desire for perfection and their need to feel thoroughly prepared before taking action. They tend to delay starting tasks until they feel they have gathered enough information, evaluated all the details, and are certain they can execute the task flawlessly.

- Over-Preparation and Analysis Paralysis: Wests often fall into the trap of over-preparing or over-analyzing before they act. They want to ensure that every angle has been considered and every potential consequence has been thought through. This can lead to analysis paralysis, where they keep gathering data and revisiting details without ever feeling ready to move forward.

- Fear of Making Mistakes: Wests have a strong aversion to making mistakes, so they often procrastinate on tasks that feel uncertain or where the outcome isn't clear. Their need for security and predictability makes them hesitant to dive into situations where they could make errors or where there's a lack of structure.

Reason for Procrastination:

Wests' procrastination stems from their fear of imperfection and their deep need for security. They often feel that there is always more data to collect or more analysis to be done before they can make a decision or take action. Their meticulous nature makes it difficult for them to move forward until they feel confident that everything is in order and that the task will be executed correctly.

- Perfectionism and Attention to Detail: Wests are perfectionists at heart. They want to ensure that everything they do is done precisely and without error, which can lead them to put off tasks until they feel completely prepared. Their high standards can prevent them from starting tasks because they feel overwhelmed by the pressure to get it exactly right.

- Desire for Control and Predictability: Wests thrive in environments where they can control the outcome and predict what will happen. They procrastinate when faced with tasks that involve uncertainty or when they feel they don't have enough information to ensure success. Their need for structure and order can cause them to delay tasks until they feel they've minimized all possible risks.

How They Handle It:

Despite their tendency to procrastinate due to over-preparation, Wests are highly effective once they feel confident about their course of action. When they do start a task, they execute it with precision and attention to detail, often producing high-quality results.

- Methodical Execution: Once Wests have gathered enough information and feel secure in their approach, they tend to follow through with tasks in a methodical and organized way. They pay close attention to every step and ensure that everything is done correctly, often resulting in high-quality work.

- Hesitation to Begin: However, they may continue to delay tasks for long periods if they don't feel fully prepared, and this hesitation can prevent them from making progress or meeting deadlines. Their cautious nature means they'd rather delay than risk making a mistake.

To Overcome Procrastination:

Wests can overcome procrastination by learning to accept that perfection isn't always possible and that sometimes action is more important than having everything completely figured out. They can also benefit from setting deadlines for themselves and learning to make decisions with incomplete information.

- Embracing Imperfection: Wests need to work on accepting that it's okay to start a task before they have everything perfectly in place. They should focus on progress rather than perfection and recognize that mistakes can be part of the learning process. By embracing a mindset of growth rather than perfection, they can reduce the pressure they place on themselves.

- Setting Time Limits for Preparation: Wests can prevent over-preparing by setting time limits for gathering information and analyzing options. Once the time is up, they should commit to taking action, even if they don't feel 100% ready. This can help them avoid falling into the trap of endless preparation.

- Focusing on Incremental Progress: Wests should break tasks into smaller, manageable steps and focus on making incremental progress rather than trying to accomplish everything perfectly from the start. By taking small steps forward, they can build momentum and feel more confident about their ability to achieve their goals without getting bogged down in perfectionism.

Overall Pattern:

For Wests, procrastination is often driven by their need for perfection and their desire to avoid making mistakes. They delay tasks when they feel uncertain or unprepared, and their attention to detail can cause them to spend too much time analyzing and preparing. To overcome procrastination, Wests need to focus on progress over perfection and recognize that sometimes taking action is more important than waiting for the perfect moment. By setting limits on their preparation time and learning to accept imperfection, Wests can become more efficient and effective in their tasks while still maintaining their high standards.

Recognizing how our survival concerns drive behavior helps us understand not only how we approach life but also how we project these concerns onto others. Whether we seek control, freedom, stability, or security, these core concerns shape our expectations and frustrations.

Let's get some therapy.

CHAPTER 19

Positional Therapy

"Do all things with love." -Og Mandino

What each position might say at therapy.

Peeking into the therapy sessions of each position gives us an inside look at what really drives each one. It's like eavesdropping on the heart and mind of North, East, South, and West—all trying to make sense of their needs, frustrations, and deepest desires. Therapy allows each position to voice their truths without judgment, peeling back the layers to reveal not only what matters most to them but also how they can better understand and connect with others.

So, let's settle into the mental couch, put ourselves in each position's shoes, and listen in. Therapy isn't just for finding personal clarity; it's a tool for unlocking empathy, helping us connect with the people in our lives, one session at a time.

North

"I'm always the one who has to step up and take control because if I don't, everything just falls apart. And I'm tired, honestly. I'm tired of having to be the one who has it all together. But at the same time, I don't trust anyone else to do it *right*. So, I take it on. I always take it on.

A lot of things are pretty obvious to me and I don't understand why people are so stupid. I just don't understand why people don't get it. I mean, I *see* the solution. It's right there. It's obvious to me!

I've been told I'm a bit too... blunt, I guess. People say I come off as intimidating or cold, but honestly, I just don't have the patience for all the emotional fluff. I don't mean to be harsh, but when things need to get done, they need to get done. I can't stand indecision. When people hem and haw and go back and forth—ugh! It drives me nuts! Just *make the call.*

It's not that I don't care. I do, deeply, actually. It's just that I care about *the outcome* more than the process, I guess. People don't see that side of me. They see the one in control, the one with the plan, the one who doesn't waver. I need certainty. I need to *know* I'm right. And if I'm not sure, I won't move forward. I can get stuck in this loop of perfectionism. It's not like it has to be perfect, I just want it my way, and then if I'm with someone I realize I have to compromise and I hate that. I don't like to be told what to do. I have plenty of ideas myself. Like, I want 100% certainty, but when does that ever happen?

And God, the pressure. There's this pressure to always be the strong one, the decisive one. I'm supposed to have all the answers, and if I don't? So, it feels like I'm failing. So, I can't stop. I have to keep pushing. But no one sees the weight I'm carrying. They just see the results and assume everything is fine because I *made it fine*. But the truth is... sometimes I wish someone else would take the lead. I wish I could trust someone else to handle things the way I would, but I can't. Not fully. Because what if they mess it up? What if they don't care as much as I do?

It's a lonely place to be. People look at me like I'm this tower of strength, but inside I'm questioning my moves. Am I doing enough? Did I make the right call? Am I failing people because I didn't think of everything? That's the hardest part—the feeling that if I'm not perfect, then I'm not enough.

But you know what? Even as I'm saying this, I already know I'm going to keep pushing. I don't *know* how to be any other way. I'm driven by this need to lead, to succeed, to take care of things. It's who I am. I guess what I want is just... for someone to understand that it's not as easy as it looks."

This perspective highlights the inner conflict of a North—how they are perceived as strong and decisive on the outside but often feel the pressure, doubt, and loneliness that comes with their need for control and perfection on the inside.

East

"Honestly, I just feel like I'm suffocating sometimes. Like, people expect me to be tied down to a plan, to stick to one thing all the time, but that's just not how I work. I need to feel free. I need to be able to move, to explore, to *do something new*. Routine? It's my worst nightmare. I can't stand the thought of living the same day over and over, you know?

But then, when I try to explain that, people just think I'm flaky. Like, I'm not *serious* or I can't commit. But that's not it! I commit to experiences. I want life to be an adventure. I want to *feel alive* every day, and for me, that means chasing the next big thing, the next idea, the next opportunity. Staying in one place, doing one thing forever... I can't. I get restless. And then the anxiety hits.

When I feel trapped, I get this itch, like, I've gotta escape. It's like, if I'm stuck, I'm missing out on something better, something more exciting. And God, I hate being bored. Being stuck in the same place with no new experiences? That's where I start to feel like I'm losing myself. I need the thrill. I need the fun. I need the *what if?* moments.

But it's more than just fun. I thrive off of energy. I feed off other people's excitement. When I'm around people who are alive, who are passionate, who are doing new things, I feel like I'm at my best. But when they expect me to follow rules or stick to some rigid plan, I just shut down. I don't want to be boxed in like that.

And okay, fine, maybe I jump from thing to thing too fast sometimes. Like, yeah, I'll admit I've got a ton of unfinished projects. I get super excited about something, dive in headfirst, and then... I lose interest.

Something else pops up, and it feels more exciting, so I go after that instead. But I don't see that as a bad thing! I just think life's too short to be tied to one thing forever. Why can't people see that?

The thing is, I know I'm all over the place sometimes. I know it can be frustrating for others when they need me to stick to something or be more, I don't know, focused? But when I feel like someone's trying to pin me down, I rebel. I need to keep things light, keep things open. I hate the feeling of being boxed in, like there's only *one way* to do something. That makes me anxious. And when I get anxious, I get... annoyed, easily.

And it's not just work or commitments—it's relationships too. I love deeply, but if I feel like someone's trying to control me or tell me what to do, I'm out. I can't handle it. I need someone who's as free-spirited as me, who's up for spontaneous adventures and doesn't need to plan everything down to the last detail.

You know what? I think people just don't get that I live in the moment. I'm *alive* in the now. I don't want to be weighed down by 'what-ifs' or 'should-haves'—I want to explore every possibility, every option. That's how I experience life. It's not that I'm avoiding responsibility. It's just that I see life as this huge, exciting playground, and I don't want to be stuck on the swings when there's a whole jungle gym to explore.

I guess what I'm really asking is... is it so wrong to want to feel *free?*"

This captures the East's inner dialogue, revealing their deep need for freedom, excitement, and variety. It also touches on their struggle with feeling misunderstood or seen as unreliable when, in reality, they just want to live fully and embrace spontaneity.

South

"You know, I just want everyone to be okay. That's really all I want. I want things to be peaceful, for people to get along, and for there to be harmony. But it feels like no matter how hard I try, I'm always stuck in the middle, keeping everyone else together while I'm barely holding it together myself.

I don't know why it's so hard for me to say 'no.' It's like, I can't stand the thought of disappointing someone or making them upset. So, I just... take it all on. I'm the one everyone turns to when they need help, and don't get me wrong, I love being there for people—I *need* to be there for people. But sometimes, I feel like I'm drowning in everyone else's needs and there's no space left for mine.

I mean, I can't even count the number of times I've agreed to do something just to keep the peace, even when I don't want to. I tell myself, 'It's fine, it's not a big deal,' but after a while, it adds up. And then I feel this... quiet resentment. Not because I don't love the people in my life, but because I feel like I'm being stretched so thin and no one really sees it. But how could they? I don't show it. I just keep smiling and saying, 'Sure, I'll take care of it.'

But you know what? Sometimes I wonder... who's taking care of me? Who's making sure I'm, okay? I guess that's the thing—I'm so focused on everyone else's feelings, their problems, their happiness, that I forget about my own. Or maybe I push it aside because I don't want to be a burden. I don't want to cause waves. I hate conflict. I'll do *anything* to avoid it, honestly. Even if that means biting my tongue or swallowing what I really want. It's easier to just go along with things than to risk upsetting someone.

And I know, I *know* that's not healthy. But in the moment, it feels like the right thing to do because the last thing I want is for someone to be hurt or mad. I can't handle that. I think it's because I feel things so deeply. If someone's upset, even if it's not directed at me, it gets to me. It's like I carry everyone else's emotions around with me. I'm always asking myself, 'Is everyone okay? Are we good?'

But here's the problem—I never ask myself if *I'm* okay. It's like I don't even consider my own needs until I'm completely burnt out. And by then, I'm exhausted. I'm always tired, always drained, because I've been pouring everything, I have into making sure everyone else is happy. And the worst part? Sometimes I catch myself complaining about how busy or overwhelmed I am, but deep down I know I put myself in that position. I took on all the responsibility because... I couldn't say no.

The thing is, I don't even know what it would look like to put myself first. That feels... selfish. And I don't want to be selfish. But I guess I need to figure out how to find a balance, how to take care of myself without feeling like I'm letting everyone else down.

Because I'm scared. I'm scared that if I don't hold everything together, everything will fall apart. But I'm also scared that if I keep holding everything together, *I'll* fall apart. I don't want to get to that point. I just... I just want some peace, for me too, you know?"

This captures the South's struggle with always putting others first, avoiding conflict, and feeling overwhelmed by the emotional weight they carry. It also highlights their deep desire for harmony and the challenge of finding a balance between caring for others and taking care of themselves.

West

"I guess... I overthink things. No, actually, I *know* I overthink things. It's just—there's always more to consider, you know? There's always another detail I haven't thought of yet, another angle I haven't analyzed. I can't just dive in without making sure I've covered everything. And people don't get that. They think I'm being slow or indecisive, but the truth is, I need to make sure I get it *right*.

It's not that I don't want to act. It's just that if I'm going to do something, I want to be fully prepared. I can't stand the thought of missing something important or rushing into something and making a mistake. I'd rather take my time and be certain than jump in half-prepared. But people? They don't seem to appreciate that. They think I'm dragging my feet, but I'm not—I'm *being thorough*.

And it's not just with decisions. It's with... everything. I'm constantly organizing making sure every little thing is in order. I swear I've made spreadsheets for things most people wouldn't even think twice about. I just need that sense of structure. I need things to be organized, to be clear, to be perfect. But the downside? I can get stuck. I know that. Sometimes I spend so much time *planning* that I never get to the actual doing. I get trapped in the details.

I'm not saying I need everything to be perfect—okay, maybe I do— but it's more about making sure everything is *right*. There's a difference. And when people pressure me to just hurry up or 'wing it,' I panic a little. Like, no, I can't just rush through things. That's when mistakes happen, and I *hate* mistakes. It's like, if I can avoid them, why wouldn't I?

But here's the thing... I don't always know when to stop. I get so wrapped up in thinking and planning and preparing that I can't pull the trigger. I worry that if I move forward, I'll miss something crucial, and then I'll be responsible for it going wrong. And that thought... it keeps me up at night. I've lost hours of sleep running over details in my head, trying to figure out if I've covered every base.

It doesn't stop at decisions either. I have this... habit of holding onto things, just in case I need them later. Like, I'll save a document from five years ago because, what if I need that information one day? I know I probably won't, but throwing it away feels... wrong, somehow. It's like, what if I'm missing something? What if that little detail comes back to haunt me because I didn't pay attention to it when I had the chance?

And don't even get me started on relationships. I mean, I *want* connection, but sometimes I analyze it to death. Like, should I say this? Should I say that? What if I say the wrong thing? And then, when I finally do say something, I'm already critiquing myself the moment the words leave my mouth. It's exhausting, honestly. I want things to flow, but I need to know what's coming next. I need the map, the plan, the structure. Spontaneity... freaks me out a bit. I don't like being caught off guard.

The irony is, while I'm obsessing over getting everything right, everyone else has already moved on. They've already made decisions, acted on them, and meanwhile, I'm still refining the details. It's like I'm living on a different timeline.

I don't know. I guess what I'm trying to say is... I want to get things right, but sometimes it feels like the world moves too fast for me to keep up. I wish I could just turn my brain off for a bit, stop analyzing every little thing, and just... *go*. But that's not me. I need the order, the structure, the plan. And sometimes? That makes me feel stuck. But without it... I'd feel lost."

This captures the inner workings of a West—how they get caught in the details, their need for precision, and their struggle to take action without feeling fully prepared. It also highlights their fear of mistakes and their desire for structure, which can lead to feeling stuck or overwhelmed by indecision.

Wasn't that intriguing? Listening in on each position's therapy session is like diving into the inner dialogue of North, East, South, and West. Each one wrestles with unique frustrations and longings. Therapy allows us to voice our truths without judgment. We get to hear the fears, desires, and challenges laid bare, giving us a clearer picture of why we act the way we do. Therapy doesn't just help us make sense of ourselves—it's a bridge to understanding others. This helps us empathize with every position, making it easier to relate, connect, and communicate more effectively with everyone in our lives.

Here are some quotes from each position about love's greatness and love's frustration.

North

Greatness:

"I feel so inspired knowing we're building something real together."

"They bring out the best in me, pushing me to keep growing."

"It's a relief to love someone who values honesty as much as I do."

"I finally found someone who matches my vision for the future."

"Being with them gives me a renewed sense of purpose."

"It's amazing to have a partner who trusts my instincts and lets me lead."

"They bring clarity and calm to my busy mind."

"I love knowing they'll stand by me no matter what."

"They see my drive, and instead of feeling intimidated, they celebrate it."

"With them, I know exactly where we're going, and I'm all in."

Frustration:

"Why isn't love as straightforward as it should be?"

"I wish I could just know exactly what they're thinking—would save a lot of time and trouble."

"I don't understand why they don't just tell me what they want. I'd get it done!"

"If they'd just be honest with me, we wouldn't have to go through all this back and forth."

"I know what I want, but it feels like I'm always the one leading the way."

"Why does everything have to be so complicated? Love should have clear steps."

"If I'm all in, why can't they be as certain as I am?"

"Sometimes, I feel like I'm carrying the relationship on my own."

"All I want is honesty and consistency—how is that too much to ask?"

"Why do we have to go through all these emotional loops? Let's just focus on making it work."

East

Greatness:

"Being with them feels like an adventure I never want to end."

"I feel alive and free, like I can truly be myself."

"They make every moment feel like a celebration of life."

"Love with them is spontaneous, fun, and always full of surprises."

"I love that they keep up with my energy and bring even more excitement."

"With them, I'm always laughing and discovering new things."

"It's so refreshing to be with someone who embraces life as I do."

"I feel like we're writing the story of us, one thrilling chapter at a time."

"They accept my wild side and add their own spark to it."

"Being with them is pure joy—they make me feel like every day is a new adventure."

Frustration:

"I just want to enjoy every moment together—why make things so serious?"

"If love isn't fun and full of adventure, what's the point?"

"I'm all about being spontaneous, but sometimes it feels like they can't keep up."

"Why do we have to label everything? Let's just go with the flow!"

"I want to explore every possibility with them, but they keep talking about 'the future.'"

"Sometimes it feels like they're trying to pin me down, and I just want to breathe."

"I don't know where this is going, but I love the thrill of it."

"Why do we have to figure everything out now? Let's just enjoy what we have."

"I fall for the person, not the plan—why can't they understand that?"

"I want someone who's ready to live life to the fullest with me, not hold me back."

South

Greatness:

"I feel safe, like I've finally found my forever home."

"They bring such warmth and comfort into my life."

"Being with them feels effortless, like we were meant to be."

"I love that they value stability and connection as much as I do."

"They're my calm in the storm and my biggest support."

"With them, love is steady, real, and deeply fulfilling."

"They make me feel seen, heard, and cherished."

"I feel like we're building a life full of meaning and trust."

"I love that our relationship is grounded and genuine."

"They've given me the kind of love I've always hoped for—stable, sincere, and loyal."

Frustration:

"I just want to feel connected, like we're really there for each other."

"Why is it so hard for them to just be present? I don't need big gestures—just real moments."

"I'd rather we both feel secure than rush into anything."

"Love should feel comfortable, like home. Why all the drama?"

"I'm happy to be their rock, but sometimes I need them to be mine too."

"Why can't we just talk things out calmly? I don't want to argue."

"I wish they could see how much I care, even in the small things I do."

"All I need is loyalty and understanding—no need for anything complicated."

"Love is about consistency and support. Why make it a roller coaster?"

"I want a steady love, one that doesn't shake every time there's a storm."

West

Greatness:

"I finally found someone who values commitment and stability as much as I do."

"They bring peace and reassurance to my life."

"I love that they're just as thoughtful and intentional as I am."

"With them, I feel truly seen, understood, and respected."

"They make love feel structured, solid, and dependable."

"I feel like we're creating something lasting, step by step."

"They respect my need for clarity and provide it without hesitation."

"Love with them feels like building a foundation that will last a lifetime."

"I trust them completely, and that feels incredible."

"They make me feel secure, like we're a team that can weather anything."

Frustration:

"I just need to understand where we're headed—love shouldn't be a guessing game."

"If we're serious, then let's make a real plan together."

"I love when things make sense between us, like pieces fitting perfectly."

"Why is everyone so focused on the 'spark'? What about consistency?"

"I'd rather take things slow and build something real than rush and lose it all."

"I don't mind going deep, but let's make sure we're on the same page."

"Love should be dependable; if I can't rely on it, what's the point?"

"I'm all for commitment—if they're willing to put in the same thought and care."

"It's the little things, the details, that show me how much they care."

"I want a love that's steady and intentional, not full of empty promises."

These quotes give us a peek into what each person really wants from love, showing us what makes them feel valued, happy, and at ease in a relationship. They highlight how each one defines a fulfilling connection, whether it's through shared adventures, a solid sense of partnership, emotional depth, or thoughtful stability.

For some, love is about growing together toward shared goals, where both partners feel driven and aligned. Others light up when they find someone who can match their enthusiasm for life, keeping things spontaneous and exciting. Some feel most at home with a partner who brings warmth, stability, and a calm presence. And for others, it's all about a dependable, intentional love where commitment and trust are foundational.

These perspectives show us the unique ways each person feels secure and appreciated in love, and they reveal what they'll naturally prioritize in a partnership.

If you want to get better at love faster the next chapter is for you.

CHAPTER 20

Get Better at the Game Faster

In this chapter, I've compiled a short series of exercises and activities for self-reflection or to work on with others. You can use this as a way to explore deeper and share in this experience with others.

The exercises and activities are designed to enhance your understanding and connection with individuals across all positions, whether it's your mate, your friends, your siblings, or your family members. Doing these activities is eye-opening and cathartic. You get to express the way you see things, and you get to see things from someone else's point of view. Empathy and perspective-taking are crucial for appreciating the diverse approaches embodied by the 4Cross Love Framework. Do them all, one, or as many as you wish.

If you would like some help in your investigation, please make an appointment with me at www.4crosslove.com/appointment I would love to help you with some of the clues you may be questioning.

Exercise and Activities

These exercises and activities encourage you to step outside your comfort zone, fostering empathy, understanding, and appreciation for the diverse approaches and perspectives within the 4Cross Love Framework so you can learn to play better, faster.

1. Strengths and Challenges Analysis

Purpose: To identify and leverage personal strengths and address challenges.

Activity: Make a list of your strengths and challenges based on your 4Cross Love Framework position. Discuss with your partner how these traits affect your relationship. Create a plan to maximize strengths and improve challenges, with actionable steps to follow.

2. Shared Goals Setting

Purpose: To align personal and relationship goals.

Activity: Sit down with your partner and discuss your individual goals and shared goals. Identify how your 4Cross Love Framework positions influence these goals and create a plan to support each other in achieving them. Regularly review and adjust these goals as needed.

3. Gratitude Exercises

Purpose: To cultivate appreciation and positivity in relationships.

Activity: Write down three things you appreciate about your partner and how they relate to their 4Cross Love Framework position. Share your list with your partner, and discuss how these positive traits enhance your relationship.

4. Mindfulness Meditation

Purpose: To improve emotional regulation and self-awareness.

Activity: Practice mindful meditation. Focus on observing your thoughts and emotions without judgment. Reflect on how your 4Cross Love Framework position influences your reactions and strive for greater self-awareness.

5. Relationship Check-Ins

Purpose: To maintain open communication and address issues proactively.

Activity: Schedule a check-in with your partner to discuss the state of your relationship. Use these sessions to openly share feelings, concerns, and appreciations, considering your 4Cross Love Framework positions. Focus on constructive feedback and mutual support.

6. Learning Together

Purpose: To foster growth and shared experiences.

Activity: Discuss the 4Cross Love Framework and how applying it has affected your view on love and your relationship. This shared learning experience can strengthen your bond and deepen your understanding of each other.

7. Role-Reversal Storytelling

Purpose: To embody and appreciate another position's viewpoint.

Activity: Share a recent challenging experience, focusing on your feelings and thoughts during the event. Then, switch roles, retelling the other's story from the first-person perspective, trying to capture the emotions and thought processes as if they were your own. This exercise encourages deep listening and empathy, enabling participants to walk in someone else's shoes.

Example:

Person A (North Position): "Last week, I felt really frustrated when you forgot our anniversary. I had planned a special evening, but it seemed like you didn't care. I felt hurt and unappreciated because I value our relationship deeply and expected you to remember this important date."

Role-Reversal Retelling

Person B (East Position): "Last week, I forgot our anniversary, and it ended up causing a lot of hurt. I didn't mean to forget it; I've been so caught up with work and other things that it slipped my mind. When I realized what happened, I felt really guilty and worried that you would think I don't care about our relationship, which is far from the truth."

Reflections

Person A (after hearing Person B's perspective): "I didn't realize how much you were juggling and how bad you felt about forgetting. I was so focused on my own hurt that I didn't see your guilt and concern."

Person B (after hearing Person A's perspective): "I understand now why you felt hurt and unappreciated. I should have been more mindful of how important our anniversary is to you and to us as a couple."

This relationship-based example helps both partners understand each other's feelings and perspectives, fostering empathy and improving communication in the relationship.

8. Empathetic Listening Circles

Purpose: To practice active listening and empathy in a group setting.

Activity: Sit in a circle and share your thoughts and feelings about a specific topic or issue, one at a time, without interruption. Listeners are tasked with reflecting back what they heard to ensure understanding and validation, focusing on understanding the speaker's emotional content and perspective rather than preparing a response.

9. Creative Expression Workshop

Purpose: To explore and express the perspectives of different positions through art.

Activity: Create art pieces (drawings, poems, short stories) that represent how you imagine the world looks through the eyes of another 4Cross Love Framework position. Sharing these creations with the group allows for a discussion about the thought processes and emotions that informed your work, facilitating empathy and creative understanding.

10. Conflict Resolution Practice

Purpose: To practice handling conflicts according to 4Cross Love Framework positions.

Activity: Choose a common conflict scenario. Role-play the situation, each person embodying their 4Cross Love Framework position. After the role-play, discuss what strategies worked and how understanding each other's positions helped resolve the conflict.

Example Conflict Scenario: Decision on Weekend Plans

Conflict: Person A (West) wants to spend the weekend planning and organizing the house, while Person B (East) wants to go on a spontaneous trip out of town.

Role-Playing the Situation

Person A (West): "I think we should stay home this weekend and focus on organizing the house. We have a lot of things that need to be sorted, and it's essential to get everything in order. This will help us be more efficient in the long run."

Person B (East): "I understand that organizing the house is important, but we've been working hard all week. I think it would be refreshing to take a spontaneous trip and have some fun. It will help us relax and come back with more energy."

Discussion: Strategies That Work

Compromise and Balance: Person A suggests dedicating Saturday to organizing the house and spending Sunday on a spontaneous day trip. This balances both needs for structure and spontaneity.

Empathy and Understanding: Both parties take time to understand each other's perspectives. Person A acknowledges the need for relaxation, and Person B recognizes the importance of organization.

Clear Communication: They communicate their needs and concerns clearly without blaming each other, focusing on finding a solution that addresses both positions.

Post-Role-Play Discussion

Person A (West): "Understanding that you need a break and some spontaneity made me realize that we can plan our organization tasks while also making time for fun. I see how this balance can actually make us more productive and happier."

Person B (East): "I see now how important it is for you to have things organized and how it affects our efficiency and your mood. Balancing our weekend between organization and fun seems like a good way to address both our needs."

Conclusion: Through practicing effective conflict resolution by embodying their 4Cross Love Framework positions, leading to a mutually satisfactory solution. Understanding each other's positions fostered empathy and clear communication, helping them resolve the conflict smoothly.

Speaking of conclusions…let's get to it.

Conclusion

This final part is not just an ending but a beginning—the start of a more aware, more intentional, and more proactive phase of your relational life. It's about taking everything you've learned and translating it into actions that enrich not only your romantic relationships but all your interpersonal interactions.

At the beginning of every season of the *Love Is Blind* series, I am filled with hope and excitement that all the couples will find their perfect match. I envision them discovering not just a partner but their person—the one who truly understands and complements them. I imagine them feeling that unmistakable zing of connection and chemistry, leading to a deep, enduring love.

I guess I am a hopeless romantic, and with the perspective of The 4Cross Love Framework, I find myself hopeful that all of our intentions to find and share true love are possible. I love this show. I hope it goes on forever, and I truly hope they use the 4Cross Love Checklist to help them.

More than anything, my hope is that you find a romantic partner and a best friend for life—someone who will stand by you through thick and thin, share your dreams, and support your goals. I'm rooting for you to win the game of love and achieve a relationship built on trust, mutual respect, and profound emotional intimacy.

I believe that with the 4Cross Love Framework and Checklist, it's more than hope. It's a reality.

The key to finding your person on this journey is going to be your ability to take responsibility for your position and uncover the nuances in your game of love, allowing your finesse to shine through with a sprinkle of your own cleverness. If you have ever played a game, whether it's tennis, chess, or boxing, you know that the secret to winning is through practicing and finding your own special way to play. You will start to unveil your own game of love using the 4Cross Love Checklist.

If there's one thing I seem to get often when introducing the four positions in the game of love, it's "I don't really fit into one of those personalities perfectly, I'm kind of all of them."

You're right. You do play all of them, but I promise you when push comes to shove, and your biology is triggered, it isn't your personality; it's your positional concern. Personality tests don't definitively tell you anything, so you can be all over the place, but you are upset for a definite, perturbing, consistent reason.

Not identifying and claiming your position gives you an excuse to do what you want, whenever you want, without being held accountable for your actions in the game of love.

In a sense, you're feeling caught. And you don't like to feel caught because all of your secrets about how you operate are revealed. Secrets you didn't even know you had been even scarier. The unknown but wholly responsible self can be a scary person to confront.

Not taking responsibility for your position in the game of love would be like entering into a game of basketball and saying, "I don't really fit into any of the positions, so I'm going to play on my terms." Or you are a doctor, and instead of following the rules (procedure and protocol), you decide you're going to do it your way. Or you are a lawyer, and instead of following the practices of law, you decide you are going to do it your way. And the list of games we are all playing goes on and on. That's not to say you can't have your own personal flare; of course you do. You are unique, but in order to play the game of love and win, you need to play your positions and adhere to the rules of the game. You don't see any random chess pieces on the board. A deck of cards is arranged the way they are for a reason.

Here's the thing. Yes, you can play basketball all by yourself and win. There's no one to guard you, you don't have to pass the ball, you can shoot from anywhere whenever you want. Heck, you can play all the positions on the court, but until you figure out that you play the best in one position for a reason and that it's way more fun when you play with others effectively and then learn to play the game with some finesse, you will be blind to the game of love.

Like any game, we must practice, make mistakes, learn, and grow. Until then, you won't win anything but a game by yourself, alone, where nobody really cares. You can convince yourself that they do, but nobody cares about you until you care about understanding them.

I believe, like our blood types, the four positions are in our biology, and we're going to have to work harder than randomly answering a subjective personality test based on how we want to be seen, what job we're applying for, what relationship we're trying to get out of, or the cute gal or guy you're trying to get a date with.

Learning how to use 4Cross takes commitment, time, and effort. This is not a star sign to realize much of nothing or a love language to illiteracy. I believe it's the playbook for the game of love. You are going to have to learn to play with others effectively while at the same time being yourself.

Unveiling Your Game

As you delve deeper into the intricacies of your own love life, you will begin to understand the subtle dynamics that influence your interactions and relationships. Just as a chess master anticipates moves and a tennis pro refines their swing, you will learn to recognize and navigate the realities of your romantic engagements. The 4Cross Love Checklist will guide you through each step with precision.

Fine-Tuning Self-Awareness

Reflect on your experiences, be honest about your preferences, and embrace your authentic self. Use the 4Cross Love Framework to identify your strengths and areas for growth. This will help you approach relationships with confidence and clarity, knowing what you bring to the table and what you need from a partner.

Mastering Positional Awareness

Recognize the positions of those you interact with to tailor your approach and foster better communication and understanding. Whether your potential mate is a North, East, South, or West, use this knowledge to anticipate their needs and respond appropriately, adapting your interactions to engage effectively.

Balancing Different Forms of Attraction

Evaluate the balance between physical, emotional, intellectual, and positional attraction in your relationship. Use the 4Cross Love Checklist to ensure that your relationship is built on a solid foundation. Cultivate each form of attraction to create a well-rounded and fulfilling connection.

Aligning Interests and Values

Engage in careful questioning and honest conversations to uncover shared interests and aligned values. This will help you find common ground and mutual aspirations, creating a sense of partnership and companionship. Think of it as working together in harmony toward a shared goal.

Effective Communication

Use the 4Cross Love Checklist to assess and improve your communication skills. Focus on mastering clear, empathetic, and respectful dialogue to resolve conflicts, express your needs, and deepen your connection. Treat this as refining your techniques and strategies for better outcomes in your relationship.

Practicing Patience and Persistence

Approach the journey of love with patience and persistence. Use the insights from the 4Cross Love Checklist to stay focused on continuous growth, even during challenging times. Recognize that every experience is a step toward greater understanding and fulfillment.

Embracing the Journey

Embrace the journey with an open heart and a willing spirit. Apply the principles of the 4Cross Love Checklist to navigate the complexities of relationships with grace and wisdom. Celebrate milestones, learn from setbacks, and cherish moments of connection as part of your ongoing growth together.

In conclusion, the nuances of love are where true mastery lies. With the 4Cross Love Checklist as your guide, you will unveil the subtle dynamics of your romantic life, fine-tune your self-awareness, master positional awareness, balance different forms of attraction, align interests and values, grow together in your communication, and practice patience and persistence. Embrace the journey, and you will find that the game of love is not just a quest for partnership but a path to personal growth and fulfillment.

In the end, winning the game of love isn't about crossing the finish line first or amassing the most points. It's about the stories you gather along the way, the laughter that fills the air, and the warmth of knowing you're not playing this game alone.

As I look back on my own journey of love, whether it be through family, friends, pets, my husband, my daughters—and now my daughters thinking about the gift of love, marriage, and children—I am struck by how much it consumes my life. It's with me everywhere I look, in every thought and action I have, because every thought and action lead back to a decision about all the people and animals I love in my life.

Love really is everything, no matter what you have, what you do, or how you look at it.

I want more family, more friends, more pets. More love.

My understanding of the 4Cross Love Framework has given me a depth of personal grace that nothing else in my life has ever come remotely close to. It gives me the strength, courage, and confidence to appreciate all the love in my life and give more back.

Farewell, but not goodbye. The journey continues, and the game of love awaits. May you play it with wisdom, grace, and an ever-renewing sense of awe for the magic that unfolds when hearts connect.

Shelly LaVigne – Love Investigator

Should you seek more guidance, you can make an appointment with me at- 4CrossLove.com/appointment